EDWARD H. HILTON.

THE TOURISTS' GUIDE TO LUCKNOW.

	PAGE.
CHAPTER I.—A Brief History of Oudh and its Rule under the Native Government, up to the time of annexation of the Province by the British in 1856	1
CHAPTER II.—A narrative of the startling events at Lucknow in 1857, with a graphic account of the Investment of the Residency	17
CHAPTER III.—A short Biography of the Kings of Oudh, with a geographical sketch of the Province	137
CHAPTER IV.—A Guide (with Maps of City and Cantonments) to the places of interest in Lucknow	155
CHAPTER V.—A Guide to the Residency, with Plans of the Intrenched Position and Cemetery	185

BY ONE OF THE BELEAGUERED GARRISON.

FIFTH EDITION.

REVISED AND ILLUSTRATED.

The Naval & Military Press Ltd

Published by

The Naval & Military Press Ltd
Unit 5 Riverside, Brambleside
Bellbrook Industrial Estate
Uckfield, East Sussex
TN22 1QQ England

Tel: +44 (0)1825 749494

www.naval-military-press.com
www.nmarchive.com

In reprinting in facsimile from the original, any imperfections are inevitably reproduced and the quality may fall short of modern type and cartographic standards.

ILLUSTRATIONS.

	To face page
Portrait ... ... *Frontispiece.*	
Sir Henry Lawrence	21
Mr. George Schilling	28
Major-General Sir John Inglis, K. C. B. ...	53
Major-General Sir Henry Havelock, K. C. B. ...	93
Major-General Sir James Outram, G. C. B. ...	94
Sir Colin Campbell	107
Mr. Kavanagh	108
Wajid Ali Shah	153
Lesser Chutter Munzil	167
Khurshaed Munzil	180
The Ruins of the Residency ... — ...	187
Group of loyal Native Defenders of the Garrison, who were present at the inauguration of the 32nd Duke of Cornwall's Light Infantry Memorial in the Residency, Lucknow, 5th April 1899 ...	Appendix D.
General Claude Martin	Appendix E.
Plan of the Intrenched Position	End of Book.

OPINIONS OF THE PRESS.

"THE book entitled 'The Martiniere Boys in the Residency' to which we referred the other day as having been presented by the author—Edward H. Hilton—to the Countess of Dufferin, on the occasion of Her Excellency's visit to the Residency,—is now before us in a neat illustrated wrapper, displaying two of the most historical buildings in LUCKNOW, viz., the College itself and the remnants of the house which gave its name to the British intrenched position during the ever memorable defence known as the most glorious of all the annals of British valor and renown in India. Mr. Hilton's book is a simple narrative of all that occurred in LUCKNOW during the eventful epoch of 1857. He describes the outbreak of the Mutiny in the Oudh Capital, and the protective measures that devolved on Sir Henry Lawrence in consequence of the same. The part taken by La Martiniere Boys in the stirring incidents of the five months' siege are described lucidly and truthfully by an eye-witness who was himself one of the beleagured garrison. Mr. Hilton has done honour to himself and to his College in becoming the historian of events, which show that the British school boy is capable of vieing with the bravest and best in the hour of danger and trial, and is willing to undergo privations and risk his life for the honour and glory of ' Old England !' The task undertaken from *esprit de corps* has been well performed, and is a noble tribute to *Alma Mater*. There is much that is original in the book, interspersed among interesting excerpts from the best sources, which make its pages attractive reading, and we commend the volume as a useful record of the period and events of which it treats. It embodies much within a small compass, and presents valuable information in a cheap and handy form. While no Martiniere boy will be without a copy of the book, we believe it ought to find a place on the book-shelf of every Anglo-Indian having asscociations connected with the great Sepoy Rebellion. The style and get up make the book a suitable ornament for any drawing-room table."—*The Express.*

A contemporary thus describes the part taken by La Martiniere Boys during the investment :—

"The startling events of the Mutiny of fifty-seven have made Lucknow a word which is not only a monument to the courage and endurance of those who there made a glorious defence against the overwhelming hosts of the fanatical enemies of England, but is also a lasting memorial of British power in India. The 'Defence of the Residency' is without parallel in Indian history. That building, and the surrounding houses, forming a weak, irregular, and incomplete enclosure were maintained for five months against fearful odds. This was the only spot then possessed by the British in the whole kingdom of Oudh, and the eyes of all India were anxiously turned towards the intrepid garrison till its partial relief was accomplished by General Havelock on the 25th September, 1857. In the chain of posts which formed the British line of defence, the 'Baillie Guard' gate is, perhaps, that best known ; but that most perilous guard of this frail fortress was the terrible 'Cawnpore-battery.'

"In close proximity to this post of danger was the position held bravely throughout the siege by fifty boys of the Martiniere, who, in addition to military duty, gave general assistance as hospital attendants, signallers, and in a variety of other ways. Many of these noble little fellows grew to manhood, and are now members of the Oudh Rifle

Volunteers.* They were all decorated with the Mutiny Medal, and received a bar attached to it for the 'Defence of Lucknow'" (*vide* Appendix A).

"THE MARTINIERE BOYS IN THE RESIDENCY."

"THE above title seems somewhat a misnomer for what is really a very excellent LUCKNOW GUIDE and TOURISTS' *vade mecum*, of which a second edition has just been issued by Mr. E. Hilton, the author and compiler. True enough, the reminiscences of the 'Old Boy' of the Martiniere form a very interesting chapter in the book, but it is now so amplified in many material respects that the *brochure* might very properly be re-named, and thus, perhaps, attract the 'globe-trotting' class more generally than it is apt to do under its present designation.

"We have noticed the previous edition, and now need merely say that the work is the very best of its kind that has hitherto been published, and although there are still some trifling errors of description, this veritable 'Guide' to the many notable buildings in Lucknow and neighbourhood cannot be too greatly commended for its general historical accuracy and the care which has evidently been taken to make it really useful to visitors to this celebrated city. There are some good illustrations, an interesting plan of the Residency grounds at the time of the beleaguerment, and a lithographed map of Lucknow City and Cantonments, all of which will prove very useful to visitors."—*The Express*.

NOTE.—Some years ago the compiler of this little work issued a small pamphlet giving his reminiscences of the Residency at Lucknow in 1857.

This pamphlet confined itself to the description of the incidents which had come under the writer's personal observation; the writer himself being then a student of La Martiniere College, the College boys, as might have been expected, figured most prominently in his narrative, and the pamphlet was accordingly entitled "The Martiniere Boys in the Residency." It was very generously received by the public, and was favourably reviewed by the Press.

Some of the opinions then expressed will be found re-printed above, and the various testimonies to the appreciation in which the book was held encouraged the author to amplify the next edition by giving a fuller account of the siege, and adding short biographies of the Kings of Oudh, and an account of the state of the Province whilst under their rule.

A brief description of the places of interest in Lucknow was also included and, as these different additions continued to be maintained, amplified and revised in subsequent editions, the work became a Guide as well as a History, and it was thought advisable to change the title to that which it now bears.

---

* The following remark by Major-General W. Hill, C. B., Inspector-General of Volunteers, on his inspection of the Corps on 15th February 1902, appeared in the Oudh Volunteer Rifles Regimental Orders :—

"The three Companies of Cadets of the Martiniere School are the best trained and set up Cadets I have seen in India. The Principal of the School (Mr. Sykes) formerly commanded the Oudh Volunteer Corps, and takes a keen interest in volunteering, and probably this will account for the efficiency of the Cadets" (*vide* Appendix B.)

PREFACE.

THE Fifth Edition of the *Tourists' Guide to Lucknow* is published with various emendations and much additional information. It may now be considered a thoroughly up-to-date publication, and is offered to the public in the greatest confidence.

The Maps of the City and Cantonments are as accurate and reliable as possible. With this edition is issued a plan of the Residency Cemetery, showing the position of the graves, with a list of the names of those interred therein.

I feel much indebted to the Rev. Thomas Moore (deceased), formerly Civil Chaplain of Lucknow, for generously permitting me to make use of his works. These have been of especial value to me in compiling the Guide to the Residency and plan of the Intrenched Position.

I have also to acknowledge my indebtedness to the authors of the volumes indicated in the sub-joined list, and other writers :—

General Sleeman's Tour through Oudh.
Mutinies in Oudh, by Gubbins.
Lucknow and Oudh in the Mutiny, by Genl. McLeod Innes.
Siege of Lucknow, by Rees.
Diary of the Siege of Lucknow, by Lady Inglis.
Russel's Diary.
Mutiny Memoirs by Colonel A. R. D. Mackenzie, C. B.
The Oudh Gazetteer.
History of the Indian Mutiny, by Colonel Malleson, C. S. I.
Life of Havelock, by Marshman.
Sir Henry Lawrence, the Pacificator, by Genl. McLeod Innes.
Great Battles of the British Army.
Medals of the British Army.

Lucknow, 1905.   EDWARD H. HILTON.

CHAPTER I.

A BRIEF HISTORY OF OUDH BEFORE THE ANNEXATION.

1. To enable the reader to form some idea of the state of affairs in Oudh before that eventful period in the annals of British India, known to all History as the revolt of the Sepoy Army in 1857, * it will be necessary to give, by way of introduction to my narrative, the following particulars, taken from reliable sources, of a few Kings of Oudh, whose misrule, having become a public scandal and a reproach to the Paramount Power, resulted in the annexation of the Province by the East India Company in February 1856.

2. The founder of the Oudh dynasty which has become extinct by the ex-King's death at Garden Reach, Calcutta, on the 21st September, 1887, in his sixty-eighth year, was Saadat Khan, a Persian, who, coming as a merchant from Nishapur, in Khorasan, attained to high power and influence at Delhi, and received the appointment of Súbádár (Governor) of Oudh from the Emperor, Muhammad Shah, of Delhi, in 1732, a position which he retained until his death in 1739. The Capital remained at Fyzabad till 1775, when Asaf-ud-daulah removed it to Lucknow, and the rulers retained the title of Nawab Vazir, or Chief Minister, of the Empire.

---

* By the year 1857, exactly hundred years had passed since Clive had won the battle of Plassey (23rd June, 1757), and thus laid the foundation of the British Empire in India. The centenary of the foundation of this Empire, instead of being kept as a time of general rejoicing, was fraught with one of the greatest calamities that ever befell the English nation.

"The mutiny," writes Lord Roberts, "was not an unmitigated evil; for to it we owe the consolidation of our power in India, as it hastened on the construction of roads, railways, and telegraphs so wisely and thoughtfully planned by the Marquis of Dalhousie, and which have done more than anything to increase the prosperity of the people and preserve order throughout the country."

The first Indian Railway was opened in 1853; and railways and telegraph-lines began rapidly to spread over the whole country.

3. Gazi-ud-din Haidar was the first person to obtain the title of King in 1819. It was during his reign that Lucknow was visited by Bishop Heber in 1824. It then possessed a considerable population, crowded together in mean houses of clay, traversed by lanes of the filthiest description, and so narrow, that even a single elephant could not pass easily. "The principal street was of commanding appearance, wider than the High Street at Oxford, but having some distant resemblance to it in the colour of its buildings, and their general form and Gothic style. Swarms of mendicants occupied every angle and the steps of every door. Of the remaining population, all were armed—a sure index of prevailing turbulence and general insecurity of life and property. Grave men in palanquins, counting their beads and looking like *Mullahs*, all had two or three sword-and-buckler lackeys attending on them. People of consequence, on their elephants, had each a *sawari*, with shield, spear and gun; and even the lounging people of the lower ranks in the streets and shop-doors had their shields over their shoulders and their swords sheathed in one hand.

4. The mal-administration* of the kingdom under Native Rule was proverbial, but it grew more intolerable during the reign of the late King, Wajid Ali; and, after many remonstrances and much deliberation, the kingdom was made a province of British India. It will thus be seen that the annexation of Oudh, though thought at the time to be a fatal act, was rendered obligatory on the British Government in order to relieve the five millions of suffering inhabitants from tyranny and oppression, brought about by the natural indolence of the King, who permitted the administration to fall completely into the hands of worthless minions, by whose misrule the condition of the kingdom grew worse.

---

* If ever there was a device for insuring mal-administration, it is that of a Native Ruler and Minister both relying on foreign bayonets, and directed by a British Resident. Even if all three were able, virtuous, and considerate, still the wheels of Government could hardly move smoothly If it be difficult to select one man, European or Native, with all the requisites for a just administrator, where are three, who can and will work together, to be found? Each of the three may work incalculable mischief, but no one of them *can* do good if thwarted by the others. It is almost impossible for the Minister to be faithful and submissive to his Prince, and at the same time honest to the British Government.

5. The profligate Court of Lucknow, however, had sunk into a hopelessly feeble state long before Wajid Ali Shah ascended the throne in 1847, for in 1831 Lord William Bentinck had called upon his predecessors for reforms, which were, however, never introduced. It may here be added that all communications between the Governor-General and the King had to pass through the Resident, who represented British interests, and for whom a Force was maintained, officered from the Line of the Bengal Army, the cost of which was a charge upon the revenues of Oudh.

"In April 1831, Lord William Bentinck, while on a tour in the Upper Provinces, paid a ceremonial visit to Lucknow, and, at a private interview, severely remonstrated with the King, Nasir-ud-din Haidar, on his dissolute habits, and threatened to take over the management of the kingdom unless the desired reforms were effected. This was repeated in the beginning of 1835, but the warning was unheeded by the King, whose time was wholly engrossed among the five European associates of his dissipation, *viz.*, the barber, (de Russett, whose son, a merchant of this name, was killed in the Cawnpore Massacre of 1857); tutor (Wright); painter and musician (Mauntz); librarian (Croupley), and Captain Magness."

6. In October 1847, Lord Hardinge, in a personal interview with the King, Wajid Ali, solemnly assured him that the British had, as the Paramount Power, a duty to perform towards the cultivators of the soil, and that, unless the King adopted a proper arrangement in the Revenue and Judicial Departments of his Government so as to correct abuses now existing, it would be imperative on the British Government to carry out the orders of the Court of Directors. Two years were specified for carrying out the necessary reforms.

7. His Majesty's character and habits were not, however, such as to encourage the prospect of improvement. Nothing could be more low or dissolute. * Singers and females, provided

---

* The Oudh Rulers were weak, vicious and dissolute, but they have seldom been cruel, and have invariably been faithful and true to the British Government.

for his amusement, occupied all his time. The singers were all *Domes*, the lowest caste in India. These men, with the eunuchs, became the virtual Sovereigns of the country. They meddled in all State affairs, and influenced the King's decisions in every reference made to him. This resulted in the misrule which prevailed, and with which Colonel Sleeman reproaches the King in a letter, dated August, 1853—" Your Minister has dismissed all the news-writers, who formerly were attached to *Amils* of districts to report their proceedings, on the ground that such officers are unnecessary, so that you can never learn the sufferings of the people, much less afford them redress. In regard to affairs in the city of Lucknow, your eunuchs, your fiddlers, your poets and your Majesty's creatures, plunder the people here, as much as your *Amils* plunder them in the distant districts."

8. Since the Government had lost faith in Wajid Ali Shah ever being able to bring about the desired reforms, the Governor-General, Lord Dalhousie, directed Colonel Sleeman, who was Resident at the Court of Lucknow in 1851, to make a tour through the country, and, after personal inspection, to report upon its actual state. The account he furnished was a continuous record of crime, misery and oppression. Large tracts of fertile land were over-grown with jungle, the haunts of lawless characters, who levied blackmail at will on travellers and others.

9. Petty chiefs had established themselves in isolated forts from whence they set the King's authority at defiance ; and the Royal troops were constantly being ordered out into the district for the purpose of bringing such refractory land-holders, as withheld the state revenue, under subjection. After some slight resistance the Garrison would capitulate, and the King's troops, having ransacked the country in the neighbourhood and along the line of march, would return to the Capital, bringing with them the Government dues, or so much of them as they were able to extort from the defaulters, who were terribly mal-treated for their temerity, before being released, in order to act as a deterrent to others similarly disposed. It was impossible to

conceive a greater curse to a country than such a body of disorganised and licentious soldiery.

To such an extent had this element of armed independence established itself that, in the year 1849, there were in Oudh 246 forts, or strongholds, mounted with 476 pieces of cannon, all held by landholders, of the first class, chiefly Rajputs. Each fort was surrounded by a moat and a dense fence of living bamboos, through which cannon shot could not penetrate, and men could not enter except by narrow and intricate paths. These fences were too green to be set on fire, and so completely under the range of matchlocks from the fort, that they could not be cut down by a besieging Force.

10. The revenue was collected by *Amils*,* aided by the 100,000 soldiers in the service of Zemindars,† of whom half were in the King's pay. The *Amils* and other public functionaries were men without character, who obtained and retained their places by bribing Court officials. They oppressed the weak by exacting, very often, more than what was due, but those who had forts, or by combination could withstand the *Amils*, made their own arrangements. The revenue was thus gradually diminished. Numerous dacoities (highway robberies), or other acts of violence attended with loss of life, were annually reported, and the reports of hundreds of others that occurred used to be suppressed by the corrupt officials. In short, neither life nor property was safe under this semblance of a Government, and there was no alternative but for the British to take over the administration.

11. Owing to these causes the country was in a state of perpetual unrest, so that it cannot be wondered that the peaceful inhabitants longed for a change. Colonel Sleeman used to be literally besieged along his entire route by the villagers who had some grievance to relate or wrong to be redressed. He gives a pitiful detail of the numerous applicants who crowded to him for help and restitution. Every day, as he travelled throughout

---

* Collectors of revenue.
† Landed proprietors.

the country, scores of petitions were presented to him, "with quivering lip and tearful eye," by persons who had been plundered of all they possessed, or who had their dearest relatives murdered or tortured to death, and their habitations burned to the ground by gangs of ruffians, under landlords of high birth and pretensions, whom they had never wronged or offended. For this misery the native officials of the King of Oudh were answerable, besides the Talukdar,* who not only oppressed the peasant by heavy exactions, but also endeavoured to deprive him of his proprietary right in the soil.

12. Under Native Rule the Talukdars of Oudh were not mere middle-men, employed to collect revenue from cultivators, but heads of powerful clans and representatives of ancient families; they were, in reality, a feudal aristocracy, based upon rights in the soil, which went back to traditional times and were acknowledged by their retainers. At the time of annexation, 23,500 villages, or about two-thirds of the total area of the Province, were in their possession.

13. Colonel Sleeman, † though averse to annexation as a system, stated in his report that, with all his desire to maintain the throne in its integrity, past experience did not permit him to entertain the smallest hope that the King would ever carry out any system of government calculated to ensure the safety and happiness of his subjects. He did not think that, with a due regard to its own character as the Paramount Power in India, and the particular obligation by which it was bound by solemn treaties to the suffering people, the Government could any longer forbear to take over the administration, and to make some suitable provision, in perpetuity, for the King when dethroned.

14. On every side the necessity for interference in the affairs of Oudh was most pressing, but the Marquis of Dalhousie,

---

*The term Talukdar means holder of a Taluka, or collection of villages, farmed out to him by Government, to whom he is responsible for payment of the land revenue assessed.

†Disabled by ill-health, Colonel Sleeman quitted India at the commencement of 1856, and died on his voyage to Europe. He was succeeded at the Lucknow Residency, by General Sir James Outram.

though determined to annex the Province, was compelled to postpone action for the present, being then engrossed by the war with Burma and the preparations for a coming struggle with Persia.

Subsequently, the Governor-General drew up a comprehensive minute in which he denounced the shameful abuse of power that had existed for years in Oudh, and stated that inaction on the part of the British Government could no longer be justified. He, however, thought that the prospects of the people might be improved without resorting to so extreme a measure as the annexation of the territory and the abolition of the throne; hence he proposed that the King should retain the nominal sovereignty, while the entire civil and military administration should pass into the hands of the Company. The Home authorities, however, resolved upon annexation, involving the absolute extinction of Oudh as a Native Government, and the final abrogation of all existing treaties with it, a measure which was at length decreed and announced to all the Empire by a simple Proclamation, dated Fort William, the 11th February, 1856.

15. Prior to announcing the annexation, Lord Dalhousie, still acting with caution in a matter of such moment, had appointed Colonel (afterwards General Sir James) Outram, Resident in Oudh (1855), with instructions to make another thorough inquiry into the condition of the people.* His report was in substance the same as those which had been submitted by his predecessor; and the Indian Government then resolved that this condition of chronic anarchy, which had reduced the people of Oudh to extreme misery, should no longer be permitted to exist.

16. Seeing that it was hopeless to expect reforms from the native ruler, a treaty was proposed to the King, by which the civil and military authority of Oudh would be vested in the British Government solely and for ever, and the title of King of Oudh continued to Wajid Ali and his lawful male heirs; it provided for his being treated with due respect, and, under

---

* Colonel Outram's successor was Mr. Coverly Jackson.

the treaty, he would have retained exclusive jurisdiction within the walls of the palace at Lucknow, except as to the infliction of capital punishment. The King was to receive an allowance of twelve lacs a year for the support of his dignity, besides three lacs for palace guards. His successors in the title were to receive twelve lacs a year, and his collateral relatives were to be provided for separately. He was allowed three days to consider, but refused to sign the proposed treaty, upon which refusal the Government formally annexed the Province and introduced its own system of administration.

17. The Resident then took over the government of the country; and a detailed account is given below of the interview, immediately before this occurred, between him and the King at the Zard Kothi Palace, on the morning of February 4th, 1856:—

"General Outram, accompanied by Captains Hayes and Weston, proceeded at 8 A. M. to visit His Majesty by appointment. The approaches to, and the precincts of, the palace were unusually deserted; the detachments of artillery on duty at the palace, together with the detachments of His Majesty's foot-guards, were unarmed, and saluted without arms; the artillery was dismounted, and not a weapon was to be seen amongst the courtiers and officials present to receive the Resident on his entering the palace. The Resident was received at the usual spot, by His Majesty in person, with the customary honours.

"During the conference, in addition to the Prime Minister (Nawab Ali Naki Khan), His Majesty's brother (Sikandar Hashmat), the Residency Vakil (Munshi-ud-daulah), his Deputy (Sahib-ud-daulah), and the Minister of Finance (Raja Balkishan), were present.

"The Resident, after assuring His Majesty that, from kindly consideration to his feelings, he had been induced to forward, through the Minister, a copy of the Most Noble the Governor-General's letter, two days ago, to afford the King ample time to peruse and reflect on the contents of His Lordship's letter, now felt it his duty, in pursuance of his instructions, to deliver to His Majesty in person the Governor-General's letter in original. His Majesty, after attentively perusing the letter, observed that he had already been made acquainted with its purport and contents, not only by the Minister, but by the copy of the letter which the Resident had been good enough to transmit, and for which the King expressed his obligation. After a brief pause, His Majesty turned towards the Resident, and said: 'Why have I deserved this? What have I committed?' The Resident replied that the reasons which had led to the new policy, were explicitly, clearly and abundantly detailed in His Lordship's letter to His Majesty, and that he was unable to discuss the subject, or to deviate in any way from the tenor of the instructions with which he had been honoured; but the Resident had little doubt that, on mature reflection, the King would readily acquiesce in the proposals made by the British Government. His Majesty should consider how amply and liberally the Government had provided for His Majesty's maintenance. The King's titles, honours, rank and dignity would be scrupulously preserved and transmitted to His Majesty's descendants, in the male issue, in perpetuity. His Majesty's authority would be absolute in his palace and household, always excepting the power of life and death over the King's servants and subjects thereunto appertaining. His Majesty's relatives and confidential servants would likewise be adequately provided for; and the Resident had every reason to hope that His Majesty's good sense would induce him to meet the wishes of Government. The Resident was bound, in the solemn discharge of his duties, to announce to His Majesty that the Treaty of 1801 no longer existed.* The systematic oppression and misrule which had existed in Oudh ever since its ratification, the violation of

---

* "By the Treaty of 1801, The Honourable East India Company engaged to protect the sovereign of Oudh against every foreign and domestic enemy, while the sovereign of Oudh, upon his part, bound himself to establish such a system of administration, to be carried into effect by his own officers, as should be conducive to the prosperity of his subjects and calculated to secure the lives and property of the inhabitants.

"The treaty had been wholly disregarded by every successive ruler of Oudh, and the pledge which was given for the establishment of such a system of administration as should secure the lives and property of the people of Oudh, and be conducive to their prosperity, had, from first to last, been deliberately and systematically violated."

all the solemn obligations which the rulers of Oudh had faithfully bound themselves to perform, as one of the high contracting parties to that Treaty, had necessarily caused its infraction, and rendered it imperative on the British Government to adopt a policy which would secure the lives and properties of His Majesty's suffering subjects. That policy had been commended by the Honourable the Court of Directors; it had been sanctioned and approved of by Her Majesty's Ministers unanimously; and the Most Noble the Governor-General of India had been directed to carry into effect the measures alluded to prior to His Lordship's departure from India. Under these circumstances, the Resident was persuaded that His Majesty would readily acknowledge that the Governor-General had no authority whatever but to give effect to the commands of the Home Government, and with this view had directed that a Treaty should be prepared for submission to His Majesty, which, embracing every suitable, adequate and ample provision for His Majesty's maintenance, and omitting nothing which could in any degree redound to the King's honour, titles and dignity, transferred the administration of the government of Oudh into the hands of the East India Company.

" His Majesty received the treaty with the deepest emotion, and handed it to Saheb-ud-daula, with directions that it should be read out aloud; but that confidential servant of the King, overcome by his feelings, was unable to read but a few lines; on which the King took the Treaty from his hands, and carefully perused each Article.

" His Majesty then gave vent to his feelings in a passionate burst of grief, and exclaimed—

" Treaties are necessary between equals only : who am I now, that the British Government should enter into treaties with me ? For a hundred years this dynasty has flourished in Oudh. It has ever received the favour, the support and protection of the British Government. It has ever attempted faithfully and fully to perform its duties to the British Government. The kingdom is a creation of the British, who are able to make and to unmake, to promote and to degrade. It has merely to issue its commands to ensure their fulfilment: not the slightest attempt will be made to oppose the views and wishes of the British Government: myself and subjects are its servants."

"His Majesty then again spoke of the inutility of a Treaty; he was in no position to sign one. It was useless; his honour and country were gone, he would not trouble Government for any maintenance, but would proceed to England, and throw himself at the foot of the Throne to entreat a reconsideration of the orders passed, and to intercede for mercy. The Resident begged His Majesty to reflect that, unless the King signed the Treaty, he would have no security whatever for his future maintenance, or for that of his family; that the very liberal provision devised by the British Government would evidently be reconsidered, and reduced; that His Majesty would have no guarantee for his future provision, and would have no claim whatever on the generosity of the Government. The Resident's instructions were concise, clear and definitive; the resolution of the Government irrevocable and final; and the Resident entreated the King to consider what evil consequences might alight upon His Majesty and family by the adoption of any ill-judged line of conduct. The Prime Minister, Nawab Ali Naki Khan, warmly seconded and supported the Resident's advice; and protested that he had done everything in his power to induce His Majesty to accede to the wishes of the British Government. Hereupon His Majesty's brother exclaimed that there was no occasion for a Treaty. His Majesty was no longer independent, or in a position to be one of the contracting Powers. His office was gone, and the British Government was all powerful. His Majesty, who was moved to tears, recapitulated the favours which his ancestors had received at the hands of the British Government, and pathetically dwelt upon his helpless position. Uncovering himself, he placed his turban in the hands of the Resident, declaring that now his titles, rank, and position were all gone, it was not for him to sign a treaty or to enter into any negotiation. He was in the hands of the British Government, which had seated His Majesty's grandfather on the throne, and could, at its pleasure, consign him to obscurity.

"The Resident felt himself unable to act in any other way than up to the tenor of his instructions, and assured His Majesty that at the expiration of three days, unless His Majesty acceded to the wishes of the British Government, the Resident would have no alternative but to assume the government of the country.

"After some further conversation, and the expression of the unalterable reluctance of the King to sign the treaty then and there, the Resident intimated that no further delay than the three days could be permitted, and then with the usual ceremonies and honours, took his leave of the King."

18. The King declined to accept the deposition* as a final act. He surrendered his rule to Sir James Outram, and enjoined on all his subjects to pay him due obedience; and then set out for Calcutta, ostensibly *en route* to England to plead his cause before Her Majesty. But he was not permitted to proceed beyond Calcutta, where he settled down in Garden Reach.† A provision of twelve lacs of rupees (£80,000) per annum was made for him (this he formally accepted in October, 1859), and a separate allowance was sanctioned for his collateral relations. When the King's departure from Oudh was decided on, there was a great deal of controversy about the choice of an Agent to act for His Majesty. The King's advisers also immediately set about efforts for his restoration, and shortly after, with this object, the King's brother, H. H. Prince Mirza Sikandar Hashmat Bahadur, accompanied by the ex-King's mother, set out for England on a royal deputation to the Queen, but their mission having failed, they settled in Paris, where they both eventually died.‡

---

* Notice of his deposition was given on the 4th February, 1856, and Wajid Ali Shah ceased to reign from the 7th.

† Garden Reach is one of the suburbs of Calcutta.

‡ The Queen of Oudh went to England in the steamship *Ripon*. She arrived at Southampton on the 20th of August, 1856.

19. A contemporary thus pathetically describes the departure of the ex-King from the capital :—

DEPARTURE OF THE KING FOR CALCUTTA.
Lucknow, the 14th March, 1856.

"The King left his Palace yesterday evening at eight o'clock on his way to Calcutta, whence he wishes to proceed to England. He has arrived this morning at Cawnpore. I was present at the time he came out of the Palace gates, and the scene which I then witnessed will ever be forcibly impressed on my mind. He at first wished to go out by the north gate, but hearing that a crowd of people had collected at the east gate to witness his departure, he changed his mind, and passed through the midst of them, though in a closed carriage, in company with his son and principal wife. The enthusiasm of the people was immense; to me it was surprising, for I believed natives incapable of displaying so much feeling. The air resounded with shouts—*Badshah salamat* (greeting to thee, Oh King ;) *Badshahat phir bani rahe* (May your kingdom again be established!) *Landhan se hukum a jawe*, (May the order arrive from London!) [I suppose to overturn the present state of affairs.] *Badshah salamat, salamat!* was heard everywhere. Then deep curses were imprecated on the heads of the *Firangis*, and I felt anything but comfortable at that time. Indeed, I thought it prudent then to take myself off, for I thought it very possible that I might become a victim to a multitude exasperated against the Europeans. The King's wives, concubines, and female palace attendants crowded into the closed turrets and houses surrounding the enclosure and set up a wail, long and continued, a wail heart-rending in the extreme. All were affected, and tears streamed down many cheeks."

20. The journey to Calcutta took exactly two months, His Majesty spending some time at Cawnpore and Allahabad before he embarked for Calcutta in the Steamer *General MacLeod*, which arrived there, with His Majesty on board, on the 13th May, 1856. For a year after coming to Calcutta the

King lived under no restraint, but the outbreak of the Mutiny in 1857 destroyed the last hope of his being restored to his kingdom. He was then made a State Prisoner* in Fort William† and afterwards provided with the well-known residence at Garden Reach, near Calcutta, where he spent the remainder of his days. Here he maintained a large establishment and lived with some show of regal splendour upon the munificent pension awarded him by Government.

21. After the annexation of the Province affairs wore a serene aspect, which seemed to augur well for the future. The settlement of the country was progressing favourably and the people appeared satisfied with the new arrangements; but this state of tranquillity was not fated to last long, for as the year advanced, elements, though not of immediate danger, manifested themselves. It was suspected that the King's emissaries were actively at work inciting the people to hostility; and none were more inimical to the British at that time than the discharged soldiery of the Native Government, which may be put down at about 60,000. These men fostered the hope that the native *raj* (reign) would be restored, and they were prepared for any enterprise having for its object the attainment of this cherished wish. These were the characters let loose upon Oudh who scattered the seed of disaffection towards the new Government throughout the land, and doubtless swelled the ranks of the mutineers when the rebellion broke out.

22. At that time Lucknow was one of the most flourishing cities in India. The central part was very densely populated, and the scenes in the principal streets were most lively. Mounted cavaliers, clothed in Cashmere stuffs elaborately embroidered with gold, and preceded by attendants carrying gold and silver mounted sticks, swords, spears and wands of office, passed to and fro in a continuous stream. Certain dignitaries, seated in open palanquins (a covered litter suspended from poles by which it is borne on the shoulders of men), richly painted and gilded,

---
* The King was liberated on 9th July, 1859.
† The Fort was built by the English in 1696, and was named after the reigning English sovereign, William III.

mingled in the throng, followed by their armed retainers and with, occasionally, a mounted escort, their horses richly caparisoned in red and green trappings: others, perched aloft on the backs of elephants, were seated in gracefully carved *haudahs** which were, in some instances, of silver. The attendants of the more wealthy inhabitants included the various races from all parts of India; and the effect produced by their diversified costumes was extremely picturesque.

23. The kingdom of Oudh, as has been shown, was annexed in February, 1856; and British administration was scarcely established, and the chaos of the past reduced to order, when the revolt of the Native Army arrested progress, and ultimately plunged the country into a worse condition than it was before.

The people were once more incited to lawlessness, and by June 1857 all authority was lost in the Province. In consequence of the impending danger, the military were ordered to garrison the Residency, the rendezvous selected for all non-combatants loyal to the British cause, who flocked thither and so materially aided in the defence of the place that it now stands a monument of England's supremacy in the East!

The Right Hon'ble the Earl of Canning, G.C.B., G.C.S.I., Governor-General of India, expressed his admiration of the defence of the Residency in the following words:—

"There does not stand recorded in the annals of war an achievement more truly heroic than the defence of the Residency at Lucknow.

"There were events that made a deeper impression on the minds of the English public; military exploits more grand and comprehensive; episodes more fatal, more harrowing; trains of operation in which well-known heroic names more frequently found place—but there was nothing in the whole history of the Indian Mutiny more admirable or worthy of study than the defence of Lucknow by Brigadier Inglis and the British who

---

° A *haudah* resembles a sedan chair placed on the back of an elephant.

were shut up with him in the Residency. Such triumph over difficulties has not often been placed upon record. Nothing but the most resolute determination, the most complete soldierly obedience, the most untiring watchfulness, the most gentle care of those who from sex or age were unable to defend themselves, the most thorough reliance on himself and on those around him could have enabled that gallant officer to bear up against the overwhelming difficulties which pressed upon him throughout the siege. He occupied one corner of an enormous city, every other part of which was swarming with deadly enemies. No companion could leave him, without danger of instant death at the hands of the rebel sepoys and the Lucknow rabble; no friend could succour him, seeing that anything less than a considerable military force would have been cut off ere it reached the gates of the Residency; no food or drink, no medicines or comforts, no clothing, no ammunition, in addition to that which was actually within the place at the beginning of July, could be brought in. Great beyond expression were the responsibilities and anxieties of one placed in command during eighty-seven of such days—but there was also a moral grandeur in the situation, never to be forgotten."

CHAPTER II.

REMINISCENCES OF THE INVESTMENT OF THE RESIDENCY.

1. In January, 1852, when I was twelve years of age, I joined La Martiniere College as a student, and at the time of the outbreak in 1857, I was one of the senior boys of the College, to the staff of which institution my parents belonged: hence I became pretty well conversant with passing events. The doubts that began to arise in the minds of the people at this station Lucknow respecting the allegiance of the native troops in Oudh and elsewhere, were confirmed by the newspapers, from which we learnt of the general resistance made by the sepoys (native soldiers) to the use of the greased cartridge.

"This was the precursor of a storm which had loomed in the horizon ever since the beginning of the year 1857—a storm which was so soon to desolate the fair fields of Upper India. This mighty tempest, raised by the millions of India, was to sweep irresistibly the handful of European intruders who lay supinely with full confidence in the conquered nation.* They needed a living agency. This was essential and one, too, where constant movement would occasion no surprise; but just such emissaries as they required were ready to hand in the *faqirs*, or wandering saints of Hindustan. No account of India, or of the Sepoy Mutiny,* would be complete which did not include a proper description of these *faqirs*. They are the saints of the Mahomedan and Hindu systems. These holy men, with their dishevelled hair, naked bodies, and painted breasts and foreheads, are constantly roving over the country, visiting shrines, making pilgrimages, and performing religious services

---

* Except in Oudh, the rising was strictly a Mutiny, not a rebellion, *i. e.*, it was an insurrection of traitorous soldiers of the Native Bengal Army, and was rarely joined in by any other part of the population, except through fear or under compulsion.

for their disciples. The Sepoys greatly honored and liberally patronized these spiritual guides."*

"Then emissaries of evil, on the stage appear,
   In garb of *goshain*, mendicant, or *faqir*.
"These wolves in sheep's clothing, wander far and near,
   In sepoy lines they find a willing ear.
"In swine and kine, a subject fit they find,
   To fire the Moslem, or the Hindu mind.
"The fat of pigs, ground bones of cows, they are told,
   With "*ghee*" and "*atta*" are in the market sold.
"Then as if to make assurance doubly sure,
   They ask the sepoy is your "*kartus*" as before?
"Suspicion roused, the sepoys find it's true,
   The cartridge issued, is not what they knew.
"Their sense of seeing sure they cannot doubt,
   This is with "*grease*" the other was without!
"They fancy then the problem solved at last,
   'Tis but a device, to take away their caste!
"When once convinced, they murmur, then refuse,
   The obnoxious cartridge, now they will not use!"

2. The mutinous 19th and 34th Native Infantry had for this reason been disbanded at Barrackpur, a Military Cantonment, about 16 miles from Calcutta; and, since many of the men of this Regiment belonged to Oudh, whence the largest proportion of soldiers for the Native Army was then drawn, it was apprehended that on their return to the Province, they would be the first to disseminate disaffection throughout the land.†

"An ill-judged policy at this juncture then,
   Let loose on India twice ten hundred men.
"These lawless hordes, from martial discipline exempt,
   Like fallen Lucifer, their faithful brethren tempt.
"Throughout the land, these troubled spirits went,
   Spreading apace the seeds of discontent."

---

* In 1856 the Russian war was over, and the Enfield (muzzle loading) Rifle, which had been used with such success in the Crimea, was introduced into the Indian Army, of which the cartridges had to be greased before they were put into the rifle to load it; and the sepoys were falsely told by these wicked men that the cartridges had been greased with the fat of pigs and cows, so as to defile both the Musalmans and Hindus.

† It is a significant fact that of 200,000 sepoys in the British Army at the time of the outbreak 40,000 were from Oudh alone.

At this time the native troops occupied various positions in Lucknow, and were a source of great anxiety to the Officers of Government and all loyal British subjects, who regarded them with evident distrust.

3. We were aware that the feeling of the native troops was far from good at Meerut, where a School of Musketry had been formed for the instruction of the sepoys in the use of the Enfield Rifle.* We had heard of the disturbances which had broken out at various stations in Bengal immediately after those at Barrackpur and Berhampur had been suppressed. Rumours of incendiary fires at Agra, which signalled the coming troubles, had reached us and helped to agitate considerably the minds of the Europeans at Lucknow—the capital of a deposed King—where with its multitude of armed inhabitants and discharged soldiery of the Native Government, the disaffection, at this time —the beginning of May, 1857—was very alarming!

That the inhabitants of Lucknow would rise against us was a very probable event, notwithstanding the false reports of their universal contentment. We had done very little to deserve their love and much to merit their detestation. Thousands of nobles, gentlemen and officials, who during the King's time had held lucrative appointments, were now in penury and want, and their myriads of retainers and servants thrown out of employ, of course. Then the innumerable vagabonds and beggars, who under the Native Rule infested the city and found bread in it, were starving during British administration.

The native merchants and bankers who, while Wajid Ali was on the throne, made large profits from supplying the luxurious wants of the King, his courtiers, and the wealthy ladies of the thronged harems, found no sale for their goods; and the people in general, and especially the poor, were dissatisfied because they were taxed directly and indirectly in every way.

The tax upon opium especially caused immense discontent throughout the country, but particularly in the city. Opium

---

* Three musketry schools were established in India for teaching the sepoys the use of the new Rifle; one school was established at Dum-Dum another at Meerut, and the third at Sialkot.

was an article as extensively used in Lucknow as in China, and the sudden deprivation of this drug was most severe upon the opium-eaters.

Then there were fanatics in the city who made use of religious enthusiasm to influence the minds of their co-religionists still more against us. It was these "idle hands" that Satan employed to do much of the mischief wrought during the fearful rebellion of 1857, an event which consummated their own ruin, and sent scores of them to the gallows.

4. In consequence of information telegraphed from Calcutta, Raja Man Singh, an influential landed proprietor in the Fyzabad District, was arrested by order of the Chief Commissioner, and placed in confinement in his fort at Shahganj. Sending for the British authorities, the Raja warned them that the troops would rise, and offered, if released, to give the Europeans shelter in his fort. Seeing the critical state of things, Colonel Goldney released him and Man Singh at once commenced to put the fort of Shahganj in order and raise levies. Matters looking very ominous at Fyzabad, the civilians sent their families to Shahganj, where they were sheltered for a few days, when Man Singh,* either from zeal, or pretended fear of the mutineers, desired them to depart. He, however, provided boats for them on the Gogra, to which they were escorted by night, and a party of Man Singh's levies accompanied them some way on their journey. They all reached the station of Dinapur in safety.

"Though loyalty is a magnificent virtue, it is usually rendered by untutored people to those who have the power to coerce and enforce it. The incidence of events during the mutiny generated in the native mind a great question as to which Cæsar they should render tribute. This thought was paramount throughout a considerable period of the war, and so long as the success of British arms was in doubt, the natives as a mass were alternately ready to be controlled or to jib,

---

* The unveiling of the statue of the late Maharaja Sir Man Singh, K.C.S.I., by Sir James Digges LaTouche, K.C.S.I., Lieutenant-Governor, United Provinces of Agra and Oudh, took place on the 13th August, 1902, at the Kaisarbagh Baradari.

SIR HENRY LAWRENCE, K. C. B.

according to the turn of events. For this fluctuation they cannot be altogether blamed. For their wise comprehension in being finally on the winning side, without having compromised themselves, they may be praised to the full."— *Indian Daily Telegraph.*

5. Most fortunately for us, at this juncture, there was one equal to the occasion at the Capital. I allude to the late Sir Henry Lawrence, who arrived at Lucknow on the 20th of March, 1857. Sir Henry was then only 50 years of age, but he looked an old man, for his face bore traces of many years of toil beneath an Indian sun, and the still deeper marks of a never-ending conflict with self. His eyes, over-hung by massive craggy brows, looked out with an expression in which melancholy was strangely blended with humour; his thin wasted cheeks were furrowed, and this, with a long scanty beard, added to his care-worn look of age. On noticing the state of affairs, Sir Henry actively set about making preparations for the defence of Lucknow, as he was not the man to be an idle spectator of the movements among the native troops then ripe for rebellion.

6. The first thing Sir Henry did was to apply by telegraph to Calcutta, the seat of Government, for unlimited power in the Province of Oudh, of which he was Chief Commissioner; and it was unhesitatingly conferred on him by the Governor-General, Lord Canning, who knew that Sir Henry was not likely to abuse it. This was a step in the right direction, leaving the Chief Commissioner unfettered to cope with any emergency that might arise, as he thought proper, without referring to Head-Quarters, a reference which would otherwise have been necessary.

7. The native regiments at Lucknow were all the while most anxious for some pretext upon which to break out; and an excuse was soon found in the following incident, by which the men tried to make out that the Government intended to destroy their caste and religion. When a feeling of discontent has once taken root, small matters, though not tending to the injury of the discontented, are readily magnified.

8. Dr. Wells, of the 48th Native Infantry Regiment, stationed at Mariaon Cantonments,* on the occasion of one of his visits to the regimental hospital, is stated to have incautiously applied to his mouth a bottle of medicine with a view to testing its contents. There is good reason for believing that he only smelt the bottle. Anyhow this act was construed into a deliberate attempt to break the caste of the men. The consequence was an outcry among them, and a refusal to touch any of the medicines prescribed for them. A few nights after the Doctor's bungalow was fired, but he fortunately escaped unhurt with the loss of his property only. It was suspected that the incendiaries were the sepoys of his own regiment, but as no proof could be obtained, punishment could not be inflicted.

9. It now became apparent that the regiment was disaffected. The men were suspected of intriguing with the relatives of the ex-King residing in the city, and tampering with men of the military police, but the officers of the regiment refused to credit these reports and rejected all suspicion of the disaffection of their men. It seems strange on looking back that these many warnings should have passed unheeded and there should have been no suspicion amongst the officers serving with native regiments that discontent was universal amongst the sepoys, and that a mutiny of the whole Bengal Army was imminent. But at that time the reliance in the fidelity of the native troops was unbounded, and officers believed implicitly in the contentment and loyalty of their men. Their faith in them was extraordinary. Even after half the native army had mutinied, and many of the officers had been murdered, those belonging to the remaining regiments could not believe that their own particular men could be guilty of treachery. Seeing this state of things, Sir Henry vigorously applied himself to concentrate his military resources, which, at the time of the first occupation of the Province by the British, had to be located in buildings that were found the best available for the accommodation of troops; but, unfortunately, these places were widely apart and inconveniently situated.

---

* The old British Military Cantonment, called by the natives Mariaon was built in the reign of Nawab Sadat Ali Khan (1789-1814).

10. The Chief Commissioner's head-quarters were at the Residency. About the Residency were closely clustered several buildings which formed the residences of, and afforded accommodation for, the offices of the Judicial and Financial Commissioners, the Civil Surgeon, and others. The Treasury was also located here, and a Company of the 48th Native Infantry guarded it and the Residency. The sepoys occupied a curved line of buildings outside the principal gate leading to the Residency, to which the name of "Baillie Guard" was given.* About a mile and a half eastward was placed the only European Infantry in Oudh, Her Majesty's 32nd Regiment.

11. The 32nd Regiment, under command of Lieutenant-Colonel Inglis, marched into Lucknow on 27th December, 1856, relieving H. M.'s 52nd, under Lieutenant-Colonel Campbell, the first British Regiment to garrison Lucknow after the annexation of Oudh.† At that time Mr. Coverly Jackson was Chief Commissioner. He was succeeded by Sir Henry Lawrence. Mr. Gubbins was Financial Commissioner, Mr. Ommaney, Judicial Commissioner, Major Banks, Commissioner, Mr. Martin, Deputy Commissioner, Captain Carnegie, City Magistrate, and Doctor Fayrer, Residency Surgeon.

The men of the 32nd Regiment occupied the Chaupar Stables (now known as *Lawrence Terrace*) as their barracks. The officers were scattered about the station; some occupied the houses along the road leading directly from Hazratganj towards La Martiniere. The rest lived in apartments of the Chattar Manzil Palace and Khursheid Manzil, which last was the Officers' Mess-house.

---

* When Nawab Asuf-ud-daulá, after transferring the seat of Government from Fyzabad to Lucknow (1775) resided in his palace, the Daulat Khana, the Resident was accommodated in one of the buildings attached to it, but when Sádat Ali Khan made the Farhat Bakhsh his own dwelling-place, he built the Residency close to it. At first no military guard was attached to the Residency, but when Colonel Baillie was Resident in Oudh, a guard of honor was appointed, and a barrack built for it by Sádat Ali, close to the gate of the Residency enclosure, which thus obtained its world-famed name of the "Baillie Guard," the name by which the natives called our intrenchment.

† One Company of the 32nd, under Captain Moore, principally married men, with their wives and children, a few of the 84th, and some Artillery, all under the command of Sir Hugh Wheeler, were massacred at Cawnpore.

12. East of the Mess-house and close to the river, is the Kadam Rasul, an old tomb built on high ground which was converted into a powder-magazine and was protected by a native guard. In this neighbourhood were the lines of the 3rd Regiment Military Police, which furnished all the Civil guards at Lucknow. The Tarawali Kothi, or Observatory, now the Bank of Bengal, was occupied by the Civil Courts, and other buildings in the neighbourhood by the European officials.

13. About one mile from the Residency, up-stream, are the Daulat-khana and Shish Mahal, which in 1775 formed the palace of King Asuf-ud-daula. Two miles higher up is the Musa Bagh Palace, where the 4th and 7th Regiments of Oudh Infantry were stationed. The head-quarters of Brigadier Gray, who commanded the Oudh Irregular Force, were in the Daulat-khana. In the Shish Mahal was the Magazine, where a considerable number of stand-of-arms, as well as 200 unmounted guns belonging to the Native Government, were deposited. Many of the guns were of large calibre, cast for the Oudh Government by General Claude Martin.

14. Before the siege began these were all brought in and laid out on the low ground close to the Redan Battery.* This battery was by far the best we had in the line of defences. It was defended by soldiers of the 32nd Regiment, under the command of Lieutenant Sam Lawrence. It mounted two 18-pounders and a 9-pounder, which commanded the road up to the Iron Bridge.

Such was the disposition of troops on the south-side of the river.

15. Three miles north of the Residency, across the river, was the old Cantonment of Mariaon. Here the officers resided in thatched bungalows, while the European and Native troops occupied thatched barracks. At a further distance of a mile was the new Cantonment at Mudkipur, where the 7th Regiment Native Cavalry, was stationed, the 2nd Regiment of O. I. Cavalry

---

* On that memorable day, the 20th July, the enemy advanced within 25 paces of this battery, but was repulsed with heavy loss.

being also located on the left bank of the Gumti, on the site now occupied by the Upper India Couper Paper Mills.

The whole Force in Mariaon and Mudkipur Cantonments is given below:—

European Artillery	... 1 light horse battery.
Regular Native Artillery	... 1 „ bullock „
Oudh Irregular „	... 2 „ horse batteries.
Regular Native Cavalry	... 1 regiment.
„ „ Infantry	... 3 regiments, *viz.*, the 13th, 48th and 71st.

16. This faulty and irregular distribution of troops was chiefly due to the fact, as before stated, that when Oudh was annexed, barracks had not been built; and as the near approach of the annual rains made the speedy construction of new buildings impossible, the places found most capable of adaptation to military requirements had been occupied. Such was the state of things at the beginning of May, 1857. At this period the condition of the province was comparatively tranquil.

17. On the 3rd May the mutiny of the 7th Oudh Irregular Infantry was the first startling event.[*] This regiment was stationed at Musa Bagh, a garden residence of one of the late King's wives, which formed one of the prettiest suburban retreats of King Asuf-ud-daula. The men refused to use their cartridges on the plea that they had been tampered with. Their officers found it necessary to assemble the men, in order to point out to them the absurdity of the fears they entertained for their religion. They used every effort to convince the incredulous sepoys of the falsity of the pretences by which their religious prejudices had been aroused, and told them that if they still refused to trust the Government, and allowed suspicion to take root in their minds and to grow into disaffection, insubordination and mutiny, their punishment would be sharp and certain. But the passions of the men had been roused;

---

[*] The Mutiny broke out in Lucknow on 30th May; Bareilly, 31st; Sitapur, 3rd June; Mullaon, 4th, Muhamdi and Fyzabad, 8th; Sultanpur and Daryabad, 9th; Salon, Secrora, and Gouda, on 10th June, 1857.

their feelings had been so excited that they could no longer control them; they were beyond the power of reason; they felt satisfied that their caste was to be taken by means of cartridges, and their excitement persuaded them that these were the fatal messengers.

18. All attempts to restore the regiment to obedience having failed, Sir Henry Lawrence resolved to disarm them. This was necessary, for the mutineers lost no time in seeking the aid of the 48th Native Infantry in Cantonments. A seditious letter addressed to that regiment, was intercepted and delivered to the Commanding Officer, Lieutenant-Colonel Palmer. It ran: "We are ready to obey the directions of our brothers of the 48th in the matter of the cartridges, and to resist either actively or passively." Without any delay the European Infantry and Artillery, two regiments of Native Infantry, and the 7th Native Light Cavalry, were ordered to proceed to the lines of the mutineers, distant about 7 miles from Mariaon Cantonment. Darkness had set in, but so prompt had been the movement that the 7th O. I. Infantry were taken by surprise. They were instantly ordered to form up in front of their lines. In the presence of a force so imposing they were overawed into obedience. Just then the Artillery portfires* having been lighted, a sudden panic seized the men. Mad with terror, they rushed frantically away. The ringleaders and most of their followers, however, were secured and put in irons pending trial. On the following day the prisoners were tried and discharged. Sir Henry Lawrence publicly rewarded those sepoys of the 48th Regiment who had not only resisted the temptation to mutiny, but had loyally apprised their superior officer of the attempt by surrendering the letter addressed to the regiment by the men of the 7th O. I. Infantry. Having thus vigorously put down the first overtact of mutiny, Sir Henry Lawrence applied himself to conciliate the native soldiery by every means in his power.

---

* Portfire is a composition of nitre, sulphur, and mealed powder, drive into a case of strong paper, cloth, and the like, used for firing cannon, now superseded by the friction tube.

19. In the yearly part of May the news of the mutiny of the native regiments at Meerut, and the massacre of Christian people in several stations in Upper India, were current among the boys in the College. This intelligence was indeed alarming; we all felt that a great calamity was at hand, in which Oudh was almost sure to suffer. Sir Henry now began to consider what was to be done in the event of an insurrection, as he was not certain what effect the intelligence would have on the minds of the native community when it became known.

20. The Treasury in the Residency, containing several lacs of rupees, besides a large amount deposited in Company's paper, was up to this time guarded by a company of sepoys of the 48th Native Infantry. On intelligence being received of the seizure of the city of Delhi with its Treasury and Magazine, and of the revolt of all the troops at that station, it appeared to Sir Henry that the time had arrived for taking effective measures to protect the Residency and the treasure.

Accordingly, on the 17th May, a company of H. M.'s 32nd Regiment and four guns were ordered into the Residency. The rest of the regiment was removed from the Chaupar Stables into the Cantonments of Mariaon. The bridge of boats was moved nearer to the Residency and brought under control, whilst a selected body of sepoys was detached to occupy the Machhi Bhawan. The Civil Lines were thus left unprotected, consequently the European residents in the vicinity removed their families into the Residency.

21. The removal of the European Regiment to Mariaon Cantonment was considered necessary as a check to the native troops there, and also with a view to prevent any intrigues between the sepoys and the disaffected in the city of Lucknow, who were not considered likely to rise in a body unless they were backed up by the native soldiery. The Native Infantry, Cavalry, and Artillery were then located in Cantonments. These were kept in check by the 32nd Regiment and European Artillery, so that they could not effect a junction with the city people without first hazarding a battle. This they were loath to do.

22. Sir Henry made the best possible distribution of the few reliable men under his command, completing his arrangements with that rapidity and energy which always distinguished him. He provided not only for the protection and the fortification of the Residency and Machhi Bhawan, but also of the Mariaon Cantonment.

23. We still continued to occupy La Martinìere, and, in consequence of the impending danger, our active and energetic Principal, Mr. George Schilling,* determined to do all in his power for the preservation of the youths entrusted to his charge. Considerable stores of wheat, *dal*, † rice, *ghee*, ‡ &c., were collected by my father, under the orders of the Principal, and placed in the small rooms situated above the second-floor of the central building, which was then, and is now, used as the principal dormitory. Among these stores were a large number of earthen vessels filled with water in case of emergency. The frequent bursting of these, and the consequent unwelcome midnight-baths, were the first tastes we had of the effects of the mutiny. The centre building was barricaded with bricks, sand bags, boxes of old books and crockery. Although it would appear ludicrous to suppose that this means of defence would have resisted the action of Artillery, yet it would have proved rather a hard matter to obtain admission to any of the upper floors as the staircases leading to them were protected by solid iron doors, which in themselves were impregnable. Perhaps it is not generally known that this castellated mansion is well adapted to sustain a siege. With

---

* Among the schemes for the pacification and civilization of Oudh in 1858-59, it was proposed to establish an English landed aristocracy. When this singularly romantic and quixotic plan was determined on, Lord Canning was on a visit to Lucknow. Mr. Schilling happened to call on the Viceroy, who, struck with his straightforward carriage, and remembering his gallant conduct during the siege, said to Sir R. Montgomery, " Why should not we make Mr. Schilling a Talukdar ?" Thus it came to pass that the Principal of La Martiniere College became a Noble of Oudh. The estate which was given to him was worth about £30,000 (4½ lacs of rupees) ; the right of sale was eventually included, and on the proceeds thereof he lived happily and much respected in Upper Norwood, England, where he died in 1896.

† Split pulse.

‡ Clarified butter.

Mr. George Schilling.

all the arrangements we made for sustaining a defence, it was not decreed that such a body of defenders, many lads under twelve years of age, would be called upon to fight, and it was just as well, otherwise there would have been a sad tale to tell. The Artillery that we had at our disposal consisted of a few gingals* mounted on the bastions. The small arms consisted of the now obsolete flint musket, the effective force of which was uncertain and the explosive force of flint, when struck sharply on steel, was doubtful. Irrespective of these means of defence we had bricks and stones accumulated on the first story, to throw down on the enemy should they approach near enough to try and effect an entrance. The wings continued to be used as class-rooms, but the boys were instructed to make for the centre building as soon as they heard the sound of the alarm-bell. This bell—which is still to be seen in the vaults of Constantia, and which was the hour-bell of the colossal clock placed in the north turret by the benevolent founder, General Claude Martin†—was put under the charge of the boy, who, for the time being, acted as look-out. As might be expected, the false alarms were neither few nor far between, and yet were never without some supposed justification. At one time a rabble of grass-cutters' tats was mistaken for a regiment of mutinous *sawars*, and, on another occasion, a dust-storm was supposed to be the forerunner of a hostile attack.

24. Sir Henry Lawrence's next move was to decide upon a place in which he could concentrate his ammunition and military stores, and which could be utilized as a place of refuge in case of attack. For this purpose the Machhi Bhawan, a castellated structure, north-west of the Residency, formerly inhabited by the dependants of the King of Oudh, was selected. The repairs of the place were begun at once and the adjacent native buildings were ordered to be razed. As soon as it was determined to convert the Machhi Bhawan into a fortification, the magazine and stores from the Shish Mahal and Kadam

---

* A light gun mounted on a carriage so as to be carried easily by men or animals.

† A short biography of this public benefactor will be found in Appendix E.

Rasul were removed into it. The Oudh Irregular Light Horse Battery was also ordered there from Mariaon Cantonment and served to augment the garrison. Some defensive works were likewise begun at the Residency, but they were slight, and were confined to the most exposed positions, and chiefly intended as a protection against any sudden rising of the city people. At the time of the mutiny the Chief Military Officer in Oudh was Brigadier Handscomb, who was subordinate to Sir Hugh Massey Wheeler,* Major-General, Commanding the Cawnpore Division.

25. After the suppression of the Mutiny of the 7th Oudh Irregular Infantry, Sir Henry Lawrence was invested with full military powers, and the rank of Brigadier-General was conferred upon him. From the 20th May he assumed command of all the British troops in Oudh. Telegraphic communication was not up to this time interrupted, and messages were constantly passing and repassing between Sir Henry and the authorities in the N.-W. Provinces. The accounts received from Agra were unfavourable; the natives in the district were reported to have thrown off all Civil authority. The horrible outrages committed by the inhabitants of some of the largest cities upon defenceless women and children, were not, however, shared in by the masses of the citizens, but were the work of *badmashes*, or loose characters, who abound in all large native towns. These revel in a time of riot or disorder, and it was not surprising that, as soon as Civil power was at an end, we should have suffered so severely at their hands.

26. There were others who strove to stem the torrent of sedition and violence in trying to preserve order among the populace. They were men of influence and character, whose efforts in this direction were not actuated by avarice or ambition. But beyond their own family circle and

---

* Sir Hugh Wheeler was, with others, treacherously massacred at Cawnpore on the 27th June, 1857, but 210 women and children of his party were reserved for future destruction. On the 15th July, the date of the defeat of the insurgents by Sir H. Havelock's small army, the Nana Saheb resolved to wreak his vengeance on the helpless women and children in his power, and they were then ruthlessly butchered by his order.

dependants, their counsels and warnings were unheeded—in fact despised—and rapine and murder took place in the day in the streets of Lucknow. The rabble seized on opulent men and kept them under restraint until such time as they were ransomed by their friends.

27. The strong Brigade of native troops, consisting of the 1st, 53rd and 56th Bengal Native Infantry, with the 2nd Light Cavalry, at Cawnpore, were also reported to be disaffected. Subsequently, on 3rd June, these four regiments mutinied; and shortly afterwards, on the 9th June, General Wheeler's urgent application to Sir Henry for aid was received. But as the provisional council, acting temporarily for Sir Henry Lawrence, whose health had just then given way, held that they could not spare a man from the Machhi Bhawan, or the Residency, it was mournfully but unanimously decided that aid could not be rendered.

28. The Mahomedan festival of the *Id-ul-zuha*** fell on the 24th May, and it was expected that an outbreak would take place on that day, when they sacrifice many cattle. It was thought that, inflamed by the sight of blood, they might now attempt an onslaught on all Europeans and Christians to add to the hecatomb. Nothing, however, occurred and the festival passed off without any disturbance, although there were abundant symptoms of ill-feeling among the populace, leading to the belief that a mutiny could not long be averted. It was,

---

* This festival is intended to commemorate the sacrifice by Abraham of a ram, which, by the interposition of Providence, was provided for him as a substitute for his son Isaac (they believe it to have been Ishmael) whom he was about to immolate at God's command, for which he became the father of a great nation—the now despised Jews, also the Arabs who trace their descent to Ishmael (the son of the bondwoman by the Patriarch) whom they regard as their great progenitor. Mina, situated on an elevated spot six miles east of Mecca, is an immured oratory containing a small slab dissevered. Mahomedans believe this to be the veritable spot where Abraham offered up his sacrifice, and that the stone was broken through the violence of the blow. It is a significant fact, however, that in no other place within the precincts of Mecca is it considered lawful to offer up sacrifices. The number of animals slaughtered there on the *Bakr-Id* Festival (the 10th of Zilhijja) is about 70,000.

Mecca is the centre of Islam, and Medina the adopted home of the Prophet, where he is buried. These two places are the resort of hundreds of thousands of pilgrims from all parts of Asia and Africa.

therefore, thought necessary that the ladies residing at Mariaon should be removed into the Residency. Accordingly, on the 25th May, they all came in, and were accommodated in the houses of those officers who were residing within the intrenchment.

29. Up to this time no further act of mutiny had been committed at Lucknow, and Sir Henry clung to the hope of averting the impending storm by conciliation, and thought that the offer of increased pay might keep the native soldiery faithful; but this idea was abandoned, as it was afterwards considered that the offer to increase the pay of the native regiments would be attributed to fear, and that the time, when a conciliatory policy might have proved successful, had gone by. No man in India, perhaps, viewed the approaching storm with clearer eyes than Sir Henry Lawrence, and no cooler head and readier hand than his surveyed its progress. The garrison of Lucknow would surely have suffered but for his foresight and determination.

30. Just before the outbreak a most absurd rumour was circulated in the city of Lucknow and believed in, to the effect that the authorities had procured a great quantity of bone dust to mix with the flour and confectionery sold in the bazar, with the intention of destroying the castes of the populace. This, of course, caused great excitement, notwithstanding that every effort was made by the Government to prove the falsity of such a report. Though all accounts which were received from native sources described the inhabitants of Lucknow as, in the main, well affected towards us, yet there was another class in Oudh who were undoubtedly hostile to the British rule, and who were much to be feared, *viz.*, the discharged soldiery of the Native Government. Of these there could not have been less than about 60,000 when Oudh was annexed, as already stated.

31. The majority of the Princes and Chiefs of India displayed throughout this perilous time, a noble spirit of fidelity to the British Government, in many cases arming their retainers and giving every assistance to the authorities in resisting the outrages of the mutineers; the most prominent

amongst these loyal Chiefs were the Maharaja Scindia of Gwalior, the Maharaja of Jaipur, those of Kapurthala, Patiala, and many other great Sikh Rajas and Sardars. The chief leaders of the mutinous soldiers, who instigated them to commit so many atrocities, were those who hoped to gain by the anarchy and disorder which would follow the subversion of the British Power; amongst these the most active were the miscreant Dhundu Pant (called the Nana Saheb), the adopted son of Baji Rao, the last Peshwa of Poona, afterwards infamous as the author of the Cawnpore Massacre, who hoped to regain the former power of the Maharattas; whilst the old King of Delhi and his sons entertained a foolish hope of being able to restore the glories of the Moghal dynasty.

32. At the beginning of 1857 the number of European troops in Bengal and the North-Western Provinces, scattered amongst a population of about fifty millions, is stated not to have exceeded 5,000, and nearly all the treasuries and arsenals were without the protection of Europeans. The European Force was very unequally distributed, a preponderating number being employed in garrisoning newly acquired territories. When the mutiny broke out Lord Canning* found that for the 750 miles between Calcutta and Agra there was only a single European regiment, stationed about half-way, at Dinapur.

33. This numerical disproportion had occasioned anxiety and the subject was brought before the Home Government, and only to the extent of three regiments was granted in 1853. Under the pressure of the Crimean war two regiments from India had been demanded, which provoked a vehement protest from the Governor-General. Despite this protest, two European regiments were transferred in 1854. They were never replaced; and when the mutiny broke out, another important fraction of the European Force was engaged in the Persian expedition.

One of Lord Dalhousie's last acts in India had been to lay on his Council table a series of Minutes, the general purport of

---

* Lord Canning succeeded Lord Dalhousie in 1856.

which was a reduction of sepoy regiments, an increase of European regiments, and of the European Officers with native regiments.

The warning was unheeded. The subject dropped out of notice; and the outbreak of 1857 found the Government with an European Force wholly inadequate to meet the barest requirements of the situation.

34. In a lecture which General Lord Roberts recently gave at meetings of the Royal Scottish Geographical Society in Edinburgh, Glasgow and Dundee, His Lordship stated that in his opinion the mutiny was mainly due to the following causes:—

(1) "The preponderance of native compared with British troops in India, the numbers in 1857 being 230,000 of the former against 34,000 of the latter.

(2) "The doubt raised in the minds of the native soldiers as to the invincibility and relative superiority of their British comrades by events which occurred during the first Afghan war, terminating in the disastrous retreat from Kabul in the winter of 1841-42.

(3) "The manner in which the sepoys had been pampered by their Officers and the Civil Government, until they began to think that they were the masters rather than the servants of the ruling Power.

(4) "The excessive age of the general staff and regimental officers of the Indian army, due to their promotion under a strict system of seniority, without any age limits for the several ranks.

(5) "The want of 'go' in the majority of the regiments owing to the system under which the more active and enterprising officers were taken away from their own corps for the more attractive and better paid duties appertaining to the irregular service and to Political and Civil employ.

(6) "The various annexations which had taken place during the second quarter of the present century, and measures of administrative reform, such as the introduction of railways

telegraphs, and other civilizing agencies, had produced feeling of alarm and unrest in the ignorant native mind, and had thus prepared the way for the mutiny. The issue of Enfield cartridges, alleged to be greased with a mixture of cow's fat and lard, the one being as obnoxious to the Hindu as the other is to the Musalman was, I believe, the spark which ignited the smouldering feeling of discontent."

35. The annexation of Oudh was said to be the main cause of the mutiny in this Province, and not, as some regarded it, a religious outbreak of the soldiery caused by our interference with their caste prejudices and religion. No doubt the minds of the natives had been for some time alarmed on the subjects of caste and religion. But although their religious fears might have been excited, and the native soldiery might have been discontented and inclined to mutiny, yet had there been a sufficient number of British regiments in the country, the sepoys would never have dared to break into insurrection.

36. While the impending danger was treated with indifference in Calcutta, Lord Elphinstone—the Governor of Bombay—fortunately for the interests of India, was fully alive to the magnitude of the crisis. Before the outbreak at Meerut he sent a pressing request to Sir James Outram to send back all the European troops from Persia without any delay, peace having been concluded with that country. His letter was accompanied by a communication from the Governor-General authorising Sir James to use his own discretion in the matter; and he determined, at once, to send back every European regiment, with the exception of the Artillery, retaining the native troops till the treaty was ratified and Herat evacuated.

37. At the time of the outbreak, India was so denuded of European troops that the entire power was left in the hands of the natives, who, seeing but a handful of Europeans opposed to them, considered themselves sure of success, and organized this vast conspiracy, which was to extinguish the British rule and race in India by **one general massacre** To this idea has been chiefly attributed the outbreak of the mutiny in India. Indeed, it would be difficult to find, in the history of any

nation, a similar instance of the revolt of an army of a hundred thousand men against a well-established Government, whose only fault was that of having manifested too great a deference to their prejudices and humours. There is no previous example of an army thus proclaiming a war of extermination against its indulgent masters and requiting their kindness by acts of the most atrocious barbarity.

38. In order to convey a correct idea of the difficulties which had to be overcome by the Government and the danger which threatened the European community at Lucknow, the strength of the military force available at the time in the Capital and its environs is detailed below :—

Native infantry, regulars	2,400
,, ,, irregulars	1,600
Police	800
Native cavalry, regulars	600
,, ,, irregulars	600
Mounted Police	900
	6,900

Artillery, two batteries.
Europeans, H. M.'s 32nd 700
,, ,, 84th, one weak Company.

39. On the night of Saturday, the 30th May, 1857, the date on which the mutiny broke out at Mariaon Cantonment, I was in charge of the Choir boys sent from La Martiniere to assist the Rev. H. S. Polehampton* in the Sunday services at Cantonments. That night, as usual, Mrs. Polehampton was conducting the Choir practice. We were in the midst of chanting the Magnificat when suddenly the bugles sounded the alarm. After finishing the Magnificat, the practice was brought to a close. The Rev. H. S. Polehampton took the Choir boys to his house and gave us the choice of remaining there or proceeding to La Martiniere at once. As our elephants were waiting,

---

* The Rev. H. S. Polehampton was wounded on the 8th and died of cholera on the 20th July, 1857. After his death, the entire duties of the Garrison devolved on the Rev. H. P. Harris ; how he performed them can only be appreciated by those who witnessed and benefited by his ministrations.

I preferred to take the boys home, and twelve of us set off on our moonlight journey of about six miles. Near the Iron Bridge we passed some sepoys marching with fixed bayonets, but, to our great relief, they took no notice of us whatever. Who they were, whether friends or foes, and whither they were going, we could not tell, nor cared to know, but with all possible speed we pushed along, fearing every moment an attack by the mob, as we had to pass through the most crowded streets. We arrived unmolested at the Hazratganj gate (since demolished), opposite the site of Eduljee's shop, when a *sawar* (native cavalry man) with drawn-sword, rode up and ordered our *mahaut*, or elephant driver, to halt. Seeing, however, that his horse would not come near our elephant, I told the *mahaut* to go on. After a little exchange of abusive epithets, the *mahaut* proceeded on, and the obstructive *sawar* took his departure after a few farewell flourishes of his naked sword by way of menace. On arriving at La Martiniere we found every one on the top of the building looking at the far-off flames of the burning bungalows in Cantonments, and we received the hearty congratulations of all on what they considered our providential escape.

The particulars of the outbreak are as follows:—

Immediately after dusk, the sepoys of the 71st Native Infantry turned out and commenced firing, whilst some of their number made straight for the Officers' Mess-house; on the way they were met by a party of the 7th Light Cavalry, who were also going in the same direction, which proved that the destruction of the officers had been deliberately planned. The mutineers were, fortunately, disappointed of their prey. The officers, being on the alert, had left the Mess-house upon the first shot being fired. It was providential that the outbreak did take place before the plot was ripe, for had the conspiracy been matured and burst forth suddenly, as is believed was the intention, there is too much reason to fear that it would have been a success. The Mess-house was set on fire.

40. Sir Henry and his staff immediately proceeded to the European Camp, where there were 300 men of H. M.'s 32nd Foot and six guns. With the guns he swept the parade-ground

of the 71st Native Infantry, and fearing that the mutineers might make for the city, Sir Henry placed two guns and a Company of the 32nd on the road leading to it. The discharge of grape soon cleared the parade and drove the sepoys back into their lines. Brigadier Handscomb, who was commanding the troops in Cantonment and had gone out to quell the insurgents, was shot dead. A portion of the 48th Native Infantry was marched to the Residency; these were the men we passed near the Iron Bridge mentioned above. The 7th Light Cavalry patrolled the main streets of Cantonments during the whole of that night, but could not stop the general plunder and destruction of house property, which was set on fire by the mutinous sepoys. The 32nd Regiment kept their position all night.

41. At daylight next morning, Sir Henry placed himself at the head of the Force, and learning that the mutineers had retired on Mudkipur, followed them thither. Crossing the parade ground our men came upon the body of Cornet Raleigh, a young officer, who, left sick in his quarters, had been murdered by the sepoys! At the same moment the mutinous regiments were discovered drawn up in line. Their attitude appeared to Sir Henry to betoken an intention to charge the guns. That officer consequently at once directed the guns to open fire on the distant line. This prompt action decided the matter and the enemy broke and fled precipitately. A day or two afterwards a number of city *badmashes* (bad characters), on their way to join the mutineers, were intercepted and, on returning to the city, they commenced an outbreak, but by the efforts of the Police, were completely defeated and dispersed. Numerous arrests followed this affair, and several executions were effected. These executions took place near the Machhi Bhawan Fort, the gallows being commanded by the guns on the ramparts, which were always kept loaded with grape-shot. Thus closed the month of May at Lucknow.

42. In the beginning of June the native troops at Secrora were ripe for mutiny, but Mr. C. J. Wingfield, Commissioner of the Bahraich Division, was enabled to place confidence in the

friendliness of the Raja of Balrampur, Drig Bijai Singh,* and to arrange that the European officers should seek refuge with him when the crisis came. This was done, and, after a few days' stay at Balrampur, the whole party, under an escort, reached the Gorakhpur district in safety.

43. "While busy preparing the defences with which Sir Henry was surrounding the Residency and the other houses near it, so as to form intrenchments, and make the best of our position, we were joined by the few Europeans who had escaped from the massacres at other stations in Oudh. The news they brought deepened the gloom of the situation. Reports of the dead bodies of Europeans, among them three ladies, lying by the roadside a few miles out, were brought to us, and the fiendish cruelty to which they were exposed received a fearful illustration, when one day, some natives brought to the Residency the body of an English lady, which they found lying on the road-side cut up into quarters! These unfortunate people were evidently making for the Residency when they were overtaken and thus cruelly murdered and mutilated by the sepoys." Up to this time it had not been decided whether both posts, i. e., the Machhi Bhawan † and the Residency, should be held, or one only, but, after some deliberation, the abandonment of the former and the concentration of the Force at the latter was decided upon. This resolution was formed on the report made by the Engineers to the effect that the Fort was untenable; that its walls would not resist Artillery; and that the large masonry drains underneath it would afford the enemy great facilities for undermining the Fort.

44. A few days later, large quantities of shot and shell with gunpowder, heavy guns and provisions, began to be removed from the Machhi Bhawan into the Residency. Still very considerable stores were left in the Machhi Bhawan, and the works there were actively continued, so that Sir Henry evidently intended to retain both the posts, which are about a mile apart.

---

* During the whole course of the rebellion, this young Raja remained staunch to the British cause, and, at its close, he was well rewarded for his fidelity by Government, which bestowed on him high titles, in addition to an extensive grant of land contiguous to the Nepal Terai where his estates lie.

† Machhi Bhawan is situated about one mile north-west of the Residency.

Since the Machhi Bhawan Fort was regarded by the natives as impregnable and they had a salutary dread of our guns playing upon the city, the retention of this Fortress, for some time longer, was a wise measure, as it served to keep the city people in check after the native troops in Mariaon Cantonments had revolted.

45. The next thing considered necessary was the disarming of the native troops, which was done about the middle of June, and many of the men were sent on leave to their homes. Their arms were brought in and stored in the Residency buildings. About this time the Intelligence Department was organized to forward despatches to out-stations; and *Sawars* (Native Cavalry troopers) used to be sent out to patrol the main lines of road in order to get accounts of passing events. There were also several native scouts employed for the same purpose. By these means information of the movements of the mutineers in the interior of the province continued to be obtained up to the time of the investment.

46. On the first rumours of mutiny and massacre, Mr. Schilling, acting on the advice of the Reverend Mr. Polehampton, had removed the guard of sepoys from Constantia and had procured, in their stead, a guard of Her Majesty's 32nd Europeans. On the 12th June, the 3rd Regiment of Armed Police, commanded by Captain Adolphus Orr, mutinied. Their barracks were situated on the new road leading past the Moti Mahal Palace and Khursheid Manzil, the building now occupied by La Martiniere Girls' School. Captain Orr, though he had removed his family into the Residency, still occupied his own house near the Police Lines. He and his father-in-law, Mr. Symes, who was a teacher in the College before the outbreak, were at home when the news of the disturbance was brought to them by a faithful sepoy. They had just time to mount their horses and escape to the Residency, when the mutineers rushed in and plundered the house, after which they directed their steps to the Khursheid Manzil, which was then ransacked.

47. Crossing the canal the rebels passed between it and La Martiniere village and ultimately took up a position in the

mango tope, known as the Bandaria Bagh, or Monkey Park, on the south boundary of the College Park,* evidently intending to attack us in the night. Hardly had they done so when the Volunteer Cavalry and the Artillery from the Residency galloped up and opened on them with grape at close quarters. This threw the rebels into great confusion; and a charge from the Volunteer Cavalry scattered them in every direction, some of them even taking refuge in the trees. Just then two companies of the 32nd came up in skirmishing order, and though they could not overtake the scattered and flying main body, they brought down not a few of the sepoys roosting among the foliage.

48. The enemy, on this occasion, was about 700 strong, while the Force sent against them consisted of 220, of whom the greater part were Europeans. The Force was commanded by Brigadier Inglis, of H. M.'s 32nd Regiment. We, at La Martiniere, had a clear view of this skirmish from the top of the main building, and longed to join in the fray, but dared not leave our position, which we had to protect against any unexpected attack of the enemy. Just then our Principal, Mr. Schilling, was returning from the Residency and met the rebels passing through the Park; but he managed to escape unmolested.

49. Next morning, the 13th of June, 1857, the Principal received orders from Sir Henry Lawrence to abandon La Martiniere † and march the boys under his charge into the Residency. Leaving our stores and the greater part of our clothing at La Martiniere we marched in column to the Residency. On our way there we had to pass through the most frequented streets of Lucknow, yet we met with no molestation, though a malignant scowl was discernible on almost every native's face. Notwithstanding an order had been issued prohibiting the carrying of arms, we noticed several armed to the teeth. The only escort we had was a guard of

---

* His Excellency the Viceroy, Lord Curzon of Kedleston, G. M. S. I., G. M. I. E., held the Oudh Darbar in the Martiniere Park on the 13th December, 1899, the Viceregal tent being on the same piece of ground as was occupied by that of the Marquess of Ripon, K. G., in 1882.

† La Martiniere College is about three miles south-east of the Residency

the 32nd Regiment leading, and the senior boys, armed with muskets * bringing up the rear. Up to the 30th June, 1857, the day of the battle of Chinhut, we continued to draw our stores and supplies of clothing and other necessaries from Constantia, but, after that disastrous day, we were deprived of this resource, since all communication with the outer world was then cut off, and we were left with the bare suit on our backs, with which we had to go through the siege, and which was considered a great hardship. (See para. 126).

50. Sir Henry Lawrence allotted to us for our quarters the house of the native banker, Sah Behari Lal, which was situated at the extreme south of the intrenchment and forming one of the outposts in that quarter. It was, throughout the siege, much exposed to the enemy's fire. By the end of the siege, this house had been so battered as to become almost untenable. It was built after the usual style of native houses, having a square of one-storied buildings, with a two-storied reception-room in the centre, and, I need hardly say, it was quite inadequate to our requirements. We continued our school studies in the intrenchment till the day of the battle of Chinhut, after which the boys and masters were compelled to give their attention to other duties. On that day all our servants, except the cook and *Bhisti* † (water-carrier), left us, and thereafter the boys had to do all the drudgery usually performed by menials.

---
* The Brown-Bess was the only weapon used by the boys during the siege till the arrival of the first relief, when the Enfield Rifle was distributed. Sir Frederi k Roberts (now Field-Marshal Lord Roberts), the late Commander-in-Chief, in his address to the Simla Volunteers, made the following remark with regard to the former weapon :—"It seems that, with the old Brown-Bess, you might stand at the foot of Ludgate Hill and fire at St. Paul's with little chance of hitting it more than once in five hundred shots." After which His Excellency told an amusing anecdote of a distinguished Peninsular Officer, who offered to stand as a target all day long, provided the distance was 300 yards and the marksman promised to aim correctly. The range of the Brown-Bess is about 80 yards. This clumsy and cumbersome weapon was worthless against an enemy armed with superior weapons. Another fault was the over heating of the barrel in rapid firing. The bare portion of the barrel became more difficult to hold than a hot potato. The carbine I had in the siege has been carefully preserved by me up to the present time.

† The *Bhisti* was shot on the 21st of September, and the cook deserted a few days after. The mark of the cannon ball, which killed the former, is still to be seen on the wall of the well in the Martiniere Post.

51. Sir Henry Lawrence's exertions to provision the Garrison were unceasing. The Commissariat Department was constantly at work; getting in, from the district and elsewhere, grain, which, with a large quantity of *ghee* and oil, were stored within the precincts of the Residency. The swimming-bath on the east of the General Hospital was filled with wheat. Stores of firewood and charcoal were also laid in; and the racket court was filled with fodder for the oxen. Fortunately, we possessed an abundant supply of excellent water from numerous masonry wells within the intrenchment.

52. About the middle of June the fortifications of the Residency began in earnest; defences capable of resisting the assault of Artillery were now being rapidly thrown up. At the time when the blockade was commenced only two of our Batteries were completed; parts of the defences were yet in an unfinished condition; and the buildings in the immediate vicinity, which gave cover to the enemy, were only very partially cleared away. The greatest annoyance we received was from the native buildings which, in close proximity, surrounded us on all sides, and which, as soon as the siege began, were filled with the enemy's sharp-shooters, from whose ceaseless fire the Garrison suffered more than from any other cause.

53. The gunpowder, which was brought in from the Machhi Bhawan, had been buried, before the commencement of the siege, in the lower Residency grounds,* on the east, outside our line of defences. This spot was afterwards found to be too exposed as, on 3rd July, the enemy had got near to it and set fire to some fodder stacks and tents which were close by. Lieutenant Aitken, of the 13th N. I., who commanded the Treasury and Baillie Guard Gateway, with a few others of his party, went out and cut down the tents, though a bright moon was shining and the spot was commanded, at a short distance, by the enemy's loopholes and the flames made every object more clearly visible. During the siege all the powder-barrels were exhumed and removed to the Begam Kothi,

---
* In the beginning of July this was abandoned as untenable. It was neutral ground during the siege until re-occupied after General Havelock's entry.

within the intrenchment, and deposited in the cellar there, where it was protected from the shells of the enemy. The treasure (23 lacs) buried in front of the Residency, east of the site on which the Lawrence Memorial now stands was, however, allowed to remain undisturbed.

54. On the morning of June 28th, 1857, Major Banks, the Commissioner, and Captain Carnegie, the City Magistrate, were deputed, with a military force, to secure and bring into the Residency, from the King's Treasury in the Kaisar Bagh, the large amount of State jewellery, valued at no less than £800,000. This included a richly-ornamented throne, crowns studded with gems, and a variety of necklaces, armlets, rings, and native ornaments. These were brought in late on the same day.* The cases in which the jewellery was found were decayed with age, and fell to pieces when it was attempted to remove them. During the siege the room in which these precious articles were kept was broken into and a large quantity of jewels were stolen.

55. By the 26th June many of the mutinous corps were known to have assembled at Bara Banki, a station 20 miles east of Lucknow. Great excitement prevailed in consequence, among the wealthier classes in the city, who were afraid of being plundered by the rebels. On the 29th June news was received from the scouts, that the enemy's advance-guard of about 600 men had arrived at Chinhut, a large village within seven miles of the Residency, on the Fyzabad road, and situated on the banks of a very extensive *jhil*, or lake, close to which stood a hunting lodge † of the former Kings of Oudh. Upon this being reported to Sir Henry he ordered out a reconnoitring party of Sikh Cavalry, who confirmed the report given by the scouts. Sir Henry resolved to attack the enemy next day,

---

*The carts containing this jewellery arrived so late that they could not be unloaded that night, and as the Residency was invested from the morning of the 30th, the carts remained unladen for several days. After we had recovered from the first shock of the investment, the carts were unladen and the jewellery placed in a room in the main building of the Residency.

† This chateau was built in the reign of King Asaf-ud-daulah (1775-97). Owing to its dilapidated condition, it was razed and the materials sold by auction, on 17th July, 1891.

and, with this object, he withdrew the troops from Mariaon Cantonments into the Residency and Machhi Bhawan at sunset of the same day. Early on the morning of the 30th, he marched out to oppose the enemy's advance with the following force:—

ARTILLERY.

4 Guns of 4th Company, 1st Battalion Bengal Artillery (now 22nd Battery, Royal Field Artillery,) under Lieutenant F. J. Cunliffe.

4 Guns of Lieut. Alexander's O. I. Battery.
2 ,, of Ashe's O. I. Battery, under Lieut. Bryce.
1 eight-inch howitzer, under Lieut. Bonham.
Major Simons in command of the whole.

CAVALRY.

Radcliffe's European Volunteers, numbering 36 sabres.
The Sikh Cavalry, under Captains H. Forbes and G. Hardinge, about 80 sabres.

INFANTRY.

H. M's 32nd Foot	... 300
13th N. I., under Major Bruce	... 150
48th N. I., under Colonel Palmer	... 50
71st N. I., Sikhs, under Lieut. Birch	... 20

56. This small Force was under the command of Sir Henry Lawrence in person, accompanied by Brigadier Inglis, and the whole body moved on confident of success. The troops, misled by the reports of wayfarers who stated that there were few or no men between Lucknow and Chinhut, proceeded somewhat further than had been originally intended and suddenly fell in with the enemy, who had, up to that time, eluded the vigilance of the advance-guard by concealing themselves in overwhelming numbers behind a thick mango-grove on the near side of Chinhut. The enemy, fifteen thousand strong, with six batteries of guns of various calibre, was found drawn up right in front of the village of Ishmailganj. The European troops and the howitzer with the Native Infantry held the foe in check for some time; and had the Sikh Cavalry and the six guns of the Oudh

Artillery been faithful, the day would have been won by the British in spite of the immense disparity in numbers. But the Oudh Artillerymen and drivers proved traitors. They overturned the guns into ditches, cut the traces of their horses and deserted, regardless of the remonstrances and exertions of their own officers. These field pieces were, however, spiked before they were abandoned.

57. The elephants attached to the limber of the 8-inch howitzer took fright shortly after the firing began, and ran off with it in the direction of the enemy. Every effort to induce the native troopers to stand by their guns having proved ineffectual, the British Force, exposed to a vastly superior fire of Artillery, and completely out-flanked on both sides by an overpowering body of Infantry and Cavalry which actually got into its rear, was compelled to retire with the loss of three pieces of Artillery and a quantity of ammunition, and with a very grievous list in killed and wounded.

> "Fell many a warrior on that dreadful day,
> Brave, generous, noble, breathed his soul away,
> But none more noble, generous, or brave,
> In battle ever found a soldier's grave."

THE BATTLE OF CHINHUT.

AN account of the battle, which was fought at the village of Ismailganj, is given below:—

The Force destined for this service assembled, from the Machhi Bhawan and the Residency, at the Iron Bridge at sun-rise, and marched to the bridge over the Kukrail Naddi,*

---

* The natives have such faith in the waters of this stream (Kukrail, or dog-river, from the Hindi word *kukur*, a dog) being a prophylactic against Hydrophobia, that they, from distant parts, resort thither immediately they are bitten; and numbers of men, women, and children may be seen, at all seasons of the year, collected on its banks, near the bridge. The person, or persons, bitten bathe in the stream and wade across it backwards and forwards seven times, feeding the dogs on either shore each time with balls of sweetened flour prepared by the *Brahmins*, or Hindu priests, who are always in attendance on such occasions. *Pujah*, or worship, is then performed, and alms distributed, which ends the ceremony and calms the fears of those concerned. This small stream joins the Gumti a little below the Upper India (Couper) Paper Mills.

which is a small stream intersecting the Fyzabad road about half-way between the Residency and Chinhut. So far the road was metalled, but beyond this the first difficulties were experienced, as the path there was the summit of an unfinished embankment of loose earth. After a halt under the blazing sun the Force moved slowly on. After proceeding about a mile and a half the videttes were fired upon from the village of Ismailganj (the actual site of the battle of 30th June) on the road to Chinhut. The troops were still in column when they were fired upon with round shot. The enemy now became visible, occupying some mango-groves. Our line was at once deployed and the guns brought into position. The howitzer returned the fire of the enemy with effect. The field pieces also fired with round shot, when the rebels moved off and it was thought that the day was won ; but, instead of retreating, the enemy only changed their position and then continued to cannonade almost simultaneously with ours, while their skirmishers kept advancing, and, in a short time, gained full possession of the village of Ishmailganj, from which they poured a deadly fire upon our men. The fire of the enemy was answered with great spirit by our men, and, after a short resistance, the retreat was ordered. The enemy kept pressing on, taking advantage of every cover to pour in a murderous fire of musketry. The heat was dreadful, the gun-ammunition was expended, and the almost total want of Cavalry to protect the rear made the retreat most disastrous. All the officers behaved well; and the exertions of the small body of European Volunteer Cavalry—only 36 in number—under Captain Radcliffe, 7th Light Cavalry, were most praiseworthy. The gallant services of Her Majesty's 32nd Regiment throughout the struggle were remarkable.

"On nearing the Kukrail Bridge* a body of the enemy's Cavalry was seen occupying the road in front. They, however, were soon driven from their position by a charge from the

---

* The Kukrail Bridge on the Fyzabad Road is exactly two miles and six furlongs from the Iron bridge ; the village of Ishmailganj five miles and the town of Chinhut six miles and four furlongs. The consecration by the Right Revd. Alfred Clifford, Bishop of Lucknow, of the cemeteries at Kukrail, took place on the 31st January, 1896, at 10 A. M.

Volunteer Cavalry. Beyond the bridge the retreat continued, covered by the Cavalry; and, in this way, the suburbs were passed through, the Iron Bridge re-crossed, and the Machhi Bhawan and Residency gained at last. It was a most melancholy spectacle to witness; and all felt the deepest sympathy for the poor wounded who were conveyed to the Banqueting Hall, which was converted into a Hospital. The place was crowded and everything in a state of indescribable misery, discomfort, and confusion. The ladies flocked around the wounded and attended to all their wants with as much solicitude as if they had been their own relatives."

> "O God! they said, it was a piteous thing
> To see the after-horrors of the fight,
> The lingering death, the hopeless suffering,
> What heart of flesh unmoved could bear the sight."

58. The pursuing enemy was stopped at the Iron Bridge by the guns of the Redan Battery, and, at the Stone Bridge, by the fire from the Machhi Bhawan Fort. They opened fire upon both posts, however, from guns which they put in position across the river; and with the 8-inch howitzer, which was captured at Chinhut, they threw several shells into the Residency. The enemy entered the city by fording the river lower down. They got into the houses adjoining at the intrenchment which were rapidly loop-holed, and before night, a fire of musketry was opened upon us. At day break next morning the enemy besieged us most desperately and closely, bringing their Artillery to bear on all the houses into which round shot and shell crashed with dreadful effect, and a rain of bullets showered on every part of our position. **From 11 a. m., on 30th June 1857, the siege of Lucknow may be said to have begun.** The defeat, the persuit, and the investment of our position had been so rapid and unexpected that it caused great confusion in the Residency. As soon as the alarm of the coming foe was spread, the servants took to flight, and the work-people, who were engaged on the defences, took the opportunity of escaping. Long, however, before all the proposed batteries were thrown up, the rebels, assembling in vast

numbers, began the blockade of the place, and everything which was at the moment outside the line of works was lost. By the abandonment of the unfinished works the west and south faces of our position had been left almost defenceless, and particularly the Martiniere post, which was protected only by a rough palisade extending along the outer front.

59. The King's Prison,* nearly opposite the Baillie Guard Gate, soon attracted our attention. The prisoners were seen making their escape, holding on by ropes let down from the high walls and windows. From the terrace of the house in the Martiniere post occupied by us, a steady fire was kept up on the liberated "Jail birds" whilst taking their flight, but it soon became too hot for us to remain there, owing to the bullets which began flying about in all directions. The enemy's guns were not yet quite in position, consequently we did not feel the full effect of them on the first day. They, however, soon established batteries, and, placing guns in position round the intrenchment, poured into it a continuous storm of shot and shell.† The deafening peals succeeded each other with a rapidity which suggested the image of unchecked vengeance falling in thunder upon our heads. The enemy also occupied in force all the surrounding buildings, and therefrom commenced a furious fusilade which was kept up *unceasingly day and night to the end of the siege*. The siege of the garrison at Lucknow, and its gallant defence, furnishes, perhaps, the most interesting episode in the history of the Indian Mutiny. It lasted for 146 days, reckoning from the 30th June to the 22nd November (midnight), the date of the complete evacuation of the intrenchment after the final relief by Sir Colin Campbell's army on the 17th idem.

EVACUATION OF MACHHI BHAWAN.

60. After our defeat and unfortunate retreat from Chinhut there were still a few hundred men in the Machhi Bhawan Fort, but this position could no longer be maintained. The

---

* This building, in which the Court of the District Judge is now located, was originally used as a Museum. The Museum has since been removed to the Lal Baradari, the Coronation Hall of the Kings of Oudh.

† The Artillery of the Garrison consisted of 25 guns and 11 mortars; against which the investing force had 33 pieces in battery.

untoward event of the 30th June diminished the whole available Force, so much that there was not a sufficient number of men to defend the two positions; and if the original intention of holding the two posts had been adhered to, both would have inevitably fallen. Sir Henry accordingly sent orders to blow up the Fort and withdraw the men into the Residency. Fortunately there was a semaphore telegraph on the Residency roof, and this was now had resort to. Captain Fulton, Engineers, accompanied by Mr. G. H. Lawrence, C. S., and a third officer, ascended to the roof to convey the message. The arrangements for the evacuation of the Machhi Bhawan were admirably carried out by Colonel (now General) Palmer, the Commanding Officer. The Force moved out noiselessly at midnight, and reached the Water-gate* without a shot being fired at them. Providentially the enemy had selected that night for plundering the city, and the two garrisons were concentrated without any loss. The arrangements for blowing up the Fort were made by Lieutenant Thomas, who fired the train so as to explode the magazine half an hour after the troops had left. The explosion did not take place till the column had safely reached the Residency. The shock was terrific; it resembled an earthquake, and created great alarm till the cause was made known to us. Thus was destroyed, on the 2nd July, 1857, the fortification of Machhi Bhawan, and with it a considerable number of guns, besides ammunition and public stores, consisting of two large and two small mortars, three 18-pounder guns and five 9-pounders, two hundred and fifty barrels of gunpowder, and as many boxes of small arm ammunition, and many lacs of percussion caps.

61. It is painful to relate the calamity which befell us at the commencement of the siege. Sir Henry Lawrence was mortally wounded at 9 A. M., on the 2nd July, by a piece of shell which nearly took off his left leg just below the thigh.†

---

* This gate was the entrance to the Residency lower garden from the north side facing the river, and hence it derived the name of "Water-gate."

† It was from a shell fired from the 8-inch howitzer, which was taken by the rebels at the battle of Chinhut, that Sir Henry received his death wound.

The shell burst in a room on the first storey of the north-east angle of the Residency, which was most exposed to the enemy's fire. Only the day previous another shell had fallen into the same apartment close to Sir Henry Lawrence and his Secretary, Sir George Couper, but without injury to either. Sir Henry had then been advised to abandon the room, which was, from its high position more exposed to the enemy's fire, but he refused to do so, as he laughingly said that he did not believe the enemy had an artilleryman good enough to put another shell into that small room. He succumbed to his wound on the morning of the 4th July, in Doctor Fayrer's house, to which he had been removed, and the Government was thereby deprived of the services of a distinguished Statesman and one of its most illustrious servants.

> " The pains of death are past ;
> Labour and sorrows cease,
> And, life's long warfare closed at last,
> His soul is found in peace.
> Soldier of Christ ! well done ;
> Praise be thy new employ ;
> And, while eternal ages run,
> Rest in thy Saviour's joy."

Three of our boys, George Roberts, John Smith, and Richard Grueber, attended Sir Henry during his illness. The first named, who was the senior boy, rendered very great service to the Doctors (Fayrer, Partridge, and Ogilvie) in procuring water for washing Sir Henry's wound, from a well in a very exposed position, and in affording such further aid as lay in his power.

62. The news of the death of our revered and beloved General cast a gloom over all ranks and classes of the beleaguered Garrison. We mourned the loss of a Chief whose unwearing efforts to protect the lives and fortunes of those committed to his care had endeared him to all who were capable of appreciating disinterested devotion to duty. Had his constitution been less shattered he might have survived the shell-wound could he have undergone amputation, but, in his enfeebled state, the utmost that could be done was to apply the tourniquet to stop the bleeding, and he lingered for two

days in the greatest agony. During this time Sir Henry remained quite collected, dictating his final instructions. How thoughtfully he dwelt on every point of importance in reference to the defence of the Garrison, and also, when speaking of himself, how humbly he talked of his own life and services. He particularly enjoined economy of ammunition and food, and expressed his deep anxiety about the fate of the women and children. "Save the ladies," he often said, and then urged that the following modest epitaph, which his tomb now bears, should be inscribed upon it after his dissolution:

HERE LIES
HENRY LAWRENCE,
WHO TRIED TO DO HIS DUTY.

May the Lord habe mercy on his soul.

An eye-witness published in the *Anglo-Indian Magazine*, the following affecting account of his last illness :—

THE LAST HOURS OF SIR HENRY LAWRENCE.*

"It is impossible to describe the feelings that overcame all on hearing, early in the morning of the 2nd July, and only two days after the commencement of the siege, the sad report, 'Sir Henry is killed!' But he was not dead. A mournful company was soon seen bearing his shattered frame across the open position from the scene of the disaster to Doctor Fayrer's house. The enemy was attacking heavily, yet many braved all, and with horror-struck faces quickly gathered around the coach of their grievously-wounded and beloved Chief, in the open verandah, where

---

* Henry Montgomery Lawrence, the son of Colonel Alexander Lawrence, was born at Matura, in Ceylon, on the 28th June, 1806. Matura is celebrated for its diamonds, and a lady at Galle one day asked Mrs. Lawrence if she had brought any with her. "Yes," said the mother, with a pride above jewels, and called in the nurse with Henry. "There's my Matura diamond!"

Sir Henry, after the usual education at local schools, obtained an Addiscombe cadetship, and there won his commission in the Bengal Artillery, which he joined at its head-quarters, Dum Dum, near Calcutta, in February, 1823.

On 9th November, 1867, Sir John Lawrence, brother of Sir Henry, made his State entry into Lucknow, an entry the pageantry of which surpassed any ever made by any previous or subsequent Viceroy or any potentate of the Kings of Oudh under the old régime.

MAJOR-GENERAL SIR JOHN INGLIS, K. C. B.

he was first laid. It was a terrible wound; the fragment of shell had struck and partly carried away the under portion of the thigh. He was quite sensible to everything around him, and during examination by the medical men, asked frequently, but calmly, how long he had to live. When one of them, more directly appealed to, pronounced with sorrowing hesitation, the fatal verdict, 'Not many hours, Sir,' he turned to the Chaplain for the Church's ministrations. The enemy (who throughout the siege had the best intelligence) would appear to have already known of our Chief's state and his place of shelter. Almost immediately after his removal from his own quarters a close continuous fire poured in on Doctor Fayrer's house, and the balls were flying thick as we gathered round to partake of what was to him, and to many others also, the last sacrament. Not one of us was touched! Yet scarcely had he been removed into an inner room and our party dispersed, when two casualties occurred at the very place where we had so lately stood and knelt: the officer in command of the guard and a private were seriously wounded.

"The Communion ended, he lay, for nearly an hour, talking during the intervals of severe pain. Who will forget the deep humility and penitence expressed by this good and noble man for the sins and shortcomings of his life, and the meek, yet steadfast faith in his Saviour? He spoke most unreservedly of those things in affectionately warning solicitude for the friends around him. He had words of counsel for all in his farewell; some he thanked tenderly for their service and affection; but it was, perhaps, still more touching to listen to his appeals for forgiveness (for who has not offended?) from others, to whom in the course of his duty, he imagined, that he might have spoken, or acted, harshly. His directions for our conduct of the defence were most decided. He appointed Major Banks* and Brigadier Inglis† as his successors in

---

* Major Banks became the senior Political Officer in Lucknow when Sir H. Lawrence died. His diary was found in the city of Lucknow, on the 3rd June, 1858, in the house of a rebel, but in a defaced condition.

† Brigadier Inglis died at Hamburg, Germany, September 27th, 1862. A monument is erected in the Residency to the memory of our gallant General.

command (the latter subordinate) and distinctly declared that it should be in military hands. Sir Henry had acted most wisely; and now, he said, that there was nothing but to fight and to endure. There was to be no thought of making terms; relief might be looked for in a month, but if two should elapse before succour came, we must still hope on ; and, rather than surrender, die to a man. The thought of the women and children he was leaving in such peril seemed to affect him deeply. God help the poor women and children ; 'Take care of the poor women and children' was his frequent cry. The fear for them, and for the future well-doing of his own foster-child—the Asylum—distressed him much. Over and over again he reiterated the words 'Don't let them forget the Asylum,' alternated with that other cry, ' The poor women and children.'

"He evidently foresaw the great difficulty of a friendly advance on our position. A Force of two thousand Europeans was the smallest, he said, that should be permitted to attempt it, and we were, by repeated messages, to impress this on the leader of the looked-for relieving troops. No possible means of securing the safety of the Garrison escaped him, even in that time of greatest personal need. We had some State prisoners of rank closely allied to those known to be amongst the most active of our foes. In case our provisions began to fail, he enjoined us to endeavour to make use of the influence of these men in obtaining supplies.

" After urging many similar likely ways of making the best of our precarious state, he turned his thoughts to more personal concerns ; and though his last words for his own dear ones were especially addressed to a near relative in attendance at his side, they had a wonderful interest for, and effect on, all those who were privileged to hear the uttered promptings of that thoughtful, tender, unselfish heart.

> To them his heart, his love, his grief were given,
> But all his serious thoughts had rest in heaven.

"No one was forgotten: brothers, sisters, friends, all remembered in that hour. Even the few faithful native servants, who were sobbing out their grief in the background, were summoned to the front, rewarded, and consoled. Nay, his very horse *(Ladaki)*, an old favorite, brought into the Residency with him, was affectionately commended to his nephew's care.

"He thought his end nearer than was said; indeed, he prayed that death might come and ease him of his pangs. The chloroform, occasionally administered, had not much effect in deadening his suffering, and, on reviving once from its partial influence, he spoke of his burial, 'Let there be no fuss about me—Let me be buried with the men : No nonsense'—'Here lies Henry Lawrence, who tried to do his duty;'—all this in disjointed sentences, speaking, as it were, to himself; and then, turning to the Chaplain (Rev. J. P. Harris) he said, ' I should like a text of Scripture added :'

"To the Lord our God belong mercies and forgivenesses, though we have rebelled against Him.' 'Isn't it from Daniel ? * It was on my dear wife's tomb.' And then, once more (after a short silence and an evident inward-dwelling on his offences), 'Don't let me be maligned ;' in reference, probably, to the fatal advance on Chinhut but two days before, which, to his oft-declared bitter remorse, he had been over-persuaded by others against his own judgment to attempt, and which, doubtless, had, by its unfortunate issue, at last precipitated the investment.

"At length he became drowsy, and we moved him into a room adjoining the verandah, barricading the doors and windows, as best we could, against the musketry fire which now literally showered in. From henceforth he was made over to woman's tender care. He never again spoke very connectedly, though he many times during that and the succeeding day, followed the Chaplain as he repeated the prayers for the sick, even when, apparently, insensible to outward things. His bodily sufferings were occasionally excruciating, though his patience and self-control were exemplary, and his grateful words and looks for those ministering to him were affecting beyond measure. Once the question was raised as to whether an

---

* Chapter IX, verse 9.

operation might not yet save his life; but his prayers against it prevailed, and, indeed, the unanimous medical opinion was, that, in this particular case, it would kill outright: He wished to die, but in peace, and in God's good time.

" And so it went on, until the morning of the 4th, when the end came, very quietly, in the midst of prayer, after some previous half-intelligible mutterings, of which the Asylum was still the chief burden. I think he was spared the trial of knowing that his nephew George, whom he loved so much, and who not long before had received his blessing, was kneeling bleeding by his side, shot through the shoulder.

" What an irreparable loss did it seem when he was really gone! His character was, perhaps, perfectly drawn by a friend, who followed him within a few days from this trial world, and who came from his post ' To see, ' as he said, ' yet once again a true Christian gentleman.' He has been called (and how truly) the ' Soldier's Friend.' That soldiers loved him cannot be doubted. The following incident will of itself prove this :—Those who had undertaken that labour of love, the preparing his body for the burial, being unable of themselves to remove it from the house, a call for assistance was made on the men working the guns outside.

" A party came, begrimed and heated from the fight, and when told the nature of the service, and for whom required, they first knelt down, subdued and sorrowing, by the bedside, and, lifting the covering sheet from his face one by one, lovingly and reverently kissed it.

" He was, as he wished, buried with the men in the same grave. Nor in his glory was he left alone ; for in the fight in which he fell many had fallen, some to share the narrow chamber of his grave, some to sleep beside him.

" While the expiring veteran was thus, with calm and steady tones, giving his last parting instructions, all around shot and shell were crashing and hostile cannons booming, and the very earth shaking under the incessant explosions."

63. His services, particularly in the Punjab, of which he was one of the earliest and most successful administrators, entitled him to a foremost place among Indian Statesmen; but even could these be forgotten, the noble institutions founded by his munificence on the heights of the Himalayas, of Mount Abu, and of the Nilgiris, which bear his name as their founder, and in which the children of European soldiers serving in India are duly cared for, would suffice to keep his memory in perpetual and honoured remembrance : though dead, his memory still liveth.

"All must to their cold graves,
But the religious actions of the just
Smell sweet in death, and blossom in the dust."

" No Military honors, " says one who was present " marked our last act to his corpse. The times were too stern for such démonstrations of respect. A hurried prayer, amid the booming of the enemy's artillery, was read over his remains, and he was buried at the same time with several others, though lowlier companions in arms." And so mournfully closed the 4th of July over Lucknow.

64. Sir Henry nominated Major Banks* his successor as the Chief Civil authority; Brigadier Inglis to command the troops of the Garrison; and Major Anderson† to command the Artillery and direct Engineering operations. Our eventual success in defending the Residency position is, under Providence, mainly attributable to the foresight which Sir Henry evinced in the timely commencement of the necessary operations, and the great skill and untiring personal activity which he exhibited in carrying them into effect.

65. The first sortie made into Johannes' house was on the 7th July; it took place at noon and was perfectly successful. The enemy, who crowded the building, made no resistance, but fled. We had one Sikh and two men of the 32nd wounded, while numbers of the *baba log*, or children (a term of endearment by which old Company's officers used to address

---

* Major Banks was shot through the head, on the 21st July, 1857, in Mr. Gubbins' post.

† Major Anderson died of dysentery on the 11th August, 1857.

the sepoys in whom they had reposed such confidence) who were found asleep and hiding in chests, were killed after a hand-to-hand struggle. We, at La Martiniere post, and officers from the Brigade Mess, acted as a covering party to the brave few who, on this and every subsequent occasion, charged the enemy on our side of the Garrison.

66. Later in the siege La Martiniere post suffered severely from the fire of the guns in Phillips' garden battery * which kept up an incessant cannonade until it demolished the range of houses on the south-east corner that had rendered us substantial protection from that quarter. Though our post was in a very exposed part of the Garrison, being only separated by a road 20 feet wide from the godowns of Johannes' house, which were occupied in force by the rebels, no boy, or master, was killed by the enemy. Two boys were certainly wounded, *viz.*, John Smith in the left thigh, and James Luffman under the left clavicle; † but, being well cared for by the teachers, they both recovered. Owing to exposure and bad food there was a good deal of sickness among the boys and masters, but only two cases ended fatally (George Reid and Carapiet Arathoon) among 50 boys during the entire period of the siege. The mortality among the women and children, especially the latter, from disease and other causes, was, perhaps, the most painful characteristic of the siege. Some parents, who had children in good health when the siege began, had not one left when it ended. Menial work fell on the ladies in consequence of the desertion of their servants. Several of them had to tend their children and even to wash their own clothes, gather their own sticks and light their

---

* This was the enemy's battery situated on the site now occupied by the Balrampur Hospital. It was captured on the 2nd October, 1857.

In 1902 a new ward, for the benefit of Europeans, was added to the Hospital, well furnished and equipped, consisting of five suits of private rooms. The funds wherewith this addition was made, were largely supplied by the liberality of the Maharajah of Balrampur. The judicious way in which the funds were expended reflects great credit on Colonel J. Anderson, the Civil Surgeon. Opposite to this, on the west, now stands the Dufferin Hospital, which was opened by His Royal Highness Prince Albert Victor, on 18th January, 1890.

† Smith was wounded on the 26th of July, and Luffman on the 8th of October.

own fires, as well as cook their scanty meals, entirely unaided, while a few, more fortunate than the rest, had the assistance of La Martiniere boys. The want of proper food and accommodation was, probably, the cause of much of the disease with which we were afflicted.

67. The boys who carried arms used to take ten or twenty rounds, go up to the top of the house in which we were located, and fire through the loop-holes at whatever seemed a fair target. There were pumpkins, and other vegetables which would have made a welcome addition to our cuisine, growing in Johannes' garden, outside the line of our defence. We found it very tantalizing to know that we must not venture to forage in this garden: for the vigilance of the enemy's marksmen was untiring, and they never lost an opportunity of picking off any member of the Garrison who was so incautious as to expose himself. Seeing that the coveted vegetables were not available for us, we did our best to make them unfit for use by the enemy, and found some diversion in firing at the gourds. This sport, however, was ultimately put a stop to by the following circumstance:— A few days after the boy Smith had been hit by one of the enemy's marksmen, known to the boys by the sobriquet of "Jim the Rifle," located in Johannes' warehouse facing our post, Luffman and myself, with the intention of avenging this, went up to the roof to try and get a pot-shot at the rascal; we both used the same loop-hole. While on the look-out, one of the lads, S. Hornby, came up to the roof with a supply of ammunition, and, while our attention was thus diverted, our mutinous opponent across the way fired at us. His bullet struck Luffman's musket, glanced along the barrel, and lodged in his left shoulder. He, as already mentioned, fortunately recovered, but we both received a very severe reprimand from the Principal, and our target practice had to be discontinued owing to the ammunition being put out of our reach.

68. On the 20th July, the memorable day of the *first* and most serious general attack, when going across the courtyard from one building to the other, a half-spent 24-pound shot passed

between my legs and struck a *bel* tree (*œgle marmelos*) which is still standing. This may be considered a very narrow escape, but in the Garrison such things were of every day occurrence. On this day the besiegers, who had probably heard of the state of affairs at Cawnpore, apparently resolved to exterminate the Lucknow Garrison also, and plucked up courage to make a direct assault. The entire position was assailed on all sides by a terrible fire of round shot and musketry, under cover of which the enemy advanced boldly to the attack. One of their standard-bearers actually reached the trenches in front of the Cawnpore battery before he was shot; some even attempted to place their scaling ladders in position, but were at once repelled. They also appeared in great numbers on our side, and several were shot down close to our defences at La Martiniere post. The result of the day's fight was cheering. The enemy had done their worst, and the engagement, which lasted the whole day, ended with a heavy loss on their side, as will be seen from the following graphic account by one of the beleaguered Garrison :—

THE
"GRAND ATTACK."*

"The enemy had now succeeded—so far as the eye could see—in surrounding us on all sides ; and were gathered in thousands, and were still gathering. We could not form, however, any accurate idea of the number against which we had to contend. According to some native accounts the number did not fall short of, if it did not exceed, 40,000 men. Other accounts again placed the figure much higher. Our strength, on the other hand, did not exceed 800—at most 900 Europeans and natives both included—and even, of this number, it is doubtful if all were physically capable of bearing arms. Of course, in such a matter implicit reliance could not be placed on native reports. The tendency would rather be to underrate, than otherwise, the strength of the force opposed to us—moreover, as matters stood at the time, it is quite conceivable that the strength of the enemy may have fluctuated during almost every moment of the

---

* During the entire period of the investment the enemy made four general attacks, but without success, *viz.*, on the 20th July ; 10th August ; 18th August ; and 5th September.

attack, as the reserves, massed in the adjoining buildings, came out and took part against us. There was nothing to prevent this, inasmuch as the distribution of the reserves at certain points was provided in the plan of operations settled for the day. Prior to the mutiny the population of the city of Lucknow was computed at 6 or 700,000 souls. There was, therefore, no limit at that period to the resources of the enemy in men as well as in material. They may have commanded 100,000 on the occasion if they chose to do so—all their strength, and all their energies were now concentrated upon the accomplishment of one object—and they left no stone unturned to secure it. All the evil-disposed—and their number was legion—as well as the rabble of the city were, apparently, associated in the attack, headed and assisted by the great body of the mutineers, regulars and irregulars, locals and police. And independently of these, thousands flocked in from the districts in quest of plunder and for other purposes. And, animated as we knew these were, by the worst of motives, and most hostile intentions, it may be well imagined·they were only too eager to avail themselves of any opportunity which might offer to take part against the Garrison, assured as they had been of ultimate success, and unbounded license. It was now apparent, at any rate, that the gathering was pre-concerted·—we afterwards learnt that it was so. All had not yet, however, reached their destination, but as time wore on the general combinations of the enemy became more and more manifest, and as each scene in the great drama was being gradually unfolded, nothing was to be seen but the movements of men, and increased energy on the part of the enemy, destined, of course, for some object, and that object did not take long in showing itself. The attack had already considerably developed, only the object of each move was now becoming more apparent. At length, when everything had been arranged and method introduced in aid of the operations, the enemy lost no time in pressing the attack with even greater vigour. Uniting as one body—losing sight of their mutual animosities for the moment—they now made frantic efforts to dislodge us. There was no mistaking the nature of the assault, as well as the spirit with which the enemy was inspired—we on our part, were in the meantime, calmly awaiting the foe. It must be admitted that, in these desperate attempts to achieve success, the enemy were not daunted for some time by the concentrated fire of the Garrison, although, considering the number of the attacking Force, and the proximity of the enemy, the fire must have told fearfully on them. This we could occasionally perceive from the number both of the wounded and dying removed from different places out of the range of the fire. The enemy was, however, not to be dismayed by failure; again and again they pressed forward—each attack appearing to be more determined than the one which immediately preceded it; on each occasion, however, only to meet with repulse, for we, meanwhile, were not idle on our side. Volley after volley ploughed through the serried ranks of the advancing foe, the effect of which was only too apparent—the enemy staggered, reeled, and then hastily retreated, taking shelter under the adjoining cover—only, however, to emerge again in greater force after a few minutes respite, thus giving us a little breathing time during the intervals of the fight—nothing now could be more terrific and more sustained than was the fire on both sides. It was continuous and incessant for hours together; the heat was overpowering. It was a July day, cloudless, the sun's rays falling full on those exposed to it. The very elements appeared to be working against us, and as the enemy gradually settled down to work, the musketry and missiles intermingled with grapeshot which came from the side of the enemy can only be likened to, and described as, so much pelting hail. The whole range of buildings too, and even three-storied, stretching along from the river's brink to Johannes' house on the Cawnpore side—this side of the intrenchment—less than 200 yards off—were full of the enemy on the day of the attack, and as they had abundance of ammunition, and were well sheltered, they flooded the Garrison with bullets. In addition to these, we had to contend against the thousands who came out and attempted to carry the intrenchment. In this state of things it was evident that no object could withstand the fire, if exposed for any time. No space, no building, no shrub, no tree, no plant escaped the withering fire. We were now in the thickest fight—a spectacle once seen never to be effaced from the mind. And now above all rose the roar of cannon and the dreadful crash of artillery, the cannon balls all the while flying in every direction, crashing through buildings, trees, and every object which lay in their course, and obstructing their passage, carrying death and destruction in every quarter. Added to all this was the din of war and the yet more terrible yells and shouts of the outside enemy as they came up, from time to time, along and within a few yards of the whole line of the intrenchment, manifesting a determination to carry everything before them.

"Such was the scene which met the gaze on all sides, as the atmosphere, clearing at intervals, gave us time and opportunity to see about us. And here, it may be observed, the noise and tumult were something awful, almost deafening. The smoke, too, which now encircled the whole place, added, if anything could add, to the horrors of the scene; it was, if possible, more dense than the worst of London fogs. In vain we tried to see. We could not do so for the thick veil which encircled and surrounded us—nothing indeed could be seen, do what you may, except at intervals, whilst the look of the atmosphere, was at once ominous and lowering. The whole panorama, at this stage, can only be described as truly appalling. We did not know at what moment the enemy might not close. They appeared so near at one time that we thought the long expected end had at last come. It was terribly trying for the time being, and nothing which we could do was sufficient to shake off the idea of the certainty of the approaching crisis. Language alone fails to convey to the imagination the mental torture of the moment—nor picture that terrible suspense—foreboding a possible catastrophe—those agonizing thoughts which durst not find expression by word or act, lest they should damp energies, or communicate to others what we endeavoured, but vainly endeavoured, to suppress in ourselves. If there remained any one way, or means of escape from this all absorbing feeling, it was in the excitement of the time, in the din of battle, as the multitude came on surging up to within the very walls of the defences. Then it was to behold a scene which baffles all description and which has fallen to the lot of few to witness. *Grand* and *majestic* beyond all compare in all its terrible outlines as the enemy advanced led by the best and bravest spirits among them, holding in their hands banners of different colors, and carrying flags which to them were symbols of certain victory, crying out at the same time " *Ali ! Ali !*" and " *Din ! Din !*"* in a tone and under circumstances which left no doubt in the mind as to the passions which swayed the multitude, and we knew what all this meant.†

"At length the long deferred crisis had arrived. And it was now felt that the time had come, in order to avert the consequences of a great and impending catastrophe—terrible to contemplate—terrible too, by reason of the consequences which would inevitably have followed failure at the critical time, for, then indeed, *a wail would have ascended which would have sent a thrill throughout the length and breadth of the civilized world.* We felt the impulse. We

Catastrophe averted.

Extract from Routledge's work.

On the 12th August, 1857, a month before the assault of Delhi, and a month after the massacre of the women and children at Cawnpore, Colonel Inglis stated his force to General Havelock, as numbering 350 Europeans and 300 Natives, in charge of 220 women, 230 children and 120 sick.

---

* *Ali* was son-in-law to the Prophet Mahomed and *Din* signifies religion, so that they were, in giving utterance to these words, appealing to *Ali* for aid in behalf of their religion.

† " The sword, " says Mahomed, " is the key of paradise and hell. A drop of blood shed in the cause of God, a night spent in arms, is of more avail than two months of fasting and prayer. Whoever falls in battle, his sins are forgiven ; at the day of judgment his wounds shall be resplendent as vermilion, and odoriferous as musk ; and the loss of his limbs shall be replaced with the wings of angels and cherubim."

Those who perish in a holy crusade are supposed to go straight to Heaven ; and all the eloquence and imagination of the Prophet were employed to paint, in glowing terms, the liberal and intoxicating joys there awaiting them. When to such liberal promises of future bliss is added the immediate prospect of present wealth, (23 lacs of rupees, besides the valuable State jewellery from the King's treasury we had in the Residency) we need not be surprised that the ruthless injunctions of the Prophet, to convert or slay, never lagged for want of willing hands to execute them.

rose to the occasion. We realized, as it were, intuitively the magnitude of the responsibility, and we girt ourselves for the great fight which was to decide the fate of so many hundreds of human beings. Everything now depended upon the display of the innate energies and resources, the fortitude, the courage of the race, the genius of the national character—for death itself, in the then state of our minds, had lost its terrors; and it would have been welcome, nay, doubly welcome, even in the worst of forms, could we only have been assured that the young and helpless, the sick and the wounded, would have escaped the fate, which we, alas! but too well knew awaited them, if we failed at the last moment to repell the assaults of a cruel, unrelenting, and uncompromising foe. It was this terrible feeling, this overpowering dread of what would be the fate of others if anything happened which preyed upon our minds, and roused in us a determination, if possible—more than human—to resist to the last, come what may, and yet not without hope in the great and righteous cause in which we were engaged.

"It was thus in the darkest hour of our trial, when almost every hope had fled, wearied and exhausted—when despair had almost seized us—that we found that we were *not alone*. Our steadfastness and faith were about to be rewarded. Our drooping spirits once more revived, for just at this juncture, in the very height of the crisis, through God's providence, the tide turned against the enemy and in our favour. And what a relief, and at such a stage. The sudden transition from the deepest despondency and despair to intense and great joy was, of course, only too obvious, though there was no open demonstration of it. In some countenances there was not even the outward expression of any change. It instilled in us, as it were, a fresh lease of life, as we saw the enemy gradually, but sullenly give way, reel, and then retreat, scattered by the fire to which they were exposed. We redoubled our efforts and those efforts

Height of the crisis, turning point.

Despair and final efforts of the enemy to recover lost ground.

were not to prove unavailing. In vain the enemy now came up to the assault. They found that they had a terrible foe to deal with. Every attempt proved abortive. Again and again they were repulsed, each time with frightful slaughter. They were now in turn in despair. They realized, for the first time, the terrors of their position. They were promised and had almost ensured victory. Failure and defeat alone awaited them. Collecting themselves again, as for one more desperate effort, they advanced again and again to recover lost ground. In their last despairing efforts—placing themselves under the leadership of men of known reputation—men who displayed a bravery on the occasion worthy of a better cause, but in vain—all in vain. These last efforts also failed and still more signally. Their very numbers proved their weakness. The strength on which they relied failed them at the very moment when success was within their reach. The enemy too had become exhausted by the very intensity of the efforts which they made to carry the position. All had proved abortive. There was nothing left now but to give way. A panic seized them, and they drew off seeking the very cover from which they had emerged, early in the morning, in the certainty of victory. But it was ordained otherwise. It was the triumph once more of Christianity over heathenism—of truth and principle over fanaticism, ignorance and superstition; and to this alone may be attributed the supremacy which our arms achieved in the end. After the final assault, we rested on our arms almost breathless from excitement and terribly exhausted by exposure for several hours to the intense rays of a July sun. Thus ended the life and death struggle of this eventful day. No other can compare to it even during the struggle of that memorable period. No other was so nearly drifting into defeat and failure; a calamity which, it may truly be said, was only averted by the interposition of a higher and unseen power.

Our victory.

"Fear not, I am with thee, O be not dismayed,
  For I am thy God, I will still give thee aid;
I'll strengthen thee, help thee, and cause thee to stand,
  Upheld by my gracious, omnipotent hand."

"When through the deep waters I call thee to go,
    The river of sorrow shall not overflow;
For I will be with thee thy trials to bless,
    And sanctify to thee thy deepest distress.

"The soul that on Jesus hath leaned for repose,
    I will not, I will not desert to his foes;
That soul, though all hell should endeavour to shake,
    I'll never, no never, no never forsake!"

Shrieks of women.

"In the interlude of the scenes which I have attempted to describe, women shrieked and men grew pale, yet, under those pale and emaciated forms was to be seen the stern determination to hold out, and fight to the last, come what may—expecting none and giving no quarter. The very presence of those who were dependent on us for their very safety—and honour—more dearly cherished than their lives—made us the more desperate and the more determined to overcome the foe, and if the worst came to the worst, we were ready to sacrifice life, and in a manner so as to deprive even death of its sting.

"Such was the feeling which animated all ranks. The part which the soldiers of Her Majesty's 32nd and 84th took in the deadly struggle, their bearing and conduct, are now matters of history. No further eulogy is needed. They have long since been classed among the 'bravest of the brave.' Never were a mere handful of Englishmen placed in such a trying position. Never did they acquit themselves better. But it was not Englishmen alone who shone so conspicuously during the terrible strife which characterized the operations of the day. The faithful natives among us emulated their European brethren. Moreover, there were a few, though very few, it is true, of other nationalities, not more than three or four, perhaps, who fought side by side with us on the occasion. Conspicuous, however, among these, was the brave and intrepid Duprat, the true type of a Frenchman. In his person France was well and nobly represented. At one period of his life Duprat

Duprat—the brave and intrepid Frenchman.

had served with considerable distinction in the French army in Africa. He was one of the survivors of Chinhut. Eventually he succumbed—one of a noble band—killed, fighting to the last. His loss, like several others, was severely felt at the time, showing how much we appreciated him, but we had one consolation at least, and that not little, in that we happened to know that the brave and gallant Frenchman died the death which so well befitted him—that of a Christian warrior. He lost everything, life, as well as all he possessed, in the cause of a State in which, may be, he had—politically speaking—no personal interest.

"Meantime in my own post the cannonade had worked its worst. Almost all the pillars which supported the portico had either been knocked down, or injured, so that the position became almost untenable after a short time. Cannon balls, not to speak of bullets, passed through every door and window—and every aperture—through rooms and places, and into recesses hitherto unknown, destroying everything in their onward course. No place was sacred or secure. All were alike exposed and searched out by the fire which the enemy brought to bear on us. A Sikh who thought himself safe, and who was firing, being under the shelter of one of the pillars, was mortally wounded, the ball piercing the pillar and carrying away his arm. And yet so deadly was the fire that we with difficulty extricated him. One by one the pillars gave way, and came down. The Artillery fire against the building never slackened for a moment; balls passed over our heads, and crossed our backs. The enemy had got the range and each ball told on the building. The Officer Commanding was thrown back, momentarily, by the mere wind of a cannon ball, for it did not touch him, which passed at the back of his head as I was sitting close to him, and almost by his side. The brave man rallied at once, and worked away as if nothing had occurred. He set us an example worthy of the man, and we did not fail to benefit by it in the trying circumstances under

NOTE.—They fired a little too high and more towards the north and centre of the portico than south, which saved us.

which we were placed. It became evident every moment, however, that the portico was gradually becoming untenable. It was no longer safe. It threatened to crush us by its very weight. The brave Sikhs became uneasy, and no wonder. We stood it as long as we could, but we found that we had no alternative, but to make a retrograde movement down-stairs. Shortly after we had taken up the new position, the fire suddenly ceased and the enemy retreated. A silence then, as of the grave, prevailed, only, however, for a time. The reaction was so sudden that we could not be reconciled to the belief that all was over. We were terribly exhausted, but were obliged to remain on duty till late in the evening. Meantime, the portico came down with a crash, as had been anticipated for some hours. The debris constituted ever after a breast-work which we held to the last, 22nd November, 1857, 12 o'clock, leaving the lights burning.

"Next morning we picked up and counted no less than 24 cannon balls in the upper portion of the building. This arose from the fact that one of the back walls, being of solid masonry, was immensely strong. The cannon balls, as they came through the portico, struck the walls, rebounded, and remained in the building.

"Many women in those days displayed heroism quite equal to that of men. In one sense they were superior. They were more patient, more philosophical, less irritable under their trials and also far more resigned. They grasped at once the position in which we were placed. The germs of those great and noble qualities displayed themselves at an early stage of our trials, and under those trials they shone forth in all their strength and splendour. These helped to throw a lustre, as it were, over the very gloom which at times seemed almost impenetrable. Their very presence, resignation, and courage—passive though it may have seemed—instilled in us spirit which had the effect of successfully carrying us through many a desperate struggle. They evinced a strength, nobility, and fortitude of character, throughout all the scenes of that memorable struggle, which

Heroism of women.

no words can adequately depict or pourtray, whilst in the display of the nobler qualities of our nature they stand unrivalled. In a word, the history of the siege of Lucknow would cease to be what it actually was—eminently the most momentous historical event of its character of any age, or period—but for the *inspiration* of woman. It was her example and presence which unquestionably had its influence, insensibly, perhaps, but not the less felt throughout the trying scenes of that memorable period—which ultimately tended so much to the success of our efforts against the continual and unceasing onslaughts of a deadly, formidable, and implacable enemy for many a weary month, whilst she was also, in many respects, the embodiment of all those graces and virtues which helped to light up some of the darkest episodes of the siege. And yet, in one sense more—in serenity of mind and complacency of deportment—she also reigned *supreme*. Several men died during the siege having become insane, no women died insane, nor, to my knowledge, did any become insane. Some men from anxiety and a variety of causes utterly indescribable, completely lost their balance of mind, and lived, as it were, a living death; and when the last hour came, passed away silently as if death to them had no terrors, and truly so, for they had long since lost the capacity or power, to all appearance at least, to realize the situation. We sympathized with them in their afflictions, and mourned their death. We could do no more. We buried them, like the rest of the illustrious dead, in silence, at dusk, and even at dead of night, to avoid the enemy's fire. A few muttered prayers, and all was over. We returned again to the work of defence.

"Such is an outline—at the same time, a very faint one—of the scenes which I have endeavoured to describe. To pourtray the reality would probably baffle all human efforts."

69. To resume my narrative I have to state that the enemy never managed to inflict a wound upon me, but about the middle of August I accidentally wounded myself. A number of us were taking rest during the heat of the day, in the

verandah of the room in the centre of the court-yard, when a badly-thrown 8-inch shell from our own mortar battery at the Post Office, instead of hitting Johannes' house, for which it was intended, lighted in our court-yard and exploded within a few yards of us. There was, of course, a regular stampede from our comfortable verandah, and, in the rush, I fell over my sister and hit my left knee against a sharp stone. Under any other circumstances the wound caused would have healed in a few days, but owing to constant duty, bad food, and the reduced condition of my general system, the sore festered and sloughed until it assumed a formidable appearance. The College Surgeon Doctor (now Surgeon-General Sir Joseph) Fayrer, when called in, told me that, unless I kept perfectly quiet, he would have to amputate the leg; and as amputation in those days meant certain death, I preferred the alternative. This wound kept me in constant pain for upwards of two months, and healed very, very slowly. The slightest scratch inflamed, owing to the bad air and want of vegetable food; and it was on this account that so few, who were wounded at all severely, recovered. Amputations were, with only few exceptions, fatal, and the least wound became serious. Much danger was experienced and several accidents occurred from our own shells. The enemy was so near our post that these were thrown to short distances and the fuses were cut down accordingly. Very frequently fragments of shells pitched from the garrison returned into the intrenched position, making in their passage through the air a very peculiar whirling noise; and it was impossible to tell from what quarter the missile was approaching.

70. Early in the month of August the Residency, which had, from the commencement of the siege, been the chief mark for the fire of the enemy, now showed great indications of dilapidation. It was pierced with shot on every side and had to be abandoned as a residence. Ensign Studdy, of the 32nd Regiment, was badly wounded by a round shot when standing at the door of the Mess-room. It will be seen from the following that even the most apparently secure apartments within the walls of the Residency were quite unsafe.

In 1899, when the 1st Battalion of the 32nd (Cornwall) Light Infantry was quartered in Lucknow, after an absence of about 42 years, I was shown the handsome Mess-plate of the 32nd Foot, which comprised a soup tureen through which a bullet had passed during the siege. The vessel and bullet were sent to Windsor Castle for the Queen's inspection, and were graciously returned with a request that they were to be kept by the Regiment as relics of the Indian Mutiny of 1857. Besides the soup tureen, I had the pleasure of inspecting many other relics of subsequent events which are in the safe keeping of the Officers of the 32nd (Cornwall) Light Infantry.

The garrison, at this time, was greatly harassed and assailed on all sides with a storm of round shot and musketry, both day and night, which resulted in many casualties.* A great number of bullets and round shot were collected by the boys in our post. Notwithstanding that many of the bullets were fired from a great distance, they fell with fatal effect in places which were considered safe. Thus the top of the houses from which we used to fire, though protected by a high parapet, was by no means safe, for many men were killed, not by bullets fired point blank, but by their falling downward through the air.

71. On the 10th of August the *second* general attack was made by the enemy, who sprung a mine in front of Johannes' house, which entirely blew down the outer room of the post we occupied, destroying also upwards of fifty feet of palisades and defences. From this outer room, which was loop-holed, the boys, as well as the masters, used to keep watch on the enemy's movements and fire whenever an opportunity offered, but, just before the mine was sprung, we were

---

* The death rate for many days averaged twenty. By the end of July, one hundred and seventy casualties had occurred in the 32nd Regiment only.

The Duke of Cornwall's Light Infantry, both Battalions, have erected a Memorial Column in the Residency grounds to fittingly commemorate the martial deeds of the 32nd Foot, which did such excellent service during the siege in 1857. Lucknow has been authorized to be borne on the regimental colours and appointments of the Regiment, which, for its gallantry, has been constituted Light Infantry; and the Officers and men were allowed to reckon one year's additional service (*vide* Appendix D).

providentially called away for Divine Service,* and thus a number of us escaped being buried in the ruins. The rooms in which were our sick and wounded now became completely exposed. The doors connecting the inner-rooms with the room blown up were open, and through these doors the enemy who swarmed in Johannes' house could be plainly seen. For sometime they neither fired nor made any attempt to advance, so that it gave us the opportunity to close the intervening doors after removing the sick and wounded to a more secure position. Johannes' house, densely occupied by the enemy and closely adjoining the line of our defences, was separated from La Martiniere post by a narrow street, only 20 feet wide.

72. The enemy soon afterwards commenced firing and, one private of the 32nd Regiment, standing on my right, who had accompanied Brigadier Inglis to the scene of the disaster, was shot in the head by a bullet passing through a door which we had just closed. The Brigadier expressed great grief at this accident, exclaiming, "Another of my brave men is gone," and immediately ordered us to fix bayonets, get under cover and guard the breach. The foe soon occupied in force all the buildings round about, from which they commenced a furious fusilade, and made several attempts to get into our Garrison, but a steady musketry fire soon made them retreat. They managed, however, to get into the *taikhana*† of the rooms in which our guard was located, and this made us feel most uncomfortable, as it rendered our position very insecure; Captain McCabe‡ of the 32nd Regiment, a gallant soldier who had won his commission from the ranks at Multan, by placing one of the colours of his Regiment on the breach, however, came to the rescue with a few

---

* Every Sunday Service was held in some improvised place for Christian worship.

† The front of the *taikhana*, or subterranean room, was lined by a range of small shops which the enemy rushed into and occupied; but after they were expelled by hand-grenades, we got into the rooms and barricaded all the outer doors.

‡ This brave officer, the gallant leader of many former sorties, was killed, on 29th September, in a sortie directed against Phillips's Garden Battery.

hand-grenades,* which were speedily dropped in their midst, through a hole which was bored through the floor. Three of the *Pandies*† were killed and the others retreated into the store rooms adjoining Johannes' house, while those of the enemy that had taken possession of the trenches of the Cawnpore Battery, with the evident intention of capturing it, had to beat a hasty retreat owing to the withering fire that was directed on them by the Officers in the Brigade Mess. The wines and stores belonging to Monsieur Duprat (Murray & Co. of the period) were kept in a cellar under the rooms occupied by the guard of the Cawnpore Battery. One day the soldiers smelt the wines and managed to open a case of champagne. After this the liquor was removed to our post and was all blown up by the explosion of the enemy's mine alluded to above.

73. On the 18th August the *third* general attack was made, and, despite the constant vigilance and exertions of the engineers, the mutineers managed this time to do serious injury by exploding a mine under the outer defences of the second Sikh square, so designated because it was principally occupied by the Sikh Cavalry and a few native Christian musicians of the Regiments that had mutinied in Cantonments. By the explosion, Captain Adolphus Orr, Lieutenants Mecham and Soppitt and one drummer were thrown into the air, but descended inside the square amidst the *débris* of the building, and escaped with little injury. The fourth, Band Sergeant Curtain, of the 41st N. I., was unhappily thrown on the enemy's side, where he was cut up by them, and the next day his headless body was seen lying on the road-side. Not less than seven men (six drummers and one sepoy) were buried under the ruins, from whence it was impossible to extricate them, owing to the tremendous fire kept up by the enemy from houses situated within ten yards of

---

* Hand-grenades, so called from the resemblance of its shape and size to a pomegranate, are usually about two inches and a half in diameter. These shells of iron are filled with powder which is fired by means of a fuse and are intended to be thrown by the hand into mines, trenches or upon besiegers mounting a breach. They burst into many pieces and do great injury.

† Sepoys being called *Pandies*, originated from the name of Mangal Pande of the 34th. N. I. at Barrackpur, who was the first man to mutiny and wound the Adjutant and Sergeant-Major of his Regiment.

The native term for Sepoy is *Telingá*.

the breach. The enemy were ultimately driven from this position by the bayonets* of H. M.'s 32nd and 84th Foot.† This explosion was followed by a general assault of a less determined character and the enemy was repulsed without much difficulty. The enemy, evidently being reinforced, now began to appear in large numbers round the intrenchment, occupying the surrounding houses and firing on any one who dared to show himself. It was impossible to move from under shelter of the houses without being fired at; and the casualties which occurred by persons passing on duty from one post to another were numerous. The Brigade Mess, Cawnpore Battery‡ and La Martiniere Post sustained the greatest injury from the enemy in Johannes' house. § The turret which led to the roof of the building was occupied by one of the late King's African soldiers who used his rifle with great precision. He was known to us by the affectionate sobriquet of "Bob the Nailer," because he nailed every man he fired at. His shots have been known even to penetrate the doors and windows of the General Hospital. This was a two-storied building, with very large and lofty rooms, standing on the same level as the Residency, and was much exposed to the enemy's fire. The doors on the north side were closed with tents and boxes filled with earth, yet many were shot inside it during the siege. The General Hospital presented one of the most heart-rending sights imaginable; and scenes of suffering which I witnessed in this place while attend-

---

* "No fact, however, has been more clearly established in the course of this insurrection than that Asiatics, whatever may be their strength, cannot resist the charge of the smallest number of Englishmen. There is something in the sight of British Infantry advancing at a run, with stern visage, bayonets fixed, determination marked in every movement of the body, which appals them: they cannot stand it—they never have stood it yet."
    In regard to the bayonet, it has been too hastily assumed that it is of no use because bayonet fighting has been so rare in South Africa. The bayonet has done great service to us in the past, and will no doubt stand us in good stead in the future against Asiatics.

† On the 3rd June, Captain Lowe returned from Cawnpore with fifty men of the 32nd and, on the 4th of June, Captain O'Brien arrived from the same station with fifty men of H. M.'s 84th Foot. These men were sent, by Sir Hugh Massey Wheeler, in return for the force lent to him by Sir Henry Lawrence in the previous month.

‡ The Cawnpore Battery was terribly exposed and cost the lives of many officers and men.

§ Johannes was the richest European merchant of Lucknow then in the Garrison.

ing the wounded and dying are indescribable. Everywhere wounded officers and men were lying covered with blood, some with mangled limbs, their faces pale and bodies almost cold. Surgeons were to be seen busy, cutting, probing the wounds, amputating and bandaging. Such scenes were common, and in time people grow callous from the continued sight of pain and suffering in the same way as they became accustomed to danger. The ladies were unremitting in their kindness; they most generously devoted themselves to the task of relieving the wants of the sick and wounded, and speaking words of comfort to the dying. The names of Polehampton, Birch, Barber, and Gall, among many others, will live in the history of this trying time. In continuation of the above may be added the names of Mrs. J. C. Parry, wife of the then Manager of the Delhi Bank, Lucknow branch; of Mrs. Erith, whose husband had been mortally wounded in Innes' Garrison during the attack by the rebels on the 20th of July; of Mrs. Bates, and Miss Alone. Of Mrs. Parry's good actions and unfailing kindness to the sick and the wounded in hospital, it would be difficult to speak too highly. Prior to the siege she had laid in a large stock of tea, and every morning and evening a *degchi* (cooking utensil) of this was prepared by her for the patients; in addition to this she used to purchase *chokar* (bran) whenever she could get it, even at a rupee a seer; this, after being soaked in water all night, was strained and made into a sort of gruel which the sick were only too glad to get. The tea and gruel would hardly be considered delicacies in these days, but were thankfully received as a welcome addition to their scanty fare by the sick in hospital, accompanied as they always were by words of kindly sympathy to the brave men who fought and bled to save their countrywomen from death, and worse than death, dishonour. Often Mrs. Parry put aside her own portion of the scanty meal which fell to the lot of each during the siege, in order to take it to some poor sufferer who needed it even more than she did. Of this lady a friend tells an amusing anecdote: "Mrs. Parry, during the latter months of the siege, suffered from sores caused by insufficient food and hardships of the time. She asked the Doctor's advice as to what she should do to get relief; he, looking very learned, prescribed a *change of diet.* 'Thank you, Doctor,' said the lady. 'I wonder you have not prescribed a *change of air*, one would be about as practicable as the other.'" Of these four ladies, all but one have gone to their rest. Miss Alone, who after the relief was married to Mr. W. B. Thompson, is still a resident of Lucknow, and lives to tell her children and grand-children stories of life during the ever memorable siege of the Residency.

74. On the night of the 20th August, Lieutenant Aitken displayed his intrepidity by a very daring act which saved us from a possible catastrophe. The enemy, eluding the vigilance of the sentries, made a pile of logs and combustibles against the Baillie Guard Gate. Lieutenant Aitken was, however, equal to the emergency. Under a heavy fire of musketry this brave Officer and some of his men removed the pile and extinguished the flames.

75. On the 21st August, the date on which "Bob the Nailer" was blown up,* I was washing my clothes in the court-yard near the well in La Martiniere post when a large fragment of shell came whizzing through the air and imbedded itself in the masonry of the well within a yard of where I was standing. This was another narrow escape and one which made me feel very queer at the time, for I heard the missile coming down but dared not move, not knowing where it would hit. Once again when five of us were digging a deodorizing pit in a corner under the large *nim* (melia indica) tree in the court-yard, which is still standing, a piece of shell came right down into the very centre of the pit, just at the moment after the boy who had dug it came out. These were all fragments from our own shells pitched from the mortar

---

* Bob the Nailer, who shot many a man in the early days of the siege, was stopped in his career by a mine which was begun from La Martiniere post and, passing under Johannes' house, blew up the latter, thus relieving the garrison of a most deadly fire from which we had suffered. The mine was begun on the 17th August, and was fired on the morning of the 21st with complete effect. Captain Fulton planned the measure, which was pushed on with unremittting exertion by Lieutenant (now Lieutenant-General) McLeod Innes, and men of the 32nd assisted by La Martiniere boys.

battery at the Post-office, which certainly proved anything but a pleasant neighbour to La Martiniere post. My father also had several narrow escapes, one of which was from a bullet which passed through the back of his chair from which he had only risen the moment before : nor was my mother without her warlike experiences. One day a 24-pounder shot from Phillips' Garden Battery * came through the wall into her room. The shot did not hit her, but one of the dislodged bricks did, striking her on the head, which embittered her very strongly against the mutineers in particular and all natives in general. Both she and my sister were, on this occasion, covered with fallen bricks and mortar.

76. About two months after the siege had begun, rations were issued to us of gun-bullock beef † or mutton, with wheat, or rice, and salt. The wheat was ground by the boys of our garrison only, and the senior lads, in addition to their own share, had to grind an extra quantity for the younger boys who were incapable of turning the hand-mill. I need hardly mention that this was the most arduous duty we had to perform throughout the siege. As the bull-beef served out to the Garrison was not fit to roast, owing to its toughness, it was generally made into stew. On one occasion, when we were standing round a large cooking pot, ready to receive our respective shares of a rather savoury stew of Commissariat beef, a large fragment of a shell came whirling through the air, struck the *degchi*, or cooking utensil, and bespattered us with its contents, so that we had to take our stew in external applications, which was not very palatable.

77. In August the entire Garrison was brought on reduced rations, which were barely sufficient to afford sustenance. The full rations at first starting were a pound of meat and a pound of flour per man ; this was reduced to twelve ounces, then to six, and after General Havelock's arrival, to four ounces. Women got three-quarter rations, children half.

---

* This battery was captured by Colonel R. Napier, on the 2nd October, 1857.
† The beef ration during the entire siege was obtained from the bullocks of No. 8 Light Field Battery.

The fighting natives received the same as the European women, except that they got no meat, receiving, instead of it, *dal* (split pulse) and *ghee* (clarified butter).

But the comparatively liberal diet was too good to last; for on 2nd October stock was taken of our provisions, when it was found that we had sufficient to last 35 days, so the scale was reduced.

After the arrival of Generals Outram and Havelock, the enemy continued to blockade us, and our gallant deliverers were now besieged along with us. They had brought in no provisions or stores of any kind, and in point of food we were worse off than even before. The number of additional mouths, owing to the very great multitude of camp followers, made considerable diminutions in our Commissariat stores; but by dint of the very strictest economy they lasted to the end of the siege.

Towards the end of the siege articles of ordinary use and consumption had become very scarce and were obtainable only at fabulous prices. I mention some of the current rates:—

Brandy	Rs. 16 per bottle, which rose to „ 20 towards the end of the siege;
Sherry	„ 70 per dozen;
Beer	„ 60 „ „
Cigars	Re. 1 each, and they rose to Rs. 3;
Country leaf tobacoo ...	Rs. 2 a leaf;
Attah (coarse flour) ...	Re. 1 per seer;*
Ghee (clarified butter) ...	Rs. 10 „ „
Sugar	„ 20 „ „
Eggs	As. 8 each;
A flannel shirt ...	Rs. 20;
A pair of boots ...	„ 12;

and all other things in proportion. That unfortunate day at Chinhut precipitated matters, and as it came so unexpectedly, people made no arrangements for provisioning themselves; many,

---

* A seer is equivalent to 2 lbs.

indeed, never dreamt of such a necessity, and the few that had, were not prepared for such a long investment. We felt a great longing for bread, which was a thing unseen and only remembered; coarse *chapatis* (unleavened cakes, the common food of the poorer classes of natives) constituted our staple fare. Except for hospital comforts, and here and there private stores, there was little else procurable in the garrison—no bread, butter, milk, eggs, vegetables, wines, beer or tobacco. The lack of vegetables was most sorely felt, and was the cause of much illness, and the want of sugar and milk was most trying to the children, amongst whom there was a great mortality. One of our masters, Mr. Wall, however, surprised us by producing a plum-cake on the anniversary of his birthday, the 15th October, which was very sparingly distributed in our post. The soldiers, who felt the loss of tobacco more severely than anything else, were put to a variety of shifts. They dried the tea-leaves left after infusion and smoked them. The guava trees, and other garden shrubs, were stripped of their leaves, which, after having been dried in the sun, were used as a substitute for tobacco. The stump of a cigar was looked upon as a luxury by many.

78. About the beginning of August firing of cannon and English music were heard in the city. We were all frantic with joy at the thought that deliverance was at hand, whereupon many climbed the highest points, regardless of danger, to see the long-expected friends coming. What bitter disappointment to find afterwards that the guns we heard were firing a salute in honour of the new King proclaimed by the mutineers.*

---

* "Brijis Kadar, a boy about 10 years of age, was proclaimed King of Oudh by the rebel soldiery. This lad was the supposed son of the ex-King, Wajid Ali Shah, but the real offspring of one Mammu Khan. The mother of this boy had originally been a dancing girl, with whom Mammu Khan, then holding subordinate charge in the Royal cook-room, had formed an intimacy. The King, hearing of the girl's beauty, admitted her to the number of his *mahals* (harems), under the title of 'Hazrat Mahal.' She received a handsome allowance, with a large establishment, of which she appointed Mammu Khan the Darogha, or Superintendent. The former intimacy was still, though secretly, carried on, and resulted in the birth of the boy Brijis Kadar."

After the capture of Lucknow by Sir Colin Campbell, the Begam and Brijis Kadar fled to Nepaul and became fugitives at Katmandu. Mammu Khan was captured and transported to the Andamans.

79. On the 5th September* the enemy made their *fourth* and last desperate assault, which was preceded, as usual, by the explosion of mines. Having exploded a large mine, a few feet short of the bastion of the 18-pounder gun in Major Apthorp's post, they advanced with large scaling ladders; these they planted against the embrasure of the 18-pounder Battery which they tried to escalade. A well-directed fire of musketry and some hand grenades, however, soon dispersed and drove them back, with heavy loss, into the adjoining houses whence they had issued. Shortly after the enemy sprung another mine close to the Brigade Mess and our (Martiniere) post, and advanced with some show of determination, but their courage soon failed them at seeng their dead which bestrewed Johannes' garden, and which bore testimony to the fatal accuracy of the fire directed at them by the officers from the Brigade Mess : whereupon they fled most ignominiously, leaving their leader among the slain. At other posts they made similar attacks, but with less resolution, and everywhere with the same result. While these attacks lasted we were subjected to a heavy fire from the enemy's batteries in different quarters, but as we kept well under cover, little or no loss was inflicted by the shower of bullets and round shot which fell in our midst. On this occasion the rebels must have suffered heavily, as they were seen, shortly after the action, carrying off their killed and wounded in cart-loads over the bridges in the direction of Mariaon Cantonments. These were the four critical periods during the investment, and had it not been for the vigilance and exertions of the Engineers (specially Captain George Fulton) and a number of the old Cornish miners of the 32nd in detecting the enemy's mines before they were completed, the assaults would doubtless have been much more numerous and might have ended in the capture of some of our most important and advanced positions.

---

* The attack on this date was especially heavy. Assaults were made on various points of the defences, and a storm of round shot and musket balls was kept up. Our men considered that the match-lockmen of the enemy had increased.

80. The State prisoners, five in number, whose previous conduct threw suspicion upon them, were located in the long room on the north side of the Hospital. The first of these was Mustafa Ali Khan, the ex-King's elder brother, who was found in confinement on the first occupation of the Province. He was reputed and generally believed to be weak-minded, and would have easily been made a tool of by designing men. Mahomed Humaun Khan and Mirza Mahomed Shekoh were two Princes connected with the Delhi family who were notorious for their intrigues. They also were confined. Nawab Rukun-ud-daulah,* one of the sons of Saadat Ali Khan, a former Nawab Vazir of Oudh, who was believed to be in correspondence with the mutineers, was one of the number. There was also the young Raja of Tulsipur,† who had been guilty of serious misbehaviour before the mutiny and was then residing at Lucknow under surveillance. The rest of the prisoners were unimportant persons, merely attendants and servants on the others. It is a noteworthy circumstance that the room where these State prisoners were kept was seldom or ever assailed by shot, or shell, and the impression was that they found some method of communicating their whereabouts, through their servants, to the enemy.

81. Fifteen of the senior boys had to do duty as soldiers of the garrison, mounting guard in their turn at La Martiniere post and standing to arms when the position was attacked. Those who did so, besides myself, were David Arathoon, William Clark, John Hornby, Daniel Isaacson, James Luffman, James Lynch, David Macdonald, Donald Macdonald, Lewis Nicolls, George Roberts, Joseph Sutton, Frederick Sutton, John Walsh, and Samuel Wrangle. Willingly did the boys throw themselves into the thick of the work. They cheerfully took the musket, and, night and day, at one of the most exposed posts, did sentry

---

* Nawab Rukun-ud-daulah died in captivity in the Residency, and was buried under the large banian tree, which is still standing, near the gate of Mr. Ommaney's Garrison.

† The Raja of Tulsipur died on the way to Alam Bagh.

duty with the soldiers. Well and nobly they did their duty and proud may those be who can point to the medal they won for their services in the 'Defence of Lucknow.'* Besides our military duty we had, also as opportunity allowed, to act as heads of sections over the smaller boys employed on various services at the different posts. The services were washing, grinding corn, pulling *pankhas*, and attending the sick and wounded in the General Hospital, and general fetching and carrying. Even the smallest Martiniere boy had to work throughout the siege; and the whole of the garrison, the ladies especially, can bear testimony to the value of their services. I myself filled the posts successively of corn-grinder, carrier of provisions, and superintendent of the boys in attendance on the sick and wounded in the General Hospital. While discharging this last duty, my father, who was at La Martiniere post, fell ill, and the Principal recalled me to our garrison to enable me to attend on him. Under the careful supervision of the teachers our post was always kept clean and neat. The senior boys had to assist in gathering wood for cooking purposes, and, after the 21st September, the date on which our *bhisti* (water carrier) was shot, the duty of supplying water also devolved upon us. Much wearisome labour and drudgery fell on the boys in consequence of the servants having deserted. We had to perform, for ourselves, other menial offices which need not be mentioned; and, in justice, it might well be said that these hardships and privations were patiently borne by one and all throughout the siege.

82. The houses of the city, occupied by the enemy, approached so closely to the line of defences, in some parts, that they afforded opportunities to the sepoys within the intrenchment of holding conversation with their brethren outside. The latter used every endeavour to induce the natives in the garrison to desert, and but for the timely arrival of Generals Havelock and Outram the native troops, who had adhered to us, would, no doubt, have deserted: nor could we have reasonably found fault with them had they done so,

---

* *Vide* Appendix B.

since there was no prospect of relief up to that time. Their desertion would have caused the most fatal depression in our own minds, as, with our diminished numbers and our continual losses, we should soon have been obliged to give up our outposts. Reduced within the narrow compass of the Residency itself, and exposed to the enemy's harassing fire from what would lately have been our outposts, it would have been utterly impossible to have held out. Nothing short of a miracle could have saved us then. Cawnpore would have been re-enacted in Lucknow, or we would have been compelled to blow up our women, children, and wounded, to prevent their falling into the hands of the insurgents, and to have died fighting on the ruins ourselves.

It will be remembered that when the three Native Infantry Regiments mutinied at the Cantonments on the 30th of May, some of the sepoys in each remained faithful. This select band shared all the labours and sufferings of the British during the siege. With scanty food, little and broken sleep, harassing exertions, daily fightings, they remained steadfast to the last. Though sorely tempted by the mutineers, who would often converse with them over the walls of the intrenchment, they never flinched from their duty. The enemy had established batteries all round the position; some of the guns were planted within 50 yards of our defences, and generally so well placed that none of our guns could bear upon them, neither could they be effectually silenced by shells, by reason of their extreme proximity to our position. About the middle of the siege the enemy was known to be short of ammunition, as shown by their often firing logs of wood, bound with iron, and hammered shot in abundance, which, at the short distances from which they were fired, were almost as effective as our own ammunition. They also threw in shells made of hollowed stone, of large size, which generally burst well, breaking into several fragments. These missiles were projected, no doubt, out of the 8-inch howitzer lost at Chinhut. During the first month of the siege the enemy's fire was incessant. It slackened usually towards sunset and was resumed, at intervals, during the night. In addition to repelling real attacks, we were exposed, day and night, to the hardly less harassing false alarms which were constantly being raised by the enemy, who frequently kept up a heavy fire, sounding the advance and shouting for several hours together without a man being visible. "We used to hear them say *chalo bahadur*,' which means 'go on brave men,' but the brave hearkened not to the persuasive accents, and contented themselves with keeping well under cover. The brave few occasionally showed themselves and were shot down." On the occasion of these false alarms we had to stand to arms and remain at our posts till the demonstrations had ceased ; and since these were of almost nightly occurrence, the whole of the officers and men were on duty night and day during the first days of the siege up to the arrival of the first relief, which was on the 25th September, 1857.

83. In addition to this incessant military duty, the men were nightly employed in repairing defences, in moving guns, in burying the dead, in conveying ammunition and Commissariat stores from one place to another, and on fatigue and other duties. Notwithstanding all these hardships, the garrison made several sorties in which they spiked a few of the enemy's heaviest guns and blew up several of the houses from which they had kept up their most harassing fire. Owing to the extreme paucity of our numbers each man felt that on his own individual efforts depended the safety of the entire position. This consciousness incited every man to defend the post assigned to him with such desperate tenacity, and to fight for the lives which Providence had intrusted to his care with such dauntless determination, that the enemy, despite their constant attacks, their numerous mines, and their incessant fire, never succeeded in gaining **one single inch of ground within the bounds of our struggling position**, which was so feebly fortified that, had they once obtained a footing in any of the outposts, the whole place must inevitably have fallen. I would here remark that, with such weak defences as we had, it would have been quite impossible for us to have held out even for a *week*, if we had been surrounded by a courageous foe. Looking at the weakness of our resources and the comparative number

of the besiegers and the besieged, it is not wonderful that Sir Henry himself, at the first moment, scarcely expected to hold out, without relief, for more than ten or fifteen days.

And if the enemy had possessed as leader a real soldier, such was the advantage of their position, so great was their superiority in point of numbers, it is possible that the earlier forebodings of Sir Henry might have been realised. A General who would have freely sacrificed his men, and whose men would not have flinched from his summons, might well have taken advantage of the disaster of Chinhut. The Residency was not, in a military sense, defensible, and must have succumbed to the determined onslaught of determined men, vastly superior in numbers to the Garrison.

But it is a remarkable fact that the mutiny produced no General amongst the mutineers—not a single man who understood the importance of time, of opportunity, of dash in war. Next to God's good Providence, whose Almighty hand all should humbly recognise in our wonderful deliverance, we owe it to the cowardice of our foe. There were several points at which a dozen men abreast might have entered our position without making the least effort, and it is surprising that the enemy did not direct his assaults at them. It was thought the mutineers feared we had mined those places where access was easy, and it may have been this belief which deterred them from attacking us.

84. I will not weary the reader with a detailed narrative of the events which succeeded the attack of the 5th September, suffice it to say, that we still underwent the same privations, sufferings, annoyances, dangers, as well as a greater loss of men daily, and the same hopelessness of relief. The siege went on as usual, with this difference only, that, about this time, the enemy, who seemed to have been reinforced and who fired with greater effect, now became more defiant, and were wont to shout, shriek, brandish their swords, and gesticulate grotesquely on the tops of houses within a few hundred yards of our position, intending to harass us by this means. Since they found they had failed in their several attempts to take the place by a

coup-de-main, they remained sheltered in the buildings around us, evidently awaiting the starvation of the garrison, depriving us of the little time left for repose by false alarms preceded by the noise of bugles sounding the assembly, and a variety of regimental calls. Occasionally their bands played familiar English tunes, which always ended with the National Anthem.

" No news from the outer world,
    Days, weeks, and months have sped,
Pent up within our battlements
    We seem as living dead.

No news from the outer world,
    Have British soldiers quailed
Before the rebel mutineers ?
    Has British valor failed ?

Through fiery heat of summer
    We've braved the rebel host,
No man amongst the garrison
    Has murmured at his post.

Through sick and deadly season
    Of steamy rain we've toiled,
And million raging fanatics
    Have from our arms recoiled.

Weary are we. Yet daily
    The hostile forces spread,
Open the deadly cannonade,
    The fatal storm of lead.

Weary and worn. Yet daily
    Harassed by false alarms,
We snatch our feverish slumberings,
    Pillowed upon our arms.

No news from the outer world,
    Days, weeks, and months have sped,
Pent up within our battlements
    We seem as living dead.

No news from the outer world,
    Have British soldiers quailed
Before the rebel mutineers ?
    Has British valor failed ?'

2.

"No news from the outer world,
    Our barricade is breached,
But not a man amongst the foe
    That gap has ever reached.
No news from the outer world,
    Our flag though rent and torn
Waves high in haughty majesty,
    Bidding our foemen scorn.

What though our ranks grow thinner
    Our courage still beats high,
Proud of our lofty lineage
    We dare to do or die.

We'll close our ranks yet closer,
    Our foemen still shall find
Our hearts know no despondency,
    Nor craven fear our mind.

Sadly we see around us
    Dear comrades we loved well,
Drop down through wasting malady,
    Or wound of shot or shell.

Sadly our hearts grow colder,
    Our home lights slowly die,
In yonder ruined cemetery,
    Our darling treasures lie.

No news from the outer world,
    Days, weeks, and months have sped,
Pent up within our battlements
    Are living and the dead.

No news from the outer world,
    Have British soldiers quailed
Before the rebel mutineers ?
    Has British valor failed ?"

                    J. B. S. BOYLE.

85. Having so long hoped, as it were against hope, for the expected relief to come and seeing no signs of a mitigation of our sufferings, many of us began to give up in utter despair, little dreaming that succour was so nigh, for, on the morning of the 23rd September, the sound of artillery in the direction of Cawnpore* was distinctly heard, thus verifying the

---

* Cawnpore, spelt as it usually is, signifies nothing, but spelt in the way in which it is written by the Hindus, Kánhpúr, the meaning becomes apparent. Kanh is a name for Krishna ; Pur stand for city. The entire word signifies "City of Krishna."

In commerce and manufactures, Cawnpore occupies an unique position in Upper India. The place is centrally situated and is served by, practically, all the Railways in India. A city so rich in commerce does not possess any pleasant places of public resort, and besides the Memorial Church and Garden there are no other places of interest.

proverb " The darkest hour of night is just before the dawn."

"No news from the outer world.
 Hark! surely now draws near
Sharp rattling sounds of musketry,
 A ringing British cheer.

Yes, news from the outer world,
 Pressing the rebels hard,
See Scotia's kilted Highlanders
 Outside the Baillie Guard.

And e'er we cease to wonder,
 They swarm our barricade,
O'er bastion and o'er embrasure,
 They make a sudden raid.

A moment's pause of wonder,
 A moment's pause—and then
Bursts forth the shout of victory,
 To greet our countrymen.

Then from each post and pillar,
 From every intrenched spot
Peals cheer on cheer of ecstasy,
 Aye from the sick man's cot!

A mighty peace sets on us,
 The glorious work is done,
Whilst hand clasps hand in sympathy,
 God bless us every one.

And forth to the outer world
 Our flag though rent and torn
Waves high in haughty majesty
 Bidding our foemen scorn.

And forth to the outer world,
 Our flag will aye proclaim,
Our duty, patience, chivalry,
 Our honor, and our fame."

J. B. S. BOYLE.

As the fire kept approaching, the commotion in the city became intense; while, within the garrison, all was exultation to know that, through God's mercy, deliverance was at hand, as foretold by the Scotch Lassie in her delirium, which is so beautifully described in the following lines by

Grace Campbell, entitled :—

"JESSIE'S DREAM."
(A STORY OF THE RELIEF OF LUCKNOW.*)

Far awa' to bonnie Scotland
Has my spirit ta'en its flight,
An' I saw my mither spinnin'
In our Highland hame at night ;
I saw the kye a browsing,
My father at the plough,
And the grand auld hills aboon them a',
Wad I could see them now !
Oh ! leddy, while upon your knees
Ye held my sleepin' head,
I saw the little Kirk at hame,
Where Tam an' I were wed ;
I heard the tune the pipers play'd,
I kenn'd its rise and fa',
'Twas the wild Macgregor's slogan —
'Tis the grandest o' them a'!

Hark, ! surely I'm no wildly dreamin',
For I hear it plainly now—
Ye cannot, ye never heard it
On the far of mountain's brow ;
For in your southern childhood,
Ye were nourish'd saft and warm,
Nor watch'd upon the cauld hill side
The risin' o' the storm—
Aye ! now the soldiers hear it
An' answer with a cheer,
As " the Campbells are a comin' "
Falls on each anxious ear—

---

* " A story is told that the first to know of the approach of Havelock's relieving force towards Lucknow was Jessie Brown, the wife of a Corporal in the 32nd Regiment. She was lying on the floor, sick with fever, her ear to the ground, when she suddenly leapt to her feet and declared that she heard the pipes of Havelock's Highland Brigade. That the 78th Highlanders had their pipes with them, as they advanced, on the memorable 25th of September, through the city of Lucknow, there can be no possible doubt. Every Officer of the old Garrison can testify to the fact, as the pipes were constantly played after General Havelock's entry and listened to with pleasure by even the usually unappreciative Southron : but that the pipes were played in the advance on that day in such a manner as to be heard by Jessie Brown or any other person in the Residency is an obvious absurdity."

> The cannons roar their thunder,
> An' the Sappers work in vain,
> For high aboon the din o' war—
> Resounds the welcome strain.
>
> An' nearer still, an' nearer still,
> An' now again 'tis " Auld lang syne,"
> Its kindly notes like life bluid rin,
> Rin through this puir sad heart o' mine ;
> Oh ! leddy dinna swoon awa !
> Look up ! the evil's past,
> They're comin' now to dee wi' us,
> Or save us at the last—
> Then let us humbly, thankfully,
> Down on our knees and pray,
> For those who come through bluid and fire
> To rescue us this day.
> That He may o'er them spread His shield,
> Stretch forth His arm an' save
> Bold Havelock an' his Highlanders,
> The bravest o' the brave!

86. On the morning of the 24th we heard the heavy guns of the relieving force. On this day there was not much firing about us, as the enemy's attention was diverted, and they could be seen busily at work removing guns to new positions elsewhere to check the British advance, but a desultory fire was kept up on our various posts during the night, evidently with the object of covering the removal of these guns. Finding that they could no longer resist the advance of Generals Outram [*] and Havelock[†] and their brave men, the enemy, becoming exasperated at their discomfiture, now wreaked a bitter revenge on the helpless European captives, men, women and children, who were brought out and ruthlessly murdered, on this date, in the open space in front of the north-east gate of the Kaisar Bagh Palace, where a cenotaph has since been erected to their memory.

---

[*] General Outram was born in 1803 and died on 12th March, 1863. His remains were interred in Westminster Abbey.

[†] Sir Henry Havelock died at Dilkusha, on 24th November, 1857, and was buried at Alambagh.

87. On the 25th July, being the 26th day of the siege, a spy named Angad,* who had been previously sent out with a message, returned with a letter from Colonel Tytler, Quarter-Master-General, informing us that General Havelock was advancing with a force sufficient to bear down all opposition, and would be with us in a few days; an anxious watch was kept for the promised relief, but the few days expired and it did not arrive. We did not then know, nor did we learn until the 29th August when Angad returned with the intimation that the relieving force, consisting of 1,500 men (1,200 of whom were Europeans) ten guns, imperfectly manned and equipped, after having fought most nobly to effect our deliverance, had been obliged to fall back three times on Cawnpore for re-inforcements and this was the last communication we received until two days before the arrival of Generals Outram and Havelock. The letter was dated Cawnpore, the 24th August, and was as follows:—

"MY DEAR COLONEL,

"I have your letter of the 16th instant. I can only say, hold on and do not *negotiate* † but rather perish sword in hand. Sir Colin Campbell, who came out at a day's notice to command, upon the news arriving of General Anson's death, promises me *fresh troops* and you will be my first care. The *re-inforcements* may reach me in from *twenty to twenty-five days*, and I will prepare everything for a march on Lucknow.

Yours very sincerely,
H. HAVELOCK, BR.-GENL."

To COL. INGLIS,
H. M.'s 32nd Regt.

On receipt of this intelligence many became so disheartened as to give themselves up to despair. Thus hopeless of life, existence became almost a burden to us.

---

* Angad was a pensioned sepoy, a native of Oudh, who was employed in the Intelligence Department by Mr. Gubbins' Assistant, Captain Hawes.

All communications were conveyed by highly-paid spies. The letters were generally written in French, Latin, or Greek, and being wrapped in a quill, or a small piece of bamboo, were carried and concealed by the spies in the most marvellous manner.

† The italics in the above letter indicate Greek characters.

Major-General Sir Henry Havelock, K. C. B.

ADVANCE OF GENERAL HAVELOCK.

"Put thou thy trust in God,
In duty's path go on :
Fix on His word thy steadfast eye
So shall thy work be done."

88. "Upon Brigadier-General Neill's arrival at Cawnpore, from Benares, he was left in command of the former place, whilst Brigadier-General Havelock. commenced his march upon Lucknow. Having crossed the Ganges into Oudh, the mutineers were encountered near Unao, on the 29th of July. The action was commenced by the 78th Highlanders and the 1st Fusiliers, with two guns. Afterwards, the 64th, commanded by Colonel Wilson, were ordered up. Patrick Cavanagh, a private of that Regiment, was hewn in pieces by the sepoys whilst exhibiting to his comrades an example of the highest gallantry. This valiant soldier, had he survived, would have received the Victoria Cross. At the narrow pass between the village and the town of Unao the mutineers were discovered in great force, but after an obstinate contest they sought safety in flight. Subsequently, the troops pushed on towards Bashiratganj, a walled town, with wet ditches, which was captured by the 1st Fusiliers, 64th and 78th Regiments.

"Major-General Havelock's force was not of sufficient strength to continue the advance upon Lucknow, cholera having broken out amongst them ; and he fell back on the 2nd August, on Mangalwar. On the 5th he again attacked the enemy at Bashiratganj, driving, them out of the town with great slaughter. Preparations were next commenced for passing over the Ganges to Cawnpore. The baggage had already been forwarded across the river, when he resolved, on the 11th, of August, to attack the mutineers a third time at Bashiratganj, where they had once more collected in great force, and again defeated them.

"Returning to their former position at Mangalwar, the troops on the 12th and 13th of August, crossed the Ganges to Cawnpore, where they arrived, nearly worn out by fatigue, sickness, and constant exposure to an Indian sun. Almost immediately, however, they struck another effective blow on the mutineers.

A large body of them had collected at Bithur, and were menacing Brigadier-General Neill at Cawnpore. Major-General Havelock, uniting his force with the former, marched on Bithur, and gained another victory. During these several encounters forty guns had been taken, and sixty more recovered for the Government. Great loss had been inflicted on the enemy, while the British casualties were comparatively small.

"The British column afterwards remained at Cawnpore waiting for re-inforcements, and on the 16th September Major-General Sir James Outram arrived with the welcome aid. The united forces amounted to no large number, barely sufficient to attempt the dangerous enterprise before them. But it was decided to advance immediately. General Outram, whose superior military rank placed him in command of the Army, declined to take it. He felt that it was due to General Havelock, and to the strenuous and noble exertions which he had made to relieve Lucknow, that to him should accrue the honor of the achievement. The Major-General, therefore, cheerfully waived his rank on the occasion, and accompanied the force in his civil capacity as Chief Commissioner of Oudh, tendering his military services to General Havelock as a volunteer.

"Brothers in arms, with equal fury fired,
Two friends, two bodies with one soul inspired."

"Accordingly the column left Cawnpore under Havelock's command, and on the morning of the 19th a force of 3,179 men crossed the Ganges by a bridge of boats, but in face of some opposition. Of these 2,388 were European Infantry, 109 European Volunteer Cavalry, 282 European Artillery, 341 Sikh* Infantry and 59 Native Irregular Cavalry. Directly the force arrived on the Oudh bank of the river a letter was received from Brigadier Inglis, written at Lucknow on the 16th of September, giving a deplorable account of our condition, expressing his conviction that our rations would not last longer

---

* The Sikhs are natives of the Punjab, Northern India, who were conquered by the British in 1849. During the mutiny of 1857 they remained faithful to the British, and helped materially to subdue the rebellion.

MAJOR-GENERAL SIR JAMES OUTRAM, G. C. B.

than the 1st October, and imploring news of Havelock's advance. Early on the morning of the 21st, therefore, the force started on its glorious mission with no thought of failure, with steady tread and set faces the force pressed forward, and on the morning of the 23rd they came in sight of the Alambagh.

"But the key of the position was the Alambagh and the adjacent buildings. These were defended by a large body of Infantry and Cavalry, and six guns. The latter were well served for a short time, but were soon silenced by our Artillery. The Volunteer Cavalry and Olphert's Horse Battery then advanced to within range of the Alambagh, the Infantry coming on in line. On nearing the Alambagh, the enemy opened fire from two guns. One of these, a 9-pounder, was posted on the high road, about 400 yards from the enclosed garden. There was a race between our Artillery and Cavalry which should take it. Captain Olphert's Artillery came up to the gun first, from which the enemy, upon seeing our charge, had at once fled, notwithstanding their large masses of Infantry and Cavalry on the right and left. A short stand was made by them about the Alambagh garden; but they were soon driven out by our Infantry, and were pursued nearly to the Canal. Our troops were then withdrawn, and occupied for the night the Alambagh position, under a heavy cannonade from the enemy.

"On the 24th the force was halted, to give the men rest, and prepare for assaulting the city; the heavy guns being, however, engaged during the whole day in replying to an incessant cannonade, which was kept up by the enemy.

89. "On the 25th the force marched at 8 A. M. for the relief of the Residency, after depositing the baggage and tents in the Alambagh under an escort of Infantry and guns, the latter, including two heavy ones, *viz.*, one 24-pounder and an 8-inch howitzer.

"From the Alambagh there was a choice of three roads. One was a continuation of the road from Cawnpore, across the Canal by the Charbagh (four gardens) bridge, and thence in a direct line for about two miles to the Residency. This was the shortest available ; but it was strongly defended. Progress here could only be attempted as a last resort.

"The second road involved a detour to the right by the Dilkusha Palace, whence troops might advance, by a circuitous route on the right bank of the Gumti, or, crossing the Gumti, might march along its left bank to an advantageous site nearly facing the Residency.

"The latter project had commended itself to General Havelock, not only as a means of avoiding the strong positions taken up by the enemy in the streets and outlying buildings of the city, but also because it seemed to present facilities for withdrawing the occupants of the Residency to the north-side of the river. But, setting aside discussion on other grounds, the season was unfavourable to this movement. Incessant rain had thoroughly soaked the earth and its effects would be felt for too long a period to admit of delaying the advance. A reconnaissance made resulted in the decision that it was impossible to move even the light field pieces across the country. This opinion was adopted, and the proposal consequently abandoned.

"The third plan was a kind of compromise, and pointed to a middle course between the other two. It was to force a passage across the Charbagh bridge, thence to turn to the right and move along the bank of the canal, for nearly two miles, to the bridge on the direct road to Dilkusha Palace, from which point a rectangular sweep of about three miles might be made. At the Charbagh bridge was the first severe opposition. The bridge was taken, the adjacent houses were stormed, and the 78th Highlanders were directed to occupy them until all the troops and baggage had passed and then to follow, protecting the rear. The main body advanced by the canal; on reaching the bridge east of Bank's house (now Government House) ; it turned to the left towards the 32nd barracks (Lawrence Terrace) : thence towards the Sikandarbagh, Shah Najaf and Moti Mahal. Between the Charbagh bridge and the Moti Mahal, the force met with very slight opposition. But at the Moti Mahal and the further advanced posts, it came under a strong fire from the Khursheid Manzil and the Kaisarbagh. It was from the Moti Mahal that the real contest began; and this was continued with deadly vigour for about three-quarters of a mile, or the whole remaining distance to the Residency. The shelter afforded by the deserted buildings of the Chutter Munzil Palace, allowed a lull to take place in the busy proceedings of that eventful day.

"Darkness was coming on and General Outram proposed a short halt to enable the rearguard with the heavy guns, baggage, and wounded men to come up. The proposition showed judgment and prudence, for the Chutter Munzil was a strong position, easy to hold and virtually communicated, by means of intervening palaces, with the Residency. Had the suggestion been adopted the safety of the rearguard would have been assured, and the entrance into the Residency enclosure could have been effected with comparatively little loss. But General Havelock, on the other hand, was desirous of pushing on without delay. The main reasons given for haste were—the straits to which the inmates of the Residency were reduced; the danger to which they were exposed from mines which might be sprung by the enemy at any moment;* the possible desertion of natives under the disappointment occasioned by failure in long anticipated relief; and the want of power in their enfeebled state to resist a new assault of insurgents, if attempted as a desperate but not unlikely venture.

"There was, moreover, the advantage to be gained by following up a success before its first effects could subside. Thus onward went the gallant and devoted band--Highlanders and Sikhs, with Havelock and Outram at their head. General Neill and the Madras Fusiliers followed—charging through a very tempest of fire. **The Residency was reached: the garrison was saved.**" But the cost was heavy.

---

* On the point of mines General Outram reported:—"We attained the Residency just in time apparently, for, now that we have examined the outside of the defences, we find that two mines had been run far under the garrison's chief work—ready for loading—which, if sprung, must have placed the garrison at their mercy."

"Without any regard whatever to what was still to follow, this junction on the evening of September 25th, though it may not have been a relief of the Lucknow Residency in the technical Military sense was a relief of the garrison in all essentials from a common-sense point of view. It was a succour in the direst straits. It was a relief from the most harrowing and agonizing dread of the ever-impending chance of a breach in the defences, without a moment's warning through which the enemy, already prepared, might rush in overwhelming numbers which nothing could withstand. Further, when the imminent accession of the sepoys from Delhi is remembered, as well as the sceptical feeling that existed in the minds of sepoys in the intrenchment, there can be little doubt that Havelock's arrival saved the garrison of Lucknow from the fate of Gordon at Khartoum.

"As our men approached the *Sher Darwaza* (now known as Neill's Gate) a tremendous fire opened upon them. General Neill, who was leading, suddenly pulling up his horse, directed his Aide-de-camp, Gordon, to gallop back and recall a half-battery which had taken a wrong road. He remained there sitting on his horse, his face turned in the direction from which he expected the half-battery to emerge, when a sepoy, who had taken post on the gate, discharged his musket at him over the parapet on the top. The bullet entered his head behind the left ear, and killed him.*

"Thus fell one of the bravest and most determined men in the British army; while of the entire force one-fourth were killed and wounded.

"The rear-guard with many wounded remained at the Moti Mahal, beyond which they were unable to pass until extricated by a force sent out the following day.

"General Outram received a flesh wound in the arm in the early part of the action near Charbagh, but nothing could subdue his spirit; and though faint from loss of blood he

---

* A masonry pillar, with a tablet, marks the spot where General Neill fell.

continued to the end of the action to sit on his horse which he only dismounted at the gate of the Residency."*

90. The 25th of September was an auspicious day for us, as having ushered in the first relieving army under Generals Outram and Havelock—a small band of heroes who fought their way, through countless hordes from Cawnpore, a distance of about 50 miles, to save us from cruel death at the risk of losing their own lives in the attempt, as too many, alas! did.

91. The guns of the relieving army were more distinctly heard on this day as they approached the outskirts of the city. The rabble were now observed flying over the bridges across the river. Subsequently the flight became more general, and hordes of sepoys, matchlockmen, and Cavalry troopers crossed the river in full flight, many throwing themselves into the river and swimming across it. A heavy fire was now opened upon the flying enemy from the Redan and Langmore's Battery near the General Hospital; and, no sooner did this begin, than the enemy assailed us on every side with a perfect hurricane of shot and shell.

92. At noon the smoke of the guns of the advancing force was seen in the city, and the rattle of musketry could be distinctly heard. Towards evening European troops and officers were clearly distinguished from the top of the Residency, where I was afterwards posted on duty to work the Semaphore telegraph by means of which General Outram communicated with the relieving force under the Commander-in-Chief at Alambagh. About five o'clock a sharp rattle of musketry was heard in the streets, and, shortly after, the column of the 78th Highlanders better known as "Havelock's Ironsides," and Sikhs, accompanied by several mounted officers, were seen charging up the main street leading to the Residency at a rapid pace, loading and firing as they passed along. The Baillie Guard Gate, then battered and broken, had been barricaded from inside by a bank of earth; and as it could not be readily opened, Generals Outram and Havelock, together with

* *Calcutta Review.*

their staff and many of the soldiers, in their eagerness to enter the garrison as well as to avoid the enemy's fire, which was now directed at this point, rushed in through the embrasure of Aitken's battery, on the right of the Gate as you enter. General Outram put up in Dr. Fayrer's house, in the room where Sir Henry Lawrence had died, and General Havelock established himself in Brigadier Inglis' night-quarters, Mr. Ommanney's house. We felt happy and grateful to the God of Mercy who, by our noble deliverers, Generals Havelock and Outram, and their gallant troops, had thus snatched us from imminent death; the pent-up feelings of the garrison now burst forth in deafening cheers, and all came forward to join in the chorus of welcome. Our joy, however, was mingled with sorrow for the many losses sustained by the relieving army in attempting our rescue, with reference to which General Havelock wrote as follows :—

" To form an adequate idea of the obstacles overcome in this advance, reference must be made to the events that are known to have occurred at Buenos Ayres and Saragossa.* Our advance was through streets of flat-roofed and loop-holed houses, each forming a separate fortress, from which a perpetual fire was kept up, but the column rushed on, with desperate gallantry, and established itself within the Residency. I am filled with surprise at the success of the operation, which demanded the efforts of 10,000 good troops. The killed, wounded, and missing (the latter being wounded soldiers, who, I much fear—some or all—have fallen into the hands of a merciless foe) amounted up to the evening of the 26th September, to 535 officers and men." Among the killed was General Neill,† ' the bravest of the brave, ' who fell almost within sight of our intrenchment. Without any relief, the garrison had kept possession of the intrenched position for **eighty-seven days**, supported by some native officers and

---

* After a most heroic defence by General Palafox, Saragossa, N. E. of Spain, was taken by the French in 1809, from the inhabitants who resisted until worn out by fighting, famine and pestilence.

† Colonel Inglis was appointed on the 26th September, 1857, to the brigade left vacant by the death of General Neill.

soldiers and discharged pensioners advanced in years. We could hardly believe it when we were told that our friends had entered the garrison. About dusk a few of the boys, who had strolled over to the Residency to see what was up, were attracted to a spot where dancing was going on to the music of two Pipers of the 78th (Ross-shire Buffs, or Seaforth Highlanders, as they are now called). This display of exuberant feeling was, however, soon put a stop to by order of General Havelock, who evidently did not think this a fitting time to indulge in such revelry, as the enemy might, at any moment, swoop down upon us.

93. "At the commencement of the siege the defending force consisted of the following troops :—

EUROPEANS.

Artillery	80
H. M.'s 32nd	600
H. M.'s 84th	50—730

NATIVES.

Sikh Cavalry	60
7th Light Cavalry	9
13th Native Infantry	250
48th „	43
71st „	117—479
Officers, British and Native	130

"Besides these trained soldiers came a large and important body of 150 Volunteers, consisting of Officers whose men had mutinied, clerks of the Government offices, merchants and tradesmen. They were distributed in parties with the regular troops throughout the garrison, and were most useful. Besides the fighting men, there were 237 women, 260 children, 50 boys of La Martiniere College, 27 non-combatant Europeans, and 700 non-combatant natives,* being a total of 2,763 persons.† There remained of the original garrison, when reinforced on 25th September, a total of 979 persons, including sick and wounded,

---

* The non-combatants were those who from age or sex were unable to defend themselves.

† A nominal list of European members of the original garrison is given in Appendix G.

of whom 577 were Europeans and 402 natives. The 32nd marched out of Lucknow, after the defence, only 250 strong, and the other Regiments suffered in proportion."

94. A few days after the first reinforcement arrived, I was sent with some of the boys, to endeavour to pick up some firewood among the captured Palaces. There we had a look at the famous *Doli* Square* and could see the mutilated corpses of our own men who had been so basely murdered by the miscreants on the day after the relief. The following will explain the circumstances under which the sad occurrence took place:—

At the time the Highlanders and Brasyer's Sikhs entered the Baillie Guard, the main body of the troops was at the Farhat Bakhsh Palace. The latter was subsequently conducted to the Residency intrenchment in safety by Lieutenant Moorsom,† of H. M.'s 52nd Foot, who acted as guide to Sir James Outram. But the rear-guard, consisting of the gallant 90th Perthshire Light Infantry (now called the Scottish Rifles), under Colonel Campbell, which had been left in the walled passage in front of the Moti Mahal Palace, was not so fortunate as to get in the same day. This regiment had with it two heavy guns, as well as the tumbrils of spare ammunition and wounded, and remained halted at its post during the night, but on the following day, Mr. Bensley Thornhill, of the Civil Service, volunteered to lead the way for the wounded. Unfortunately his knowledge of Lucknow proved deficient, as will be seen by his having guided the convoy of litters into a square enclosure near the Gate where General Neill fell, and close

---

* So-called from being the scene of the abandonment of our wounded in *dolies* (Hospital litter) near the Gate where General Neill fell.

† " Lieutenant William Moorsom was selected by the Commissioner at Lucknow to conduct a scientific survey of the city in 1856, and had executed an admirable map of a large portion of the city immediately surrounding the Residency, including the Palaces and part of the suburbs in that direction, before he left the station with his regiment. It is from the survey made by him that all the plans had been derived, which were of such essential service throughout the siege, and subsequent military operations."

This distinguished young officer was killed in action at Lucknow in the year 1858, and a monument is erected to his memory in Rochester Cathedral.

to the enemy, who opened a spattering fire from every point. The escort fell back, the *doli* bearers fled, and about forty of the wounded were instantly butchered by the mutineers.* A few of the *dolies* were forced on under the fire, and reached the Residency; and among these was that which contained Lieutenant (afterwards Lieutenant-General) H. M. Havelock,† son of General Havelock, who had been badly wounded in the arm. Others which were just entering the square were turned back, and regained the right path along the river. The loss of life on the 26th is greatly to be deplored, but the massacre of the wounded would have been averted if Mr. Thornhill had not unfortunately missed his way. The contest to which the rearguard was exposed was exceedingly severe; and the opposition which the whole force would have had to encounter the next day and the sacrifice of life would have been much greater if the movement to the Residency had not been accomplished on the evening of the 25th (*vide* page 97).

95. We began exploring the Farhat Bakhsh Palace. This building consisted of a perfect labyrinth of court-yards, inner gardens, gateways, passages, verandahs, outhouses, and pavilions. Though the boys had often been loitering there, we invariably lost our way in some of the intricacies of those buildings. Plunder was the order of the day. Everywhere might be seen people helping themselves to whatever they pleased; shawls, pieces of satin, silk, gold and silver brocade, richly embroidered velvet, saddles for horses and coverlets for elephants; the most magnificent carriages, dresses of cloth of gold, turbans of the most costly brocade, the finest muslins, splendid dresses, the most valuable swords and fire-arms of every description; books,

---

* The author of "The Romantic Episode of a Detective" comments in the following words on the neglect shown in not commemorating the gallant acts of these brave men:—

"I think England has failed in her duty, to her honoured dead, in not raising a monument in the square to the brave men who were sacrificed to the fury of savages, while helpless and wounded, in the service of their country, and unable to defend themselves. Their sad fate is terrible to think of. Asiatics are cowards when left to themselves. And cowards are always cruel to the helpless."

† Lieutenant-General Sir Henry Marshman Havelock-Allan, V. C., K. C. B., M. P., was killed by Afridis in the Khyber Pass, 30th December, 1897, whilst watching military operations.

pictures, and valuable clocks. Very soon, however, all such property was declared to be prize : and prize-agents were appointed to collect it, and plunder was prohibited. It is difficult to restrain a victorious army from depredation, but, in the present instance, the spoliation of the natives assumed a meritorious character in the eyes of the European troops. They were exasperated beyond measure by the perfidious and brutal massacre of their fellow-countrymen and women, and they considered the plunder of the town in which these atrocities had been perpetrated an act of righteous retribution, but the General was determined to subdue this propensity. For this purpose the sentry at the Baillie Guard Gate received orders to detain all property suspected to have been plundered, with the exception of crockery, which we stood in great need of and which we were allowed to take *ad libitum*.

96. In several rooms in the palace were found boxes containing nothing but crockery ; these were very soon ransacked, emptied out on the floors, part removed and the rest trodden under foot. The floors were soon covered a foot deep with broken crockery and china. Some of the sets were exceedingly handsome and embellished with the armorial devices which had been adopted by the several Kings of Oudh. In these gorgeous palaces we, who had so recently been exposed to the severest hardships, now revelled in the enjoyment of luxuries, reclining on silken couches and eating our reduced and miserable pittance of food out of dishes of the most costly and magnificent china. In the range of buildings adjoining the Farhat Bakhsh Palace, which was near the present Museum, we (La Martiniere boys) happened to discover a whole store of fireworks. This was a grand opportunity for us ; and we immediately seized the rockets and began to fire them in the direction of the enemy. One of them, however, took a retrograde movement, and, exploding in the room itself, ignited the other combustibles. We cleared out very sharp and quite unobserved by the sentries. In a few minutes the whole was in a blaze. These buildings contained valuable property of some of the Begams[*] which was all destroyed.

---

[*] Begam is a princess, or lady of high rank.

The place continued burning for some days, any efforts to put it out being impossible under the enemy's fire. The cause of this conflagration was never quite brought home to us, but the soldiers had a suspicion that La Martiniere boys were at the bottom of the mischief. One proof of their suspicion came home to me in a very forcible manner. A few days afterwards John Hornby, George Bailey, and myself, roaming about as usual, were allowed by the sentry to cross the grass plot between the Terhi Kothi (now the residence of the Judicial Commissioner) and the Chutter Munzil. The soldier averted his face in order to conceal a smile as he allowed us to pass, and we did not understand the meaning of this until we had proceeded about half-way across the plot, when we were assailed with a shower of bullets, which came whistling about our ears from a Hindu temple (since demolished) near Dilaram Kothi,* across the river, this causing a regular stampede among us lads, who profited by the lesson taught, as we never ventured to pass that way again.

97. It was the original intention of Generals Havelock and Outram, on their junction with the garrison, to withdraw the women, children, sick and wounded forthwith to Cawnpore. With this view, the provisions, the baggage, and the bulk of the ammunition of the relieving column had been left at Alambagh; and the troops came on with nothing but the clothes on their backs and only three days' food. But the obstacles to the retirement of the garrison appeared constantly to multiply. Since the force crossed the Ganges† at Cawnpore on the 19th September it had been diminished more than one-fifth of its entire strength. Without carriage, the number of women, children, sick and wounded, besides 23 lacs of treasure, and about 30 guns of various calibre, could not be removed. Taking all these circumstances into consideration, Sir James Outram came to the determination to remain at the Residency and await further re-inforcements.

---

* This building is now the property of the Maharaja of Balrampur.
† The superstition connected with the sanctity of the water of the Ganges is similar to that which induces many Englishmen to obtain water from the river Jordan for the baptism of their children, and need occasion no surprise.

98. On the re-inforcement of the pent-up garrison in the Residency and adjoining posts, by the force under Generals Havelock and Outram, the old position was extended and a new line of defence taken up, on the north, as far as the river Gumti, and eastward, so as to include the Terhi Kothi, Farhat Bakhsh, and Chutter Munzil Palaces ; these are lofty and extensive ranges of palaces, built of solid masonry, and rising nearly from the water's edge.

99. Though we had extended our positions yet we were far from being free. Contrary to expectation, the enemy, instead of abandoning the city after the arrival of Generals Havelock and Outram, continued to blockade the Residency; and our gallant deliverers were now besieged along with us. They had brought in no provisions or stores of any kind ; and, in point of food, we were worse off than before, but, by strict economy, there was sufficient to last beyond the 22nd November, when we evacuated the garrison. Space would fail to give even a brief outline of the sorrows during the next three months. Reduced to starvation, allowances of the coarsest food, many clad in rags, and crowded into the narrowest quarters, we still courageously endured. And if this was the condition of those in health, what must have been the state of the sick and wounded ? Small-pox, cholera, boils, dysentery and malarious fever added their horrors to the situation, while the iron hail of death, mingling with the drenching rain of the monsoon dropped upon us, so that the deaths sometimes rose to twenty in a single day. The siege still proceeded and the position of the garrison was scarcely less dangerous than before. Hourly the din of cannon and musketry went on, but the enemy made no attempt to advance his batteries, and we obtained considerable relief by his attacks being less frequent.

The arrival of the Commander-in-Chief, Sir Colin Campbell, * and his army, which formed the second relieving force, was now anxiously expected. That Officer, on learning

---

* Sir Colin Campbell, or Lord Clyde, who rose to the rank of Field-Marshal and the Peerage, died 14th August, 1863, in the 71st year of his age. His remains were interred in Westminster Abbey.

SIR COLIN CAMPBELL.

that the intended withdrawal of the garrison by General Outram, who assumed command immediately after the troops entered the Residency, had been abandoned as impracticable, for the reasons stated in para. 97, now hastened to place himself at the head of a force commensurate to the enterprise and sufficient to overcome every obstacle in the way of our deliverance.

FINAL RELIEF BY SIR COLIN CAMPBELL.

100. The Commander-in-Chief left Cawnpore on November 9th, and joined the troops under command of Brigadier-General Hope Grant, C. B., the same day, at camp Bani Banthra, about 9 miles from Alambagh. There being a few detachments on the road, Sir Colin deemed it expedient to wait till the 12th, before commencing his advance.

On that day he marched early for the Alambagh with a thoroughly equipped force, about 5,000 strong, including 700 Cavalry and 30 pieces of cannon. Among the 30 pieces of cannon were 8 heavy guns (24-pounders and 8-inch howitzers*) drawn by bullocks and two rocket tubes mounted on light carts. These were manned by the Naval Brigade, which was composed of 250 men belonging to the crew of the Ship *Shannon*. The 68-pounders which were brought from the *Shannon* frigate by Captain Peel, had been left at Allahabad, as it was impossible to procure the necessary cattle for their transport.

101. When it was known in the garrison that the army of relief, under the Commander-in-Chief, had started from Cawnpore, Mr. T. H. Kavanagh, a European gentleman of the Uncovenanted Service, under the guidance of one of our native spies named Kanauji Lal,† volunteered to proceed from the Residency, on the night of the 9th November, to the Camp at Alambagh to act as guide to the Commander-in-Chief, and to convey plans of the city and suggestions from Sir James

---

* The 4 howitzers were subsequently placed in the Residency, where they are now to be seen.
† Before the outbreak Kanauji Lal was a Nazir, or Bailiff, in the Court of the Deputy Commissioner of Dariabad in Oudh.

Outram regarding the route which Sir Colin should adopt in entering it. It was a hazardous undertaking, as every outlet of the garrison was closely guarded by the enemy's pickets, and the way lay through the very heart of the hostile city. Disguised as a *badmash*,* Kavanagh managed to reach the British Camp at Alambagh, a distance of about 5 miles, in safety, very early the following morning, an enterprise of consummate daring which won for him the Victoria Cross and other substantial rewards from Government.† Kavanagh took with him a code of signals, and, by means of the semaphore telegraph erected on the top of Alambagh, communication was established with the Residency.‡ The distance between the two semaphores was three miles in a direct line "as the bird flies."

102. At 9 o'clock on the morning of the 14th, Sir Colin, adhering to the plan and suggestions of Sir James Outram "to give the city a wide berth," made an extended movement from the Alambagh to the right upon the Dilkusha Palace; thence advancing upon La Martiniere College he continued the movement along the right bank of the Gumti. This detour was rendered necessary so as to avoid the enemy's batteries which lined the direct road leading through the city to the Residency.$ The advance-guard was exposed to a heavy musketry fire at the Dilkusha, which was captured after a conflict of nearly two hours. On reaching this point

---

* *Badmashes* are bad characters and was a term of opprobrium applied to the rebels other than the mutineers of the regular sepoy army. Messrs. Felix, Edward, and Alfred Quieros assisted to disguise Mr. Kavanagh. Of these three brothers the one last named is alive and residing in Lucknow.

† A highly interesting work has been written by this gentleman, showing how he won the Victoria Cross, which was conferred upon him under the Royal Warrant of the 13th of December, 1858, by which this high distinction was accorded to certain non-military persons, who, as Volunteers, had borne arms against the mutineers in India.

‡ "All necessary particulars," writes Mr. Gubbins, "being fortunately found under the head 'Telegraph,' in the *Penny Cyclopædia* in my library, the General ordered the immediate erection of a semaphore on the south tower of the Residency, and copies of the necessary instructions were sent to Alambagh."

$ The distance between the Residency and Alambagh is about five miles, the road for the first two miles running through the city, and, after leaving it, being closely bordered by gardens and detached buildings, in which the enemy had established pickets.

LUCKNOW KAVANAGH IN HIS DISGUISE.

La Martiniere came in sight. This building was held in force by the enemy, and as our men advanced a number of round shot came tumbling in amongst them. Remington's troop of Horse Artillery, Bourchier's Battery, and a heavy howitzer brought up by Captain Hardy, now came into action and under cover of their fire the 8th Foot and 1st Battalion of detachments attacked and drove the enemy across the canal. In the course of the pursuit, Lieutenant Watson (now Colonel Watson, C. B., and V. C.) of the Bombay Army, commanding the squadron of the 1st Punjab Cavalry, slew in a hand-to-hand encounter the leader of the enemy's party, a native officer of the 15th Irregular Cavalry.

103. Sir Colin now took a general survey of the country from the top of La Martiniere, where a semaphore telegraph was established, by means of which messages were exchanged with Sir James Outram at the Residency. A force having been posted for the defence of the Dilkusha and Martiniere, on the 16th the column proceeded up the right bank of the Gumti and advanced on the Sikandar Bagh, a walled enclosure containing a summer house and garden, which was strongly fortified and loopholed by the enemy. Sir Colin, with the quick eye of a soldier, saw the blunder committed by the enemy, who had now no outlet of escape. On the head of the column approaching the garden, fire was opened on it. As soon as the troops got into position, the fire of the whole brigade was concentrated on the enclosure, about 120 yards square, with walls 20 feet high, and turreted rooms at each angle.

104. In the space of a short time, Travers's two heavy guns (18-pounders) effected a breach in the south-east angle; when the place was stormed in a most brilliant manner by the 93rd Highlanders, the 53rd and the 4th Punjab Rifles, supported by a Battalion of detachments under Major Barnston. Then ensued a scene which baffles description. The enemy, hemmed in on every side and finding escape impossible fought with the courage of despair. An eye-witness relates that, when he entered the enclosure next morning, the dead lay in weltering heaps inside that fatal square, which was strewn with arms and accoutrements

of every description. Not less than 2,000 of the enemy, a compact brigade of three complete regiments, were absolutely annihilated. They were interred in deep trenches outside the enclosure.

"Although the carnage was frightful, the cowardly and savage acts of the mutineers made us look upon them not as honest foes, but as foul and cruel murderers for whom death by the sword was too good a fate and whose only fit end was the gallows. In attempting a revolt against the Government, had they confined themselves to violence against its officers they would not have placed themselves outside the pale of mercy; but the ruthless butchery of our defenceless women and children justly aroused our wrath, and we would have been less than human if we did not put forth our strength to crush them."

105. A short distance beyond the Sikandar Bagh, stands a huge masonry structure, with an expensive dome, beneath which lie the remains of Gazi-ud-din Haidar, the first King of Oudh, whose tomb it is. This mausoleum, called the Shah Najaf, was defended with great resolution by the enemy against a heavy cannonade of three hours. It was then stormed in the boldest manner by the 93rd Highlanders under Brigadier Hope, supported by a Battalion of detachments, including a Company of the 90th Perthshire, under Captain (now Viscount) Garnet Wolseley, in command of Major Barnston.

106. On the morning of the 17th the conflict was renewed; and so stubborn was the resistance that it took six consecutive hours to capture the Khursheid Munzil, the building now known as La Martiniere Girls' School, distant about two miles from Constantia, General Claude Martin's mansion, in which the boys are located. The Khursheid Munzil was defended by a ditch about twelve feet broad and beyond that a loop-holed mud wall.

About 3 P. M., after a steady cannonade, and when it was considered that men might be sent to storm it without much risk, it was taken by a Company of the 90th Light Infantry, under Captain Wolseley, and a picket of H. M.'s 53rd under

Captain Hopkins, supported by Major Barnston's Battalion of detachments, under Captain Guise, H. M.'s 90th Regiment, and some of the Punjab Infantry, under Lieutenant Powlett. Lieutenant (now Lord) Roberts * ascended the building and planted the flag of the 2nd Punjab Infantry on the west turret which announced to all the capture of the position. **The same day Generals Outram and Havelock had the memorable meeting with Sir Colin Campbell at this place.** †

" What a meeting was that ! The Iron Chief, Sir Colin, with the dust of battle still upon him, the 'good Sir James,' and the dying Havelock. Meeting, too, while the walls of the palace where they stood were still reverberating with the din of battle;—fit atmosphere for that re-union ! True knights these three brave hearts ! Each had perilled his life to rescue the helpless, and one was soon to lay his down worn out in their defence."

This important point at last in our possession terminated the desperate struggle of the day, and not only secured for us all the other positions previously taken, but ensured the relief of the Residency.

107. The advantages resulting from the capture of the enemy's strongholds were invaluable, as freedom of action was thereby guaranteed to the relieving force. Though the obstacles which still lay in the line of advance were formidable, yet Sir Colin hoped that, by the co-operation of Generals Havelock and Outram, the enemy would soon yield and it was not long before his expectations were realised, for the Tarawali Kothi (observatory), now occupied by the Bank of Bengal, was captured within a few hours after the taking of the Khursheid Manzil. After the capture of these positions a raid was made on the Moti Mahal Palace. The enemy, placed between two fires, offered but slight resistance. The advance was now vigorously pressed forward from both sides and a junction effected, the same day, with the beleaguered garrison in the Residency. The troops now occupied all the

---

* Lord Roberts was born at Cawnpore.
† A masonry pillar, with a tablet, marks the spot where the Generals met.

houses between our extended intrenchment and the Moti Mahal, including the Khursheid Manzil. **The second and final relief of Lucknow was thus accomplished on the afternoon of the 17th November, 1857.**

108. Such was the glorious issue of this prolonged contest, which cost Sir Colin the loss of 45 officers and 496 men in his endeavour to reach us. But only half the design had been carried out. To effect the retreat in security required the utmost vigilance on the part of the troops: for the enemy still held various positions, in overwhelming numbers, and the long line of road to be traversed by the garrison until it reached the Dilkusha, the base of Sir Colin's operations, was exposed to artillery fire.

EVACUATION OF THE GARRISON.

109. Preparations for evacuating the intrenched position were carried on vigorously. Every one was engaged in preparing conveyances of some sort for the removal of the ladies, sick and wounded. A large quantity of shot was thrown down wells, the rest removed. The unmounted native guns were destroyed (see para. 13). On the afternoon of the 19th November, the women and children (including La Martiniere College boys), sick and wounded, the treasure, amounting to twenty-three lacs of rupees,* and the ex-King's jewels, the serviceable guns, ordnance stores, the grain† still possessed by the Commissariat of the garrison, and the State prisoners, were safely escorted to Dilkusha Palace.

The exodus from the Residency, and the escape to the Dilkusha, will never be forgotten by those who took part therein. Many delicate women and children, unprovided with vehicles or horses, had to walk over five miles of very rough ground, exposed at one place to the fire of the enemy's musketry.

---

* At the present rate of exchange, Rs. 15 to the pound, 23 lacs of rupees would be equal to £153,333-6s.-8d.

† There had been a separate store of grain collected from various sources of which the Military Department had no knowledge. By the extraordinary foresight of Sir Henry Lawrence the large plunge bath east of the Banqueting Hall had been set apart for contributions. Whenever any rich native offered his services, Sir Henry used to take him at his word, and tell him to send in grain, hence this extra supply.

Mrs. (now Lady) Inglis behaved on this occasion in a manner worthy of her name; a *doli*, or hospital litter, was prepared for her accommodation, but she refused it, in order that the sick and wounded might be better attended to. The road to Sikandar Bagh was frightfully dangerous after we passed the Moti Mahal Palace. In one spot we were passing a 24-pounder manned by some sailors of the Naval Brigade; they called out to us to bend low and run as fast as we could; we had hardly done so when a shot from the enemy's battery, across the river, whizzed over our heads and struck a wall beyond.

The senior boys who bore arms in the garrison (mentioned in para. 81) were, however, recalled next day, by Brigadier Inglis, as all capable of carrying arms were expected to remain at their posts in the intrenchment until it was finally evacuated. This order was very reluctantly obeyed by us, as we had no desire to return to the scene of our sufferings. On the 20th, we, however, retraced our steps to the Residency, which was reached at dusk after a perilous journey.

110. After staying one night in the old garrison, Nicolls and I were sent back, on the 21st, to Dilkusha, in charge of two ponies carrying money and other valuable property belonging to the College. In the open plain between the Moti Mahal and Shah Najaf we came upon one of the Shannon guns, with which a few sailors and an Officer were replying to the fire of the enemy's gun situated in a grove across the river. Our tats obtained for us from the enemy the honor of a shot, which whizzed over our heads in unpleasant proximity, whereupon the tats kicked up their heels and went off, while we stood by the gun till the artillery fire ceased and thereafter, by the help of the sailors, the tats were captured and we resumed our perilous journey. A few of the rupees " watered the plain," but we managed to convey the greater part of the charge to Dilkusha Palace.

111. On the 20th November, to assist and cover the retreat from the observation of the enemy, the heavy guns of the Naval Brigade, under Captain Peel, were put in position in

Battery, outside the west angle of the Moti Mahal, and opened fire against the Kaisar Bagh Palace, which constituted the rebel citadel. The computed strength of the insurgents at this time amounted to 30,000 sepoys, together with 50,000 volunteers; and they possessed 100 pieces of ordnance, guns and mortars. The enemy slakened fire under this heavy bombardment, which had the desired effect of leading him into the belief that an assault was contemplated on the Palace; consequently all his attention and energies were devoted towards strengthening the defences of that place in order to resist the threatened attack. Sir Colin was not slow in taking advantage of the opportunity thus afforded him to finally evacuate the intrenchment.

Nothing was, however, allowed to disturb the ordinary appearance of things in the intrenchment until the very last moment, which was at *midnight of the 22nd November*, when, amidst the deepest silence, the entire garrison, leaving the lights burning, filed out of the Residency and passed through the advanced posts to the Sikandar Bagh, where Brigadier the Hon'ble Adrian Hope's* Brigade, with 15 guns, were drawn up and held in readiness to fall on the enemy in case he ventured to molest the retreat.

112. **The line of retreat** † was through the Baillie Guard Gate, the Farhat Bakhsh and Chutter Munzil Palaces, beyond which, after emerging near the steam engine house (since demolished), the journey was continued along the banks of the river Gumti till the Moti Mahal was reached. Passing through the courts of this Palace the convoy gained, on the further side of it, the high road leading by the Shah Najaf, which was passed on its way to the Sikandar Bagh. Between the Moti Mahal and Shah Najaf the refugees were greatly exposed to the fire of the enemy's guns placed on the further side of the river, but they passed through without any loss and arrived in safety at the Sikandar

---

* The Hon'ble Adrian Hope was shot on the 15th April, 1858, at the storming of the Fort Royea, in the Hardoi District of Oudh.

† The dotted line on the map shows the route of retreat of the garrison.

Bagh, where, after a few hours halt, the journey was resumed, over a sandy track of ground, along the outskirts of an abandoned village (Jeamow), north of La Martiniere in the direction of Dilkusha Palace, which was reached in safety. As soon as the convoy had passed the Sikandar Bagh, the troops holding different positions along the line of retreat were withdrawn, and before dawn on the morning of the 23rd the whole of the forces reached the Dilkusha Palace, which is about five miles distant from the Residency. "One Officer of the garrison had a narrow escape from falling into the hands of the enemy. The hour fixed for our departure was midnight, and before this arrived many of the garrison laid down to take some rest, making sure of being awoke when the movement began. Among these was Captain Waterman of the 13th N. I. He fell fast asleep in a retired corner of the Brigade Mess, and his friends failed to awake him. The troops had marched out of the Residency, and had cleared the palaces altogether before he awoke. His consternation on awaking may well be imagined. He was alone in the abandoned position with thousands of rebels outside who did not then know it had been deserted. Appalled by the horror of his position he followed in the track of the retiring force as fast as he could, but not until he had left the old position far behind him did he overtake the rear-guard."

113. The evacuation of the Residency was ably carried out in the face of an innumerable and insidious foe, rendered desperate with rage and vexation and burning for revenge at the numberless defeats he had sustained. So completely deceived was the enemy that he not only did not follow up the retreat but continued to fire for several hours on the old position after it had been abandoned. To General Outram was due the planning and execution of the strategical movement by which the evacuation of the Residency was accomplished.

114. One melancholy event, however, threw a gloom over Sir Colin's glorious achievement, *viz.*, the death of General Havelock, who was called away before he was permitted to enjoy the rewards which his Sovereign and country were anxious to

lavish upon him. On the 20th he had been seized with dysentery and his constitution, so shattered by over-exertion and fatigue, was unable to contend with so formidable a disease. At 9-30 A. M. on the 24th November Sir Henry Havelock* expired in a soldier's tent at Dilkusha Palace. "I die happy and contented," were among his last words; "I have, for forty years, so ruled my life that when death came I might face it without fear."

> "His closing eyes the beam of valour speak,
> The flush of ardour lingers on his cheek,
> Serene he lifts to heaven those closing eyes,
> Then for his country breathes a prayer—and dies!"

115. On the afternoon of the same day, shortly after his death, the troops began their march to Alambagh (about four miles distant, which we reached the same evening), and conveyed with them, in the litter on which he expired, the mortal remains of the noble chief, who had so often led them on to victory. "Next morning we buried him in Alambagh enclosure, under a mango-tree in whose bark his first curt epitaph, the letter "H" was carved, at a season when other index of his resting-place would have been unwise. There stood around the grave General Havelock's son, together with Sir Colin Campbell, General Outram, Brigadier Inglis, Brigadier Adrian Hope, Captain Peel, and many of his brave followers, who were gathered there to perform the last rites to one of England's noblest dead. The volleys of the firing party were the good soldiers' fittest requiem; and so Henry Havelock was buried." To avoid detection, General Outram caused the grave to be smoothed over. At the same time he directed such minute measurements to be taken as to lead to the recognition, when required, of the precise site. An obelisk now marks the spot.

> "The funeral rite is over,
> The mighty spirit's fled;
> A nation mourns in sadness,
> Brave Havelock is dead.
> The vital spark is extinct,
> We shall see his face no more:
> And we, who lately worshipped him,
> His greatness now deplore!

---

* Sir Henry Havelock was born at Ford Hall, Bishop Wearmouth, a suburb of Sunderland, on the 5th April, 1795.

"Oh! speak the word but softly,
For our bosoms sore have bled;
A nation's woes are outpour'd,
Great Havelock is dead.
The hero of so many fights
Is dead, and great's our grief;
'Twas he who earned the laurel,
And to Lucknow brought relief.

"When those we lov'd were struggling
With foes, and worse, with death;
'Twas he who saved them to us—
Now he's breath'd his latest breath.
But we'll reverence his memory,
Say how gallantly he led;
The foremost in a dozen fights—
Brave Havelock is dead.

"Oh! speak the word but softly,
For our grief is new and great;
We shall hear no more of Havelock,
Whose deeds our hearts elate.
We have lost him at a moment
When he'd gained the hope of years—
Distinction—hard fought, dearly-earn'd,
And now we mourn in tears—

"The loss of one, whose very name,
Like Gilead's soothing balm,
Brought comfort to the hearts of all,
And direst pain could calm.
Oh! speak the word but softly,
That mighty spirit's fled;
A nation mourns in sadness—
Great Havelock is dead!"

     T. C. ANDERSON, LIEUT.,
      (*12th Regt., Bengal Army*).

116. On the 25th and 26th November we halted at Alambagh, so as to allow of arrangements being made for the equipment of the column which was to remain here under the command of General Outram, with the object of keeping open the road to Cawnpore, and of avoiding the appearance of having abandoned

Oudh. For three months General Outram, with a small force of 4,000 men, 25 guns, including howitzers and 10 mortars, successfully held the place till the return, on 1st March, 1858, of Sir Colin, who came with a large army for the purpose of capturing Lucknow* and subjugating the Province. This was accomplished after he had restored order in other parts of the N.-W. Provinces where his presence was urgently needed at this time.

117. On the 27th the Commander-in-Chief having received an important message, suddenly marched towards Cawnpore, escorting with General Hope Grant's Division, the refugees, wounded, and treasure. A march of about nine miles brought us to Bunnee Bridge, where the camp was pitched for the night. The sound of heavy cannon was now heard in the direction of Cawnpore, at which we were greatly startled, for we had hoped that we had done with the alarms of war.

118. All was conjecture in the camp as to what this could mean; and it did not dawn upon us then that the hurried movement of Sir Colin, in the direction of Cawnpore, was with the object of affording help to the British troops left in the intrenchment † there to guard the passage of the river. This small force of about 2,000 men under the command of Major-General Windham, "the hero of the Redan," was sorely pressed by the Gwalior Contingent‡ who had taken possession of the

---

* It is a noteworthy fact that Lucknow was defended for 147 days by a few Englishmen and loyalists, whilst its re-capture occupied only 19, *i. e.*, 1st to 19th March ; and it is a strange coincidence that the last position taken by the British, the *Musa Bagh*, was the place where the mutiny began. (*Vide* para. 17).

† The intrenchment was constructed on the right bank of the Ganges to protect the bridge of boats crossing into Oudh. This fort was ultimately dismantled and is now the Government Harness and Saddlery Factory.

‡ The Gwalior Contingent, maintained by Sindhia under the treaty of 1843, had broken out in mutiny and joined the forces of Nana Saheb. From the intelligence received there was little doubt that in consequence of the arrival of four regiments from Oudh, and the gathering of various mutinous corps which had suffered in previous actions, as well as the assemblage of all the Nana's followers, the strength of the enemy amounted to about 25,000 men, with all the guns belonging to the Contingent, some 36 in number, together with a few guns of the Nana Saheb.

city and suburbs of Cawnpore. That arch fiend "the Nana,"* who was responsible for the tragedy enacted at Cawnpore,† was also reported to be hovering in the neighbourhood of that station at the head of a considerable force.

The sepoys‡ obtained posession of the town, and for two days General Windham had to sustain an unequal contest with

---

* "Nana Saheb, whose name will ever be conspicuous in the annals of crime as the personification of perfidy and cruelty, was the adopted son of Baji Rao, the ex-Peshwa, or head of the ancient Mahratta confederacy. In the year 1818, while at peace with the British Government, the Peshwa had endeavoured, by an act of the basest treachery, to destroy Mr. Mountstuart Elphinstone, the Resident at his court; but the assault was gallantly repelled and he was obliged to fly from his capital, at Poona, and was hunted through the country for several months, by Sir John Malcolm. His power was finally crushed at the battle of Kirkee. But just at the period when he was brought to bay, and must have surrendered at discretion, he was admitted to terms, and by an act of reckless prodigality, endowed with an annuity of £90,000. This provision he lived to enjoy for 32 years, and, after having received from the British Government a sum exceeding two millions and a half sterling, died, in 1853, at Bithur, about 16 miles above Cawnpore, which had been assigned as the place of his residence. Of these accumulations, he bequeathed a large portion to his adopted son, Dhondu Pant Nanaji, better known as Nana Saheb, who had the assurance to demand the continuance of the pension. It was as a matter of course, refused, and from that time he conceived the most bitter hostility to the English. His feelings were, however, artfully dissembled, and he freely associated with, and gave entertainments to the European community at Cawnpore, by whom he was regarded as a liberal and enlightened native nobleman. When the spirit of disaffection first appeared among the native troops at Cawnpore, the Nana manifested the most friendly disposition towards Sir Hugh Wheeler, and, at his request, afforded every assistance for the safeguard of our treasury, which remained, for several days, under the protection of 600 of his men and two of his guns. But no sooner had the sepoys at Cawnpore broken into open mutiny, and obtained the ascendancy, then he threw off the mask and took the lead of the hostile movement. Having obtained the larger share of the plunder of the treasury and persuaded the mutineers to place themselves under his command, he proclaimed himself Peshwa, and raised the far-famed national Mahratta standard. The indiscriminate destruction of the European and Native Christians, under every form of barbarity, who had not taken refuge in the intrenchment to which Sir Hugh Wheeler had retired, now became the pastime of this fiend in human shape."—*Memoirs of Sir Henry Havelock.*

NOTE.—Notwithstanding the large sum of a lac of rupees which was offered by Government, as a reward for the capture of the Nana, he made his escape, in the guise of a *fakir*, or mendicant, into Nepaul territory, where, it is rumoured, he and his brother died in the jungles during 1859. Tantia Topi, the Nana's abettor in the Cawnpore crimes, was hanged in April, 1859.

† A full account of the tragedy will be found in the book, to be had at the Methodist Publishing House in Lucknow, entitled "The Cawnpore Massacre," by W. J. Shepherd, one of the five (the other four being Captains Thomson and Delafosse, Private Murphy, and Gunner Sullivan) who escaped to tell the lamentable tale. Shepherd died, at Lucknow, on 26th July, 1891.

‡ Sepoy or native soldier, the term is of Persian origin and corrupted from sipáh

a body of the ablest of the mutineers, ten times his own number, and commanded by Tantia Topi, the only native general created by the mutiny.

119. Preceded by the 3rd and 5th Punjab Infantry, flanked by the 9th Lancers and Horse Artillery; while the rear-guard, composed of the 93rd, a troop of the 9th Lancers and Light Field Battery, we resumed our march very early the following morning, and, after a fatiguing journey, arrived late in the evening at Mangalwar, a village within a short distance of the bridge of boats over the Ganges, where we encamped, but our gallant Chief, accompanied by his staff, galloped into the intrenchment the same evening, and, by his promptitude on this critical occasion, saved the position.

"No idea can be formed of the disastrous consequences which would have ensued; in a short time the bridge across the Ganges, if not in the hands of the enemy, would have been under fire from any amount of guns that they might choose to bring upon it, perhaps totally destroyed. The army of Lucknow, burdened with its frightful train, would have been not only isolated from Cawnpore, but from the whole of India proper, and placed in the awkward predicament of being between two enemies, the Gwalior Contingent and the rebel army in Lucknow; and in a country, too, where every village was a fortified enemy's position, and no supplies were procurable. This was exactly the state of affairs Sir Colin foresaw, and therefore hastened as much as possible the withdrawal of the Lucknow garrison and his return to Cawnpore."

120. We marched unmolested from Lucknow to Cawnpore, a distance of about 46 miles, in two days. But for the rapidity of Sir Colin's movements and his superior generalship, the bridge of boats* at Cawnpore would have been lost and we should have been cut off from all communication with the

---

* The position of this bridge was a little above that of the present Railway bridge which was opened for traffic on 15th July, 1875.
The length of the bridge is 25 spans of 110 feet and 2 spans of 40 feet, or in all 2,830 running feet. It cost something over twenty lacs of rupees, which in English money would be £133,333-6s.-8d., at the present rate of exchange.

other side, for the mutineers had entire possession of the town of Cawnpore and had advanced their posts so close to the bridge as to render it difficult to cross under their heavy fire. At daylight on the 29th, the enemy opened fire on the intrenched camp and bridge of boats, but their surprise must have been great to see on the opposite bank of the river the heavy guns of the field force placed in battery to secure the bridge and cover the passage of the river. The Artillery fire from General Windham's intrenchment was directed to the same point. For some time the Artillery combat appeared not unequal, but gradually the guns of the British asserted their superiority. Then commenced the passage of the Cavalry, the Horse Artillery, and Brigadier Adrian Hope's Brigade.

No sooner had the convoy advanced than a sharp fusilade commenced and the enemy tried to destroy the bridge of boats by floating fire-rafts down the river; fortunately they did not succeed. We continued our journey and arrived without accident on the ground set apart for us. The passage of the huge convoy over the bridge, under the protection of Brigadier Greathed's brigade, was a most tedious business, occupying thirty hours, from 3 P. M. on the 29th till about 9 P. M. on the 30th, when Brigadier Inglis brought over the rear guard.

121. On the 30th November, when there was sufficient light to enable us to distinguish objects, we found ourselves located within the melancholy and battered intrenchments of Sir Hugh Wheeler, a scene of desolation which inflamed the minds of the troops with a fierce desire for revenge. We remained at Cawnpore a few days, before taking our departure for Allahabad, and were favored whilst there with a few shells occasionally—parting shots from the enemy, who were encamped, in great force, within a mile of us. Our troops were impatient to attack them, but no action could be taken until after the refugees, sick and wounded, Sir Colin's chief care, had been despatched to Allahabad.

122. The arrangements for their transit were not completed until the 3rd December, 1857, when the convoy with the

women and children, the sick and wounded of the Residency, left Cawnpore for Allahabad under a strong escort commanded by Colonel Kelly. This was a great comfort to us after the hardships we had endured in the Residency, during the **five months' investment** of that place by the rebels, beyond whose reach we had now been placed by an Almighty hand.

123. Every description of conveyance was impressed into the service for our transport, and we must have presented a curious spectacle, travelling as we did, a few in *palki-garies* and the now obsolete *buggy*, some *bahlies* (a two-wheeled springless conveyance drawn by two bullocks and resembling a pair of *ekkas* combined), others in *ekkas* (a two-wheeled conveyance drawn by a pony), and not a few in the common country cart, or *hackerie*, with a reed awning to keep off the sun and rain. All La Martiniere boys, excepting those of a very tender age, were expected to march, but I was so fortunate as to annex an *ekka* at Cawnpore in which myself and another lad (G. Paschound) travelled comfortably up to Khaga, the E. I. Railway terminus at that time, about forty miles from Allahabad.*

124. Our curiosity was excited at the first sight of a railway train at Khaga, where we arrived on the afternoon of the 7th December. All of us began to look in wonderment at the Iron Horse, but we were not allowed to indulge our curiosity long, for immediately after our arrival at the terminus we were put into ballast trucks and carried away at a fearful speed, as it then seemed to us, in the direction of Allahabad, which was reached at 3 P. M.

125. On nearing the Fort of Allahabad† we were surprised at the welcome accorded us by the military, who fired a royal salute from the ramparts, in honor of the survivors of the

---

* The first Indian Railway was opened in 1853.

† Allahabad, or the city of God, is a large Mahomedan town, situated at the junction of the Ganges and the Jumna. It was ceded in 1801 to the British by the Nawab of Oudh. The Fort was originally built by Akbar, the great Moghul Emperor, in 1575. The pillar in the Fort, which is 42 feet in height, was erected by the Buddhist King Asoka about the year 240 B. C. The Fort of Agra was also built by Akbar in the year 1566.

Lucknow garrison. The ground in front of the Fort, close to which the train halted, was crowded with the European residents, officers, ladies and soldiers: in fact, almost all the inhabitants seemed to be present to receive us, standing in great array on both sides of the train, and there was loud cheering as the engine steamed in with its living freight. When this demonstration was over, we received the congratulations of the people, and were then taken inside the Fort, where we were well cared for and provided with comestibles far more palatable than the tough steaks obtained from the old half-starved battery bullocks in the Residency.

126. Mr. Schilling, our Principal, assisted by my father, now set about preparing outfits for the boys, who were by this time in rags, having only the suit in which we stood and in which we went through the siege, for ever since the disaster at Chinhut no messenger could be sent to Constantia to bring in a supply of clothing and other necessaries which had been left there in charge of the servants (see para. 49). New clothes and bedding were then served out to us; and the luxury of a change, after five months, can well be imagined.

127. As we now presented a decent appearance, arrangements were made for our departure, and shortly after Christmas, we, *i. e.*, those connected with La Martiniere College, left Allahabad, in country boats, for Benares, where we arrived about the middle of January, 1858. Our journey down the river Ganges was slow and anything but pleasant. At Benares the boys were located in two large bungalows, opposite the Government gardens, where we resumed our studies and remained the whole of 1858, returning to Lucknow in the beginning of 1859.

128. The rest of the fugitives were conveyed, in the Steamer *Madras* to Calcutta, where they landed, in safety on the 9th January, 1858. In anticipation of their arrival the following notification was published in the Government Gazette

Extraordinary :—

RECEPTION OF THE FUGITIVES AT CALCUTTA.

"Within the next few days the river Steamer *Madras*, conveying the ladies, children, sick and wounded of the Lucknow garrison, will reach Calcutta. No one will wish to obtrude upon those who are under bereavement or sickness, any show of ceremony which shall impose fatigue or pain. The best welcome which can be tendered upon such an occasion is one which shall break in as little as possible upon privacy and rest. But the rescue of these sufferers is a victory beyond all price, and, in testimony of the public joy with which it is hailed, and of the admiration with which their heroic endurance and courage have been viewed, the Right Hon'ble the Governor-General (Lord Canning) in Council directs that, upon the approach of the *Madras* to Prisep's *Ghat*,* a royal salute shall be fired from the ramparts of Fort William. The Governor-General in Council further decrees that all ships of war in the river shall be dressed in honor of the day. Officers will be appointed to conduct the passengers on shore, and the State barges and carriages of the Governor-General will be in attendance."

129. A contemporary thus describes the reception at Calcutta which was accorded the fugitives :—

"According to arrangement, on Friday, the 8th of January, 1858, at 5 P. M., two guns from the ramparts of Fort William announced that the *Madras* was in sight, and almost every body that had horse, or carriage, rode down to Prinsep's *ghat*, where it was intimated the passengers would land. The *Madras* having, however, a heavy boat in tow, made, notwithstanding the tide in her favour, but slow progress, and as it soon became evident that she could not arrive ere the night set in, a telegraphic message was despatched to the Commander of the Steamer to anchor below Garden Reach and to come up next morning. At six o'clock on Saturday morning a crowd of

---

* *Ghat*, a ferry, or landing-place.

people assembled at Prinsep's *ghat*, but a dense fog delayed the arrival of the *Madras*, and it was not until a quarter to eight that she could be sighted. A royal salute of 21 guns from the ramparts of Fort William announced her arrival, and other salutes followed from the men-of-war on the river. All vessels on the river were dressed out with all their flags, and presented a very imposing sight. Along the steps from the *ghat* down to the water's edge was formed a sort of gangway, guarded by policemen; along the whole red carpeting was laid out such as it is customary to use on State occasions.

"At last the *Madras* arrived off the *ghat*, but owing to some cause or other, considerable delay took place before the passengers could be landed, the public, in the meantime, looking on in stern silence, as if afraid least even now some accident might happen to those whose escape from the hands of a barbarous and blood-thirsty enemy was decreed by a merciful Providence. The whole scene partook of a solemnity rarely witnessed, and, indeed, the expression on the faces of the bystanders betokened universal sympathy for those they were about to welcome to the hospitable city of palaces. Mr. Beadon, the Secretary of the Home Department, on behalf of Government; the Hon'ble Mr. Talbot, Private Secretary to the Governor-General, on behalf of Lord Canning; and Dr. Leckie, as Secretary to the 'Relief Committee,' went down to the water's edge to receive the ladies. A sudden rush towards the river, a thronging towards the gangway, and a slight whisper of voices, indicated the landing had begun. Cheers were given at first, but only slowly responded to, people evidently being too much occupied with their own reflections to think of cheering; but as the ladies and children proceeded up, people raised their hats instinctively, looking on in silent reflection. At this moment another ship in the harbour fired a salute, but it did not sound joyfully; it appeared rather like minute guns in remembrance of those whose widows and orphans were now passing on in solemn review.

"The black dresses of most of the ladies told the tale of their bereavement, whilst the pallid faces, the downcast looks, and the slow pace, bore evidence of the great sufferings they must have undergone both in mind and body. And yet how thankful must we be that they have been spared other trials, in comparison to which death itself would be a relief ! As they passed, sad reflections forced themselves upon our minds, and we asked where are those who, for the sake of saving English women and children from dishonor and death, have willingly sacrificed their own lives ? Where is the illustrious Havelock ? Where the heroic Neill ? Where so many others that have stretched forth the arm for the rescue of helpless women and innocent children ? Alas! they are no more, but their names will live for ever in the heart of every true Briton. And though there is no monument to mark the place where they sleep the everlasting sleep, their blood has marked, in indelible ink, in the bosom of their surviving brethren, the word 'retribution.' The solemn procession thus passed on and were handed into carriages which conveyed them to their temporary home. Home, did we say ? It sounds almost like mockery to call the solitary room of the widow and orphan by that name."

CONCLUDING REMARKS.

130. The drama of Lucknow may properly be divided into four acts: 1st, the defence by Sir Henry Lawrence and Brigadier Inglis; 2nd, the succour of Lucknow by Sir Henry Havelock and Sir James Outram, 25th September; 3rd, the relief of Lucknow on the 22nd November, 1857, by Sir Colin Campbell, when the hard pressed garrison were carried out from overwhelming numbers of the enemy ; and 4th, the siege of Lucknow by the British force under Sir Colin Campbell and Sir James Outram.

The foregoing illustrates briefly what transpired at Lucknow during the period of the investment of the Residency, which will always possess great interest for tourists on account of the heroic defence, during that eventful period, of a position, the nature of which it would be impossible to give a correct idea of at this distant date. "What was the position ? Let the reader imagine a number of houses, built for ordinary domestic purposes, originally separated from each other by small plots of ground, but now joined together by mud walls and trenches—the mud walls for defence from outer attack, the trenches for protection against the enemy's shells ! Such in a few words was the enclosure known to the world, from the principal building within it, as the Residency. It is true that the walls of the houses were thick, that the bricks were of that small class peculiar to India during the last century, and that they were cemented by well-tempered mortar. But even the strongest houses constitute but a poor military position. This position, moreover, was blockaded and attacked by the enemy before a single part of it had been made really defensible. The defences were naturally rough, run up under enormous difficulties, and never in their most finished state deserving the name of regular fortifications. The houses of the several occupants, and the batteries erected along the line of intrenchments came to be regarded as posts, and each of these posts was commanded by an officer." The defences were scarcely deserving the name; we merely defended a certain number of houses in the very heart of the city, with the enemy in possession of the houses adjoining. These were so near that the solicitations, threats, and taunts which the rebels addressed to the loyal native defenders of the garrison were distinctly heard by us. The line of defence between us consisted only of hastily constructed trenches and barricades (see para. 52). It was, in fact, a siege, not of a position, but of so many isolated posts, whose propinquity to each other offered an unbroken front to the enemy.

131. The ruins of the Lucknow Residency are objects of sorrowful interest which Government has preserved, these many years, with reverential care ; all the houses that played a part in the illustrious defence are now mere battered fragments of walls, broken pillars, roofless, floorless, skeletons of houses ; some of these even with few of their bones left. But good taste has forborne to do anything which can hint at the idea of restoration.*

---

* Lord Curzon's instructions have done much of the work of restoration and conservation of the ruins of the buildings within the Residency enclosure. The essential principle in the restoration being that only such should be undertaken as are necessary to prevent further delapidation.

132. The grey stones, and thick, old, native built walls, riddled with cannon shot ; the gateway that is sacred to the memory of fierce fighting, the scars of which may still be seen ; the deep *taikhanas*, or underground rooms, into which the light slants through narrow windows level at the same time with their own lofty ceilings and with the ground outside ; all these and the other remains of the Residency buildings have been cleared of *débris* which would have littered and disfigured the place. But it has, otherwise, been left quite untouched. At the present day the course of shot and shell can be traced from the shattered brick-work low down in the walls of even the deep *taikhanas*. So with the shell that killed Sir Henry Lawrence : the walls still stand which bore its direct shock, and a small marble slab records the evil work done by one of its fragments, of which the last history may be read on a broad flat tomb-stone in the cemetery.

133. For all purposes of identification the great majority of the buildings within the enclosure may be described as still standing ; and, in some cases, where those of lighter structure have gone too completely to decay to be susceptible of preservation, plain brick columns, bearing marble slabs, record the name and site. In all cases, however, the dust and *débris* that could not have been allowed to remain without spoiling the cared for appearance of the whole place, have been wisely taken away. And it is just this well tended appearance, this tenderly cared for aspect of the enclosure generally, with its trimmed gardens, swept walks, and flower beds, that throw into such extraordinary and pathetic relief the dead ruins standing all about blind and silent, yet so full of thrilling associations. Not a broken stone has been replaced when its replacement would have caused the obliteration of a fact, the concealment of an honorable wound. But not a fancy has been left unrealized which could help to make the ground itself rich with testimony of the survivor's anxious care. Nor is this made manifest by means of flowers and shrubs alone : for though the buildings which saw the terrible events of the great defence

are gaunt and desolate wrecks, there are other buildings of a later date standing close by, also sacred to the memory of battle scenes; and these good taste have kept as new looking and fresh as if they had only been constructed yesterday. I allude to the memorial monuments and the tombs.

134. Lord Northbrook's admirably thought of monument* to the loyal native soldiers who fell in the defence, though really of the other day only, looks no newer than the tall cross† erected to the memory of Major-General Sir Henry Lawrence and the brave men who fell in the defence of the Residency, or than any of the many grave-stones and memorials, stately and simple, that crowd the little churchyard. With an ingenuity that may be unconscious or accidental on their part, or more probably suggested by others, the native guides who take visitors over the Residency grounds and point out the places of peculiar interest bring the tour to an end at the cemetery. The last sensation, therefore, that the visit excites is that which rises up in sympathy with the praises lavished by their countrymen on the memory of the gallant dead, and the long-lived glory of those whose earthly lives were extinguished in the smoke and roar of the defence. You visit first the scenes of battle, and stand on places where the most eminent of the victims fell, when you realize the terror of the besieged women and the ferocity of the fighting at the most advanced batteries, and then you pass in among the solemn monuments where the emotions called up

---

* The foundation stone of this monument was laid on 7th January, 1876, by His Royal Highness the Prince of Wales, now His Majesty the King. It stands east of the Baillie Guard Gate outside the original boundary of the intrenchment. After the ceremony was over His Royal Highness expressed his desire to have presented to him all the survivors of the siege then present. This was done by Major Cubitt, V. C., one of the heroes of Chinhut.

The Duke of Edinburgh visited Lucknow during Lord Mayo's régime, and the Prince of Wales during Lord Northbrook's viceroyalty. The Duke of Connaught visited Lucknow in December, 1883.

† The foundation stone of this memorial was laid by Sir George Couper, Bart., C. B., (the then Judicial Commissioner of Oudh, and subsequently Lieutenant-Governor, N.-W. P. and Chief Commissioner of Oudh), at 4 P. M., on Saturday, the 2nd January, 1864, the Band of H. M.'s 107th Regiment being in attendance. Total height of column, including stone steps, is 35'-6". The dressing and engraving of the stone, including inscription, alone cost Rs. 4,500. (See Appendix C.)

by all these memories are sanctified by religious symbolism and recorded in stone.

135. Here now my narrative ends, not without earnest thanksgiving to that beneficent and merciful Providence who preserved us through the fearful perils by which we were so long encompassed, and caused our lot to differ from the sad fate of those who perished at Cawnpore.

The following lines, published after the Mutiny, were reproduced in the *Pioneer*. They add a pathos all their own to the touching tale of death and desolation at Cawnpore :—

CAWNPORE—1857.

With body wasted and worn,
   With a heart as heavy as lead,
A woman sat where her husband's form
   On the blood-stained floor lay dead.
Women and children, wild
   With hunger, round her pressed :
One little babe—her infant child—
   Was starving on her breast,
And thus, with weary song, she lulled
   Her dying child to rest.

   Roar, Roar, Roar,
   Oh ! that incessant din
     From the enemy's guns without,
     And our own few guns within.
Shell, and musket and gun,
   Gun, and musket and shell,
Mingle their roar with our groans and shrieks,
   And turn this place into Hell.

   Roar, Roar, Roar,
   Will these hideous guns never cease ?
   Roar, Roar, Roar ;
   Must death be our sole release ?
Must all—the good, the brave,
   The young and the old—thus die ?
Must we vainly pray our God to save ?
   To him must we vainly cry ?

   Death, Death, Death ;
   In every shape and form :
   Death, Death, Death,
   Rides on the iron storm.
He comes with the hurtling shot,
   He comes with the bursting shell,
While wounds, starvation and disease
   Do his dread work too well.

I have lost my husband dear,
　　Two brothers and their wives ;
And while my heart is wearing out,
　　Death takes my children's lives.
Death, Death, Death—
　　'Mid misery, hunger, and woe,
My last child dying, my husband dead,
　　I court thy friendly blow.

Why should I shrink from death,
　　When my dear ones all are gone ?
Their lives were ended in want and woe,
　　And why not thus my own ?
Oh husband, good and kind,
　　So dear and true to me,
Why should thy wife remain behind,
　　When death hath taken thee ?

　　　　Death, Death, Death ;
　　I hear the weary moan
Of another sobbing wife reply
　　To her husband's dying groan :
And I hear the stifled sigh,
　　Of a soldier in his pain ;
And I hear his farewell moan,
　　"Comrades, lift me once again !"

　　　　Death, Death, Death ;
　　Beneath the embankment there ;
A husband tends his wounded wife,
　　While friends kneel round in prayer.
Their tears fall thick and fast
　　On that blood-stained blood-red sod,
As their dying friend's last torture past,
　　Her soul takes flight to God.

　　　　Death, Death, Death ;
　　Yon feverish woman seems
To be happy 'mid those joyous scenes
　　Which come but in her dreams ;
But her weary wasted form,
　　Her fiercely burning head,
Proclaim that soon her troubles o'er,
　　She too must join the dead.

Last week her husband fell,
　　Shot down, close by her side,
And her aged, grey-haired mother,
　　In that burning barrack died.
Her only sister followed,
　　Struck by a bursting shell ;
To-morrow she will join them all,
　　Down in that hideous well.

Oh, were my loved ones all
　　Once more in life again,
Oh, were they only safe from here,
　　From all this grief and pain !
From all this carnage, woe and strife
　　To see them safely fly,
How gladly would I yield my life,
　　How gladly would I die !

With a body wasted and worn,
 With a heart as heavy as lead,
A woman nursed her dying child,
 With her husband before her dead.
  Death, Death, Death—
In weary tones, with gasping breath,
 'Mid misery, sickness, wounds and woe,
 'Mid the cannon's roar and the yells of the foe,
She sang this song of Death.

Her husband's corpse was thrown
 That evening into the well,
Whose black deep mouth for victims yawned,
 Like the very mouth of Hell;
  Death, Death, Death!
Her babe—the last was dead;
 Heart-broken, from that bloody floor,
 She rose and staggered to the door,
 Then passed out, to return no more;
While the stars shone overhead.

  * * * *

The cannon's roar, the foe's wild yell,—
Her own, her child's, her husband's knell—
Upon her ear unheeded fell.
The broken prayer alone she said,
 Then pressing to her bursting heart
The babe—from which she could not part—
 Into the well, with frantic start
She plunged—and joined the dead.

136. The Residency was providentially prepared for a long siege, having been provided with a large supply of provisions and ammunition through the forethought of that great and good man, Sir Henry Lawrence, who sacrificed his life there to his country's cause. His remains are interred in the Residency churchyard close by, and the simple epitaph inscribed upon his monumental stone—" Here lies Henry Lawrence who tried to do his duty "—has quickened the pulses of many a traveller who has lingered in that historic cemetery, filled with the graves of sons and daughters of the English race who perished during that long ordeal of battle.

" Here sleep the brave, who gently sank to rest,
Mourned by the virtuous, by their country blest!
Theirs is the sweet reward of praise sincere,
The kind remembrance, and the greatful tear;
For them the living rear the storied bust,
In holy reverence, sacred to their dust."

137. The passing stranger cannot but be affected reading the epitaphs over the illustrious dead ; but he must feel proud when looking up at the bullet riddled walls of the Residency, eloquent in its silence and ruin, and the shattered tower on which our country's flag waved gloriously throughout the long siege. Whilst the members of the garrison felt a noble pride in thus displaying to their assailants their resolute confidence, the sight of that symbol of British predominance filled the hearts of those assailants with fury. The flag was a constant aim of their sharp-shooters. Again and again were the halyards severed ; the flag was riddled ; the staff cut through by bullets. But as soon as darkness permitted, a new staff and new halyards were supplied. Patched up though it might be, the flag continued to the last to float defiance to the enemies of England.

> " And forth to the outer world,
> Our flag though rent and torn
> Waves high in haughty majesty,
> Bidding our foeman scorn.
>
> " And forth to the outer world,
> Our flag will aye proclaim,
> Our duty, patience, chivalry,
> Our honor, and our fame."
>
> JOSEPH B. S. BOYLE.

The visitor recalls the heroism of the garrison, which for one hundred and forty-seven days manfully defeated the incessant attacks of the thousands of rebel soldiers who encircled the intrenchment with their ring of deadly fire.

138. The hardships and misery endured by the besieged during that critical period defy description, and no adequate idea of them can be formed by perusing the foregoing narrative of my reminiscences of the investment, as even the most exaggerated account would fall short of the reality.

The following stanzas from Tennyson's heart-stirring ode may very suitably find a place in these reminiscences, as they so graphically describe the siege as it is impressed upon my recollection at the present time, although years have elapsed since the occurrence :—

THE DEFENCE OF LUCKNOW

BY

LORD TENNYSON.

1.

BANNER of England, not for a season, O banner of Britain, hast thou
Floated in conquering battle or flapt to the battle-cry !
Never with mightier glory than when we had rear'd thee on high
Flying at top of the roofs in the ghastly siege of Lucknow—
Shot thro' the staff or the halyard, but ever we raised thee anew,
And ever upon the topmost roof our banner of England blew.

II.

Frail were the works that defended the hold that we held with our lives.—
Women and children among us, God help them, our children and wives !
Hold it we might—and for fifteen days or for twenty at most.
' Never surrender, I charge you, but every man die at his post ! '
Voice of the dead whom we loved, our Lawrence the best of the brave :
Cold were his brows when we kiss'd him—we laid him that night in his grave.
' Every man die at his post !' and there hail'd on our houses and halls
Death from their rifle-bullets, and death from their cannon-balls,
Death in our innermost chamber, and death at our slight barricade,
Death while we stood with the musket, and death while we stoop to the spade ;
Death to the dying, and wounds to the wounded, for often there fell
Striking the hospital wall, crashing thro' it, their shot and their shell,
Death—for their spies were among us, their marksmen were told of our best,
So that the brute bullet broke thro' the brain that could think for the rest ;
Bullets would sing by our foreheads, and bullets would rain at our feet—
Fire from ten thousand at once of the rebels that girdled us round—
Death at the glimpse of a finger from over the breadth of a street.
Death from the heights of the mosque and the palace, and death in the ground !
Mine ? yes, a mine ! Countermine ! down, down ! and creep thro' the hole !
Keep the revolver in hand ! you can hear him—the murderous mole !
Quiet, ah ! quiet—wait till the point of the pickaxe be thro' !
Click with the pick, coming nearer and nearer again than before—
Now let it speak, and you fire, and the dark pioneer is no more ;
And ever upon the topmost roof our banner of England blew !

III.

Ay, but the foe sprung his mine many times, and it chanced on a day
Soon as the blast of that underground thunderclap echo'd away,
Dark thro' the smoke and the sulphur like so many fiends in their hell—
Cannon-shot, musket-shot, volley on volley and yell upon yell—
Fiercely on all the defences our myriad enemy fell.
What have they done ? where is it ? Out yonder. Guard the Redan !
Storm at the water-gate ! storm at the Baillie-gate ! storm, and it ran
Surging and swaying all round us, as ocean on every side
Plunges and heaves at a bank that is daily drown'd by the tide—
So many thousands that if they be bold enough, who shall escape ?
Kill or be kill'd, live or die, they shall know we are soldiers and men !
Ready, take aim at their leaders—their masses are gaped with our grape—
Backward they reel like the wave, like the wave flinging forward again,
Flying and foil'd at the last by the handful they could not subdue ;
And ever upon the topmost roof our banner of England blew.

IV.

Handful of men as we were, we were English in heart and in limb,
Strong with the strength of the race to command, to obey, to endure,
Each of us fought as if hope for the garrison hung but on him ;
Still—could we watch at all points? we were every day fewer and fewer.
There was a whisper among us, but only a whisper that past :
'Children and wives—if the tigers leap into the fold unawares—
Every man die at his post—and the foe may outlive us at last—
Better to fall by the hands that they love, than to fall into theirs !'
Roar upon roar, in a moment two mines by the enemy sprung
Clove into perilous chasms our walls and our poor palisades.
Rifleman, true is your heart, but be sure that your hand be as true !
Sharp is the fire of assault, better aimed are your flank fusilades—
Twice do we hurl them to earth from the ladders to which they had clung :
Twice from the ditch where they shelter we drive them with hand-grenades,
And ever upon the topmost roof our banner of England blew.

V.

Then on another wild morning another wild earthquake out-tore
Clean from our lines of defence ten or twelve good paces or more.
Riflemen, high on the roof hidden there from the light of the sun—
One has leapt upon the breach, crying out : 'Follow me, follow me !'
Mark him—he falls! then another, and *him* too, and down goes he.
Had they been bold enough then, who can tell but the traitors had won ?
Boardings and rafters and doors—an embrasure ! make way for the gun !
Now double-charge it with grape ! It is charged and we fire, and they run
Praise to our Indian brothers, and let the dark face have his due !
Thanks to the kindly dark faces who fought with us, faithful and few,
Fought with the bravest among us, and drove them, and smote them, and slew
That ever upon the topmost roof our banner in India blew.

VI.

Men will forget what we suffer and not what we do. We can fight
But to be soldier all day and be sentinel all thro' the night—
Ever the mine and assault, our sallies, their lying alarms.
Bugles and drums in the darkness, and shoutings and soundings to arms
Ever the labor of fifty that had to be done by five,
Ever the marvel among us that one should be left alive,
Ever the day with its traitorous death from the loop-holes around,
Ever the night with its coffinless corpse to be laid in the ground,
Heat like the mouth of a hell, or a deluge of cataract skies,
Stench of old offal decaying, and infinite torment of flies,
Thoughts of the breezes of May blowing over an English field,
Cholera, scurvy, and fever, the wound that *would* not be heal'd,
Lopping away of the limb by the pitiless knife,—
Torture and troubles in vain,—for, it never could save us a life.
Valour of delicate women who tended the hospital bed,
Horror of women in travail among the dying and dead,
Grief for our perishing children, and never a moment for grief,
Toil and ineffable weariness, faltering hopes of relief,
Havelock baffled, or beaten, or butcher'd for all that we know—
Then day and night, day and night coming down on the still-shatter'd walls
Millions of musket-bullets, and thousands of cannon-balls—
But ever upon the topmost roof our banner of England blew.

VII.

Hark cannonade, fusillade! is it true what was told by the scouts,
Outram and Havelock breaking their way through the fell-mutineers?
Surely the Pibroch of Europe is ringing again in our ears!
All on a sudden the garrison utter a jubilant shout,
Havelock's glorious Highlanders answer with conquering cheers,
Sick from the hospital echo them, women and children come out,
Blessing the wholesome white faces of Havelock's good Fusiliers,
Kissing the war-harden'd hand of the Highlander wet with their tears!
Dance to the Pibroch!—saved! we are saved!—is it you? is it you?
Saved by the valour of Havelock, saved, by the blessing of Heaven!
'Hold it for fifteen days!' we have held it for eighty-seven!
And ever aloft on the palace roof the old banner of England blew.

Nisi Dominus, frustra.

CHAPTER III.

A SHORT BIOGRAPHY OF THE KINGS OF OUDH,

WITH

A GEOGRAPHICAL SKETCH OF THE PROVINCE.

Oudh is a strip of territory extending from the base of the sub-Himalaya mountains, in a direction from north-west to south-east, until it reaches the Ganges. Its greatest length is about 270, and its breadth 160 miles. Its general character is that of a more or less undulating plain, with a gradual declination as it extends from the mountain to the river. It is intersected by numerous streams, the principal of which, inclusive of the frontier stream of the Ganges, are the Sarju, Ghagra, Chauka, Gumti, and Sai. These, with numerous lesser streams and tributaries, entering the country from the Himalayan chain and *Tarai* * forest, which separates Oudh from Nepal, and flowing gently through the country towards the Ganges, without cutting very deeply into the soil, always keep the water near the surface, and available in all quarters, and in any quantity, for purposes of irrigation. Never was there a country more favoured by nature, or more susceptible of improvement, under judicious management. There is hardly an acre of ground that is not capable of good culture. It is generally well timbered, studded with groves and fine solitary trees in great perfection. The soil is good, and the surface everywhere capable of tillage, with little labour or outlay. Considered generally, however, Oudh surpasses in natural advantages almost every other part of India—having the Ganges running along the whole of its south-west frontier, a varied and fertile soil, a genial though hot climate, and numerous facilities for irrigation and water carriage. Yet with all these natural advantages, never was there a country where anarchy and confusion so generally prevailed. An unusual blight seemed to rest upon it, and neither life nor property were secure, the cause of which is briefly explained in Chapter I of this book.

The climate of Oudh is less humid than that of Lower Bengal, and has greater varieties of temperature. The year falls naturally into three seasons—the rainy, from the middle of June to beginning of October; the cold weather, from October to March; and the hot season, from April to June. During this season hot winds blow and dust storms are

---

* *Tarai* is the malarious belt of thick *jungle* lying between the lower slopes of the Himalayas and the plains of the North-West Provinces and Bengal.

prevalent. The winter rains fall generally towards the end of December and in January, and heavy night dews are very common. The mean temperature is 77·5° F. in the shade. It ranges from 44° in January, the coldest month, to 111° in June, the hotest month. The heat proves most oppressive in the rainy season.

The average annual rain-fall is 39·37 inches.

Oudh, once a Hindu kingdom, became, under the Mogal dynasty, a Muhammadan Nawabship, then a Nawab Vazirship, then, under British protection, a Muhammadan kingdom, and lastly an Anglo-Indian Province.

Lucknow, the capital of Oudh, is situated mainly on the right bank of the Gumti,* which is navigable for many miles above the town and downwards, through its whole course to its confluence with the Ganges between Benares and Ghazipur. It is spread over an area of 36 square miles, and in population† Lucknow ranks next to the Presidency towns. It is healthily situated, being 403 feet above the level of the sea, in latitude 26°58′ N. and longitude 80°58 E. Its claim to the title of capital dates from the accession of Nawab Asaf-ud-

---

* Gumti means winding or meandering. This river takes its rise in the Pilibhit District of the N.-W. Provinces, in an alluvial tract between the Garrah and the Ghagra rivers. Its source is in a small lake or morass called the Phaljar Tal, 19 miles east of Pilibhit town, and about 605 feet above sea level. From thence the river flows in a south-eastern direction for 42 miles, when it enters Oudh, in the Kheri District, in latitude 28°11′ N., longitude 80°20′ E. Continuing in a south-easterly course for 94 miles further, it receives the Kathna as a tributary, on its left bank, and then the Sarayan. After thus meandering for 174 miles from its source it reaches Lucknow. At about 52 miles south-east of Sultanpur, the river re-enters the N.-W. Provinces, in the Jaunpur District, where it is spanned by a bridge of 16 arches. It receives the Sai river, on its left bank, 18 miles below Jaunpur, and the Nand river, also on the left bank, 33 miles lower down, in the Benares District. It empties itself into the Ganges, 5 miles below this point, in latitude 25°31′ N., longitude 83°31′ E., after a total course of about 500 miles. The Gumti is navigable by boats of 500 maunds, or about 18 tons burthen, throughout the year, as far as Dilawarpur Ghât, near Muhumdi, in the Kheri District.

† The last census took place on the 1st March, 1901. The recorded total was 264,049 persons, of which 240,649 resided within Municipal limits and 23,400 in Cantonments. The European element is unusually large. The Hindus number three-fifths of the population. Many pensioners of the British Government and of the King of Oudh reside in the city. The Lucknow Mussalmans are chiefly Shias, that being the recognised orthodox sect under the Nawabs.

The distinctive characteristics of Muhammadans and Hindus are religiously kept up. One of them is in the fastening of the outer garment. On meeting either party, though the dress is much the same, you at once distinguish the Muhammadan from the Hindu by the universal fact that the latter has his tunic (*mirzai* or *chapkan*) made to button on the right side while the Muhammadan hooks his on the left.

daula, A. D. 1775, and although destitute of any extensive trade or manufacture, it is still a place of considerable wealth, and the centre of modern Indian life and fashion, and the best school of Indian Music, Grammar and Moslem theology. Lucknow is divided into four parts :—

The first part comprises the native city, which is extensive, but meanly built, and squalid in parts remote from the Chauk, or public promenade, where everything is bright and cheerful to render it attractive to European visitors and to the native gentry who frequent the place. The buildings in many parts of the city are monuments of waste of wealth, under the native *régime*. The second contains the King's Palaces, including the residences of his Court and religious edifices; the third, the civil station, which chiefly consists of houses of the European community; and the fourth, the Dilkusha Cantonments,* which occupy the south-eastern quarter and is separated from the city by Gazi-ud-din Haidar's Canal. The old Cantonments, built by Saadat Ali Khan, was on the opposite side of the river and known as Mariaon, a name which the locality still retains. The chief points whence good views of Lucknow can be had, are La Martiniere College and Saadat Ali's Tomb, the Chutter Munzil Palace and Residency Tower, the Imambara of Asaf-ud-daula and the Clock Tower at Husainabad, from the tops of which you can obtain a beautiful panorama of the city and the surrounding country.

The present city stands on what was the sight of 64 villages, the memory of several of which is still preserved in the names of the *mohallas* built over them, but all traces of others have passed away, and their names can only be collected from ancient records. The originial centre of the city, is the high ground which, crowned by the Masjid, or mosque, of Aurangzeb, overhangs the Stone Bridge, and which is called Lakshman Tila. On this site formerly stood the village of Lakshmanpur. There is an old story that Ayodhya† (Ajodhya) was once such an enormous city, in the days when the great dynasty of the Rajput descendants of the sun held the seat of empire there,

---

* To the south of the city and beyond the canal, which forms the boundary from the railway station to the Dilkusha (Clyde) road, lie the Cantonments of Lucknow. They extend from the Rae Bareli road on the west to the Gumti river on the east, and cover an area of 9·25 square miles.

The Dilkusha Cantonments were built after the Mutiny in 1859.

†Ayodhya means "the unconquerable" city; and is the name from which the modern province of Oudh, or Avadh, has been called. It was the capital of the ancient kingdom of Kosal or Kosala, situated on the banks of the Sarju, or Ghagra. It stands first among the sacred cities of India because it was here that Ram, the greatest of the incarnations of Vishnu, was born, and from a spot on the Sarju, near Ayodhya, he is said to have ascended to heaven in the sight of his admiring and longing companions.

that it extended from its present site to Lucknow. This may, probably, be explained by the consideration that Lakshman, the deity of Lakshmanpur, was the brother and constant companion of Rama, the worshipped of Ayodhya, and that tradition, as it never separates the two persons, would be likely also to connect their cities.

There is reason to believe that Lakshmanpur was originally inhabited by Brahmins and that they were dispossessed by a family of Sheikhs who came down with the invading army of Saiyid Salar, since canonized as Ghazi Mian, the nephew of Mahmud of Ghazni, 1160 A. D. This is the earliest date of which there is any record of this event, but, though every Mussalman family in Oudh declares that they came down with Saiyid Salar, it is obvious that the Muhammadan colonization must have taken place slowly and gradually, and it, probably, was not completed for fully a hundred years.

This family of Sheikhs obtained a good deal of influence in the country, and subsequently supplied more than one member to the list of Subadars. One of their first proceedings was to build a fort, which soon became renowned for its strength. One they built occupied the site of the old Machhi Bhawan fort,* and is said to have been planned by a Hindu, named Likhna, whence the place was called Killa Likhna. As the Sheikhs prospered and increased, a town grew up around them, which, from the two names of Lakshmanpur and Likhna, got the name of Lucknow. It is impossible to give the exact date of the introduction of this new name, but it certainly was current previous to the reign of Akbar Shah.

To give an example of the prosperity of this town, the Sheikhs have a story that when, in 1540 A. D. the Emperor Humayun went down to Jaunpur to fight Sher Shah, then King of Jaunpur, and subsequently Emperor of Delhi, he retreated, after his defeat, viâ Sultanpur, Lucknow and Pilibhit, to Cashmere, and, on his way, stopped four hours in Lucknow, where, beaten and dispirited as his force was, and, therefore, probably, little able to compel obedience, they, nevertheless, collected for him, in that short space of time, Rs. 10,000 in cash and 50 horses. That such a story should obtain credence is, in itself, a proof that Lucknow was then a wealthy and flourishing town.

---

* When Asaf-ud-daula became Viceroy of Oudh, Lucknow was but a village of little importance. The Sheikhs, who had risen in rebellion against his rule, built there a castle, the Machhi Bhawan, from whence they raided the surrounding country. The Viceroy in person expelled them from their stronghold, and, being pleased with the locality, selected it as the site of his future capital, removing thither, from Fyzabad, in 1775.

We hear mention made of the title of Subahdar (Governor of a Subah, or province) of Oudh as early as 1280 A. D., but the title could not properly be given till, in 1590 A. D., Akbar Shah divided the Empire of Hindustan into 12 Subahs, of which Oudh was one. The boundaries of the Subahs differed from those of the present province of Oudh, chiefly in the fact that they included part of the Gorakhpur District, but excluded Tulsipur, and a large part of what is now the Fyzabad District. Of this Subah it is impossible to say that any one place was the capital. The Subahdars seem to have been constantly changed, seldom keeping their place more than three or four years. Most of them were Delhi favourites, who remained at Court the greater part of the year and then came down to Oudh to collect the revenue, marched about the country and, when they had got all they could, went back again.

BIOGRAPHY OF THE KINGS OF OUDH.
1.—SAADAT KHAN, BURHAN-UL-MULK, * 1732-1739.

Saàdat Khan, the progenitor of the Kings of Oudh, descended from a noble Saiyid family, was a merchant † who came from Persia to seek his fortune in Hindustan. He combined with the usual qualities of a good soldier, the rare talents required for an able administrator. His original name was Muhammad Amin. In the year 1705, while still but a lad, he arrived at Patna, to join his father and elder brother, who had preceded him thither. On his arrival, finding the former dead, he and his brother proceeded to push their fortunes at Delhi. ‡ His first service was with Nawab Sirbulland Khan, whom, however, he soon quitted, resenting a taunt uttered by his master on occasion of some trifling neglect. The youth took his way to Court, where he soon acquired favour; and having materially assisted his imbecile Sovereign in getting rid of Husain Ali, Governor of Bihar, (the younger of the Saiyids of Barha, who were at that time dragooning the King) Muhammad Amin was rapidly promoted to the Viceroyalty of Oudh, with the title of Saàdat Khan. He found the Province in great disorder, but soon reduced the refractory spirits and greatly increased the revenue. He protected the husbandman, but crushed the petty chiefs who aimed at independence.

With him the debate arose between Lucknow and Fyzabad for the rank of capital. Saàdat Khan certainly lived at Ayodhya and built a fort there: as certainly he also lived at Lucknow, and changed the name of the Fort from Killa Likhna to Machhi Bhawan, or fish-house, in allusion to the crest of a fish, which he had assumed, and which has since become a decoration on the buildings of Lucknow. Unlike his descendants, who built themselves Palaces which now fill the city, he hired the Sheikh Palaces in the fort, known as the Panch Mahala and the Mubarak Mahal, for which he paid a monthly rental of Rs. 565.

History questions the fact of Saàdat Khan having, in concert with Nizam-ul-Mulk, Subahdar of the Deccan, invited Nadir Shah's invasion, but a careful comparison of authorities leads to the belief that he was guilty of this treacherous deed. The atrocities committed by Nadir are familiar matters

---

* Burhan-ul-Mulk means Governor of the country.

† Some authorities say he was an adventurer, not a merchant. Very probably he was both.

‡ "Delhi is a large fortified city on the west bank of the River Jumna, and was at one time the capital of India. The original city is supposed to have been founded about the year 50 B. C.; and the present comparatively modern one in the year 1640. Delhi was one of the chief centres of the Sepoy Revolt in 1857, and was captured by General Archdale Wilson after a four months' siege."—*Indian Daily Telegraph.*

of history. The traitor chiefs did not escape persecutions. Nizam-ul-Mulk and Saàdat Khan were not only grossly insulted by Nadir for their treacherous conduct towards the Emperor, but were plundered and made the instruments of extorting treasure from distant provinces. Nizam-ul-Mulk, jealous of the power and ability of Saàdat, took advantage of the persecutions of Nadir Shah to execute a plan of getting rid of his rival. He affected to confide in him his own determination of suicide, and agreed with Saàdat Khan that each should take poison. The latter drank his cup empty, and left the hoary schemer without a rival in the Empire.

Saàdat Khan, who had but a few years before been a needy adventurer, and had now been plundered by Nadir Shah, was still enabled to leave his successor a large treasure, estimated at nine millions sterling. Though he accumulated so much wealth, he did not leave behind him the character of an oppressor. On the contrary, he seems rather to have respected the poor, and to have restricted his exactions to the rich. He reaped much as he had sown; his ability and management established a Sovereignty; his faithlessness brought him to a premature and ignominious end. He proved no exception to the rule, that they who are busiest in entrapping others, are themselves the easiest deluded.

Saàdat Khan was buried at Delhi.

2.—MANSUR ALI KHAN, 1739-1753.

Saàdat Khan was succeeded by his son-in-law and nephew, Mansur Ali Khan, Safdar Jang, who followed his predecessor's policy in keeping up a strong interest at Court and connecting himself closely with the Imperial Government. In 1747 he received the post which Saàdat Khan had so much coveted, and was made Vazir, or Minister of State, to the Emperor. From this date the title of Subahdar ceases, and the Governor of Oudh is called the Nawab Vazir, a combination of two titles of Nawab of Oudh and Vazir of the Empire; the latter title was bestowed by the Emperor of Delhi.

Mansur Ali Khan was the founder of Fyzabad, where he resided, besides making it his military head-quarters. He built the rampart and moat that surrounded the city and had several standing camps near it; so that it can hardly be denied that, in his reign, Fyzabad, and not Lucknow, was the Capital of Oudh. He was an able ruler, and his financial administration was successful.

The Nawab died in 1753, of fever, and his remains were removed to Delhi for interment. The mausoleum of Safdar Jang is well-known as one of the finest structures of the kind at Delhi.

3.—SHUJA-UD-DAULA, 1753-1775.

Mansur Ali Khan was succeeded by his son Shuja-ud-daula, who was appointed Vazir by Shah Alam. Of all the Oudh Nawabs he seems to have formed the largest plans for aggrandizing himself and his province at the expense of the decaying Moghal Empire. Like his predecessors he was pre-eminently a soldier, and was for a great part of his rule engaged in wars. In 1763, the English having quarrelled with their own *élevé*, Mir Kasim, Governor of Bengal, Shuja-ud-daula took the field in his favour and advanced upon Patna, taking with him the fugitive Moghal Emperor, Shah Alam II, and the exiled Nawab of Bengal. Defeated by the British, in successive battles at Patna and Buxar, the Nawab fled to Bareilly, while the unfortunate Emperor joined the British Camp.

By the treaty of 1765, which followed this event, Korah and Allahabad, which hitherto formed part of the Oudh Viceroyalty, were made over to the Emperor for the support of his dignity and expenses, all the remaining territories being restored to Shuja-ud-daula, who, reduced to extremities, had thrown himself upon the generosity of the British Government. It had been intended to deprive him of his territories, but Lord Clive, on a personal interview, reversed the decision, and reinstated him on the condition of his paying the expenses of the war.

He fixed his head-quarters at Fyzabad * and attracted commerce to the place, so that, with its great natural advantages, it very soon became a flourishing mart. It appears, however, that in the last years of his reign, when Rohilkhand had been subjugated and most of it annexed to Oudh, he fixed his residence at Lucknow as being more central. He was a ruler of great ability and energy, and was, for a great part of his reign, engaged in wars. Shuja-ud-daula died suddenly on 26th January, 1775, at Fyzabad, of which city his tomb, the Gulab Bari (rose garden), is one of the chief ornaments. He is described as being extremely handsome and endowed with great strength.

"Bahu Begam was the wife of Shuja-ud-daula; she was a native of Persia and the grand-daughter of Mirza Husain, the chief of Emperor Alamgir's kitchen. The Begam died in 1816, and the building of her tomb at Fyzabad was not completed until 1858. It cost between three and four lacs; and it has an annual income of Rs. 6,000 derived from an endowment which is spent in repairs, religious ceremonies and periodical illuminations."—*Indian Daily Telegraph.*

---

* Fyzabad is on the river Ghagra, navigable thence to Bhalia, where it joins the Ganges.

4.—ASAF-UD-DAULA, 1775-1797.

Shuja-ud-daula was succeeded by his son, Asaf-ud-daula, who transferred the seat of Government to Lucknow, which dates, from this period, its existence as a City and its rank as the Capital of Oudh. Up to this time it was merely a large town of some few hundred houses, extending no further than the area round the Machhi Bhawan. It is pretty clear that the site of the Chauk was occupied by a distinct village, while jungle covered the ground where the Husainabad and Kaisar Bagh now stand.

Under Asaf-ud-daula, the Lucknow Court reached its highest splendour. All the wealth of the State was devoted to the personal aggrandisement of its ruler and the accumulation of those materials which minister to oriental pomp. No Court in India could rival the magnificence of the Nawab-Vazir.

At his accession a new treaty was concluded confirming him in possession of Korah and Allahabad. This Nawab-Vazir ceded the districts of Benares and Jaunpur, worth 75 lacs, with a net profit of 25 lacs annually, to the British, for the better defence of his dominion, stipulating also a yearly payment of £312,000 * in maintenance of the auxiliary force. He brought about reforms in his army, which was put on a more efficient footing by the introduction of European Officers into the Military Department.

As a token of gratitude for the recovery of the King of England (George III) from a dangerous illness, Asaf-ud-daula presented the Doctor with Rs. 25,000 and distributed a similar sum in charity in His Majesty's name. This King is held in affectionate remembrance up to the present day by the natives, who are in the habit of repeating every morning this couplet as an auspicious incantation before commencing business :—

Jis ko na de Maula us ko de Asaf-ud-daula.—Whom giveth not God (*Maula*) him giveth Asaf-ud-daula.

Asaf-ud-daula seems hardly to have had any distinct plan for building, but to have allowed the city to grow up round the Chauk, chiefly to the western side of what is now the Canning Street. He encouraged merchants and traders to settle by the widest and most extravagant liberality. He spent money lavishly on public buildings and gardens, some of which are the chief ornaments of Lucknow, such as the Daulat Khana, Rumi Darwaza, Bibiapur Kothi, Chinhut House, the Great Imambara, Charbagh and Aishbagh. This last garden is now

---

* This subsidy was subsequently commuted for a territorial grant, and the Southern Duab, together with the Districts of Allahabad, Azamgarh, Western Gorakhpur, &c., were ceded to the Hon'ble East India Company, by Saádat Ali, in 1801.

the site of the filtering and distributing Station of the Municipal Water Works. His own Palace was in the building known as the Daulat Khana, the chief house, or Asafi Kothi, being named after himself. He died childless on 21st September, 1797, and was buried in his own magnificent Imambara at Machhi Bhawan.

5.—VAZIR ALI.

Vazir Ali, reputed son of Asaf-ud-daula, succeeded him and reigned for four months, but his proved illegitimacy and worthless character led the Governor-General, Sir John Shore, afterwards Lord Teignmouth, to displace him and elevate Saádat Ali Khan, the half-brother of Asaf-ud-daula and younger son of Shuja-ud-daula. Mr. Cherry, Resident at Benares, negotiated the treaty with Saadat Ali, who was then living at Benares on a pension of 1½ lacs of rupees. The new Nawab marched to Lucknow, where Sir John Shore was encamped. The Governor-General was in extreme peril from Vazir Ali's lawless soldiers, but he, with the utmost calmness, maintained his position, and the new Nawab was eventually placed on the throne, Vazir Ali being deported to Benares on the same pension of 1½ lacs a year. In 1799 Vazir Ali assassinated Mr. Cherry, at Benares, and raised a temporary rebellion, but was defeated, taken prisoner, and sent to Fort William. After many years of captivity there he was transferred to the Palace built for Tippu Sultan's family in the Fort of Vellore, where he died in 1817.

The marriage expenses of this Prince in 1795, amounted to 30 lacs of rupees, while his funeral expenses in 1817, cost but 70 rupees, a strange reverse of fortune.

6.—SAADAT ALI KHAN, 1798-1814.*

In 1798 Asaf-ud-daula's half-brother, Saádat Ali Khan, succeeded Vazir Ali and earned for himself, during his reign of sixteen years, the character of the best administrator and wisest and most sagacious ruler that Oudh had ever seen. Nawab Saádat Ali added the sum of 19,22,362 rupees to the subsidy given to the British Government, every year, on account of the auxiliary force during his predecessor's reign; and afterwards, for the greater satisfaction of the British Government, made over to the Hon'ble East India Company,

---

* About the beginning of the eighteenth century, Saàdat Ali Khan, a timid potentate, asked for protection against his own subjects, so Lord Wellesley kindly allowed a British Resident and British troops to protect him.

The Resident at the Court of Oudh, during the reign of Saádat Ali Khan, was Colonel J. Baillie, whose portrait is in the Provincial Museum at Lucknow.

certain Districts of his dominions (some of which now form part of the North-West Provinces), estimated to yield an annual revenue of nearly a million and a half sterling.

He was parsimonious in his habits, and the contrast between him and his lavish predecessor got him the name of a miser, but the fine works he executed and the steadiness with which he carried out his plan of embellishing the eastern part of the city, as his brother had done the western, prove that he was ready to spend largely where occasion required. Almost all the principal buildings between the Kaisar Bagh and the Dilkusha were built by him. He was, on the whole, a good and just ruler; had mixed in the society of British Officers and had been well trained to habits of business. No Sovereign of Oudh conducted the Government with so much ability as he did. He never remitted his vigilance over the administration; and in this way, and by a judicious selection of his ministers, he secured the prosperity of his dominions, which enjoyed almost uninterrupted tranquillity during his reign. He was the first to establish a reserve treasury in 1801 A. D., and, on his death, he left 14 crores of rupees (14 millions sterling) in it.

In the early part of his reign the King used to drink hard and to indulge in pleasures which tended to unfit him for the duties of Sovereignty, but, in 1801, he made a solemn vow at the shrine of Hazrat Abbas, at Lucknow, to cease from all such indulgences and to devote his time and attention to his duties. This vow he kept during the remaining years of his life. Saádat Ali Khan died on the night of 11th, July 1814, and was buried in the larger of the two tombs on the north-east side of the Canning College, and his wife, Khurshedzadi in the smaller.

Munauwar-ud-daula was Prime Minister of Saádat Ali Khan.

> "Where now the Pomp, which marks an Eastern Throne?
> Where is the Monarch, and his Courtiers gone?
> Yon lofty dome, in vain uplifts its head!
> It marks but the spot where rest the mighty dead!
> But the lone lamp, which trembles in the tomb,
> Is a fit emblem of the unchanging doom
> Which awaits alike, the Tyrant, and the Slave,
> The free, the generous, virtuous, and the Brave
> Like that lone lamp awhile life brightly burns
> Then smokes and flickers, and to ashes turns!"
>
> K. M. NICHOLSON.

7.—GHAZI-UD-DIN HAIDAR, 1814-1827.

In 1814 Ghazi-ud-din Haidar, the seventh and last Nawab-Vazir, succeeeded his father, Saádat Ali Khan, but beyond building his own tomb (for the decoration of which he despoiled the Imambara of Asaf-ud-daula of its furniture) and the tombs of his father and mother, he did little towards the embellishment of the city. On 8th, October 1814, Lord Hastings arrived at Cawnpore, where he was interviewed by Ghazi-ud-din Haidar, who returned to Lucknow a few days afterwards, in company with the Governor-General. He received the title of King, in 1819, from the Marquis of Hastings, who made him quite independent of the house of Delhi ; so that the imperial name of Nawab-Vazir now vanishes from history.

On the day of his coronation, jewels and pearls to the value of Rs. 30,000 were scattered over the heads of the spectators. But the increase of dignity thus conferred upon him was more than counterbalanced by the degradation which he was subjected to at the hands of his chief wife, the Padshah Begam, an imperious and furious character, whose frequent ebullitions often disfigured the King's robes and vests, and left even the hair of his head and chin unsafe.

In these domestic broils the King's son, Nasir-ud-din Haidar, always took the part of his adopted mother, the Padshah Begam.* His natural mother had died soon after his birth ; and people suspected that the Padshah Begam had her put to death in order that she might have no rival in his affections, and she had an entire ascendancy over him by every species of enervating indulgences.

The former Kings of Oudh, fearful of revolutions which might exclude their families from the succession, and anxious to make for them a more secure provision than the circumstances of their own kingdom rendered possible, were in the habit of lending large sums to the East India Company, which, in fact, were thus vested in European securities, the interest on these sums being duly remitted to the appointed heirs. Thus, for instance, Ghazi-ud-din Haidar lent to the Marquis of Hastings, in October 1814, for the purposes of the Nepaul war, two millions sterling, and received in return the Terai, or jungle country, between Oudh and Nepaul. All the interest of this money was distributed in the manner described, amongst the members of his family.

The revenue of Oudh was nominally upwards of a million and a half a year, and Ghazi-ud-din left his treasury well filled, but his son emptied it.

---

* Mussalman Sovereigns take the title of *Padshah* (protector—ruler). The first wife, the Queen, is therefore the Padshah Begam.

No event of any importance took place during the reign of Ghazi-ud-din Haidar, who was most polite in his manner. Bishop Heber, who visited Lucknow in the reign of this King, describes his Court as the most polished and splendid of its day in India.

Arts and literature were greatly encouraged during the reign of this monarch, who died a natural death, on 20th October, 1827, and, according to previous instructions, was buried at Lucknow in the Shah Najaf, on the banks of the Gumti.

Agha Mir, Minister of Ghazi-ud-din Haidar, built the Karbala near the Wingfield Park, which is now used as the Scottish Masons' Lodge (Lodge Independence) in the New Civil Lines.

8.—NASIR-UD-DIN HAIDAR, 1827-1837.

On the death of Ghazi-ud-din Haidar, in 1827, his son, Suleman Jah, under the title of Nasir-ud-din Haidar, succeeded him. He had, for his consort, a daughter of the Emperor of Delhi, a very beautiful young woman of exemplary character; but other wives were soon associated with her, amongst others, *Dulari*, a woman of low origin and disreputable antecedents. She was introduced into the Palace as wet-nurse to the new-born Prince, Munna Jan, whose mother's name was Afzal Mahal. The King elevated her (*Dulari*) to be his chief consort, under the title of *Malika Zamani*, or queen of the age; and such was her influence over him that she persuaded him to declare her son, Kywan Jan, who was three years old when she entered the Palace, to be his eldest son and heir-apparent to the throne.

When Lord Combermere visited Lucknow in 1827, he was received in true regal style by Nasir-ud-din Haidar; and some idea may be formed of the splendour of this Monarch's Court from the following sketch by an officer in attendance on the Commander-in-Chief:—

" On arrival at the Palace, we sat down to breakfast with the King and his Courtiers. The King was splendidly attired in a tunic of green velvet, and girded with a costly shawl. He wore a turban enriched with diamonds and his person was profusely ornamented with necklaces, ear-rings, and armlets, of diamonds, emeralds, and pearls. After breakfast we adjourned to the State-Chamber, an ill-proportioned, indifferent room. The throne is, however, beautifully decorated with embroidery in seed-pearl. Here His Majesty presented the Commander-in-Chief with his portrait set in diamonds, suspended by a string of pearls and emeralds."

A sketch of one of his wives, Taj Mahal, is given below :—

" Her dress was of gold and scarlet brocade, and her hair was literally strewed with pearls, which hung down upon her neck in long single strings, terminating in large pearls, which mixed with and hung as low as her hair, which was curled on each side of her head in long ringlets, like Charles the Second's beauties. On her forehead she wore a small gold circlet, from which depended large pearls interspersed with emeralds. Above this was a paradise plume, from which strings of pearls were carried over the head. She wore enormous gold ear-rings, to which strings of pearls and emeralds were attached, each pearl larger than the one above it. She had a nose-ring also, with large round pearls and emeralds; and her necklaces, &c., were too numerous to be described. She wore long sleeves open at the elbow, and her dress was a full petticoat with a tight body attached, and open only at the throat. She had several persons to bear her train when she walked; and her women stood behind her couch to arrange her head-dress, when, in moving, her pearls got entangled in the immense robe of scarlet and gold she had thrown around her."

Nasir-ud-din Haidar ultimately became estranged from the Padshah Begam, his adopted mother, whom, with her grandson, Munna Jan, he banished from the Palace and assigned apartments in the Residency.

As to this King it may be said that while unpopular with the natives he was well disposed towards the Europeans. He lived simply for pleasure, and the description of him in the " Private Life of an Eastern King " is probably not exaggerated. Vicious, debauched, dissolute, he surrounded himself with friends of the worst description, English, Eurasian and Native, and ignored the terms of the settlement by which he was allowed to govern only as long as he conducted himself and his kingdom in a proper manner. His character was just such as might be expected from the education he received from ignorant women and Court eunuchs, and it is not surprising that in his time all decency and propriety were banished from the Oudh Court. His conduct at times was so revolting that the British Resident, Colonel, afterwards Sir John, Low, was compelled more than once to decline to see him, or to transact business with his minions.

The state of his kingdom had reached so incurable a stage of decline, that nothing but the assumption by the British Government could preserve it from utter ruin.

Of the ten crores left by his father in the reserve treasury, he spent all but 70 lacs, while the nobles, dreading his vindictive spirit, had him poisoned* on the night of the 7th July, 1837. His remains were interred in the Karbala † to the south-east of the Imambara, or tomb of Malka Afak, wife of Muhammad Ali Shah, situated in Iradatnagar, north of the Gumti, and approached by the road leading over the Iron Bridge.

His minister was Roshan-ud-daula, who built the Kothi now used as the Deputy Commissioner's Cutchery.

The reader will be able, from the foregoing, to form an idea of the wealth of Lucknow at this time, and I may also mention that the ex-Minister, Agha Mir, left the capital, in October, 1830, with 800 carts and numerous camels and elephants, conveying property to the value of 25 crores, for Cawnpore, where he settled and died two years afterwards. Agha Mir was succeeded by Hakim Mehdi Ali Khan, who was re-called from Farrukhabad and appointed premier of the kingdom in 1831.

9.—MUHAMMAD ALI SHAH, 1837-1842.

As Nasir-ud-din Haidar had no legitimate son, his uncle, Nasih-ud-daula, the brother of Saádat Ali Khan, succeeded him after a violent attempt on the part of the Badshah Begam, adopted mother of Nasir-ud-din Haidar, to get an illegitimate son, Munna Jan, put on the throne. On hearing of the demise of the King, the Badshah Begam, a bold imperious woman, who had been living in seclusion at Ilmas Bagh with Munna Jan, forcibly entered the Palace with an arm'ed body of retainers and placed him on the throne: for this act both of them were deported to Chunar; here they remained as State prisoners, in the Fort, on a joint monthly pension of Rs. 2,400, which was continued to them up to the time of their death. Nasih-ud-daula took the title of Muhammad Ali Shah, and reigned only five years. With his accession commenced a period of something like administrative reform.

Muhammad Ali Shah was evidently so much in earnest in his efforts for the improvement of his kingdom, that the British Government, overlooked the glaring mismanagement still existing in parts of Oudh, and did not act on the permis-

* Two females, sisters of the King's prime favourite, Daljit, from whose hands alone the King would receive any drink, are generally supposed to have poisoned him, at the instigation of the Minister, Nasir, having called for some *sharbat* a short time before his death, which was given to him by the elder, Dhania Mahri.

† Karbala is the name of the city where Husain is buried, but it generally means the burial place of *Tazias*, which is a representation of the tomb of Husain.

sion to depose the reigning King, given by the new treaty. The King's intentions were good, and the character of the Court rose very much during his short and comparatively uneventful reign.

He was a sovereign of some ability and experience; and his steady habits and application to business rendered him a favourite with his subjects. He died, on the 16th May, 1842, and was buried in the Husainabad Imambara, which building was erected by him as a burial place for himself.

At his death he left, in the reserve treasury, thirty-five lacs of rupees, one hundred and twenty-four thousand gold mohurs, besides twenty-four lacs in Government securities—total seventy-eight lacs and eighty-four thousand rupees.

10.—AMJAD ALI SHAH, 1842—1847.

Amjad Ali Shah, son of Muhammad Ali Shah, was the next King. His was an unimportant reign of five years. He constructed the metalled road to Cawnpore and built the Hazratganj, which, at the present time, is the principal business street in Lucknow, unequalled by any similar trading centre in the Indian mofussil. It is quite possible in this centralized mart to procure every imaginable commodity as satisfactorily as in Calcutta. Conspicuous amongst other commercial houses, are the premises of the long established firm of Messrs. Murray and Company. In the reign of this monarch, likewise, was founded the Aminabad Bazar, so called after his Minister, Amin-ud-daula. It is at the present time one of the largest markets of the city. On the accession of Amjad Ali Shah, the British Government took the opportunity of pressing the reforms requisite to place the kingdom in a state of tranquillity. A limited period was assigned for effecting the requisite changes, and, in default of performance, it was intimated that the territory of Oudh would be placed under British management. The threat proved futile, for it was hopeless to expect reforms from one whose time was passed within the walls of his Palace, caring for nothing beyond the gratification of his individual passions.

He was succeeded by his second son, the ex-King Wajid Ali, as Mustafa Ali Khan, the eldest son of the late King, was physically unfit to reign (see para. 80), and his claim to the throne was, therefore, passed over in favour of Wajid Ali, who surpassed his father in profligacy and accordingly effected the downfall of his house. Amjad Ali Shah died on the 13th February, 1847, and was buried in the *Maqbara* (mausoleum) in Hazratganj, opposite the Delhi and London Bank. It was originally furnished with costly fittings, all of which were

WAJID ALI SHAH.

plundered by the Mutineers. Two of the principal chandeliers cost 5,000 dollars each. After the Mutiny, and until the completion in 1860 of Christ Church, the services of the Church of England were held in this building.

Amjad Ali left in the reserve treasury ninety-two lacs of rupees, one hundred and twenty-four thousand gold mohurs, and twenty-four lacs in Government paper—total one crore and thirty-six lacs. The ex-King, when in possession of royalty, was accustomed to spend, out of the reserve treasury, large sums over and above the whole revenue of the country.

11.—WAJID ALI SHAH, 1847—1856.

Wajid Ali, the last of the line of the Kings of Oudh, succeeded to the throne on the death of his father, Amjad Ali Shah. His chief architectural work was the Kaisar Bagh, and, having completed it, he gave himself up to voluptuousness and neglected all State matters. Everything that ministered to the craze for adornment, appetite, and luxuriousness was supplied and indulged to the highest degree possible. The Palace halls were nothing less than harems of polygamy. Few sovereigns have ever been so utterly forgetful of the duties of a governor of men, or more thoroughly steeped in selfishness and pleasure than was Wajid Ali Shah. His territories at length, from his misrule and neglect became an unequalled scene of outrage and bloodshed, and a refuge for the *dacoits* (robbers) of Northern India, who would cross the Ganges at night and plunder in the British territories all around, making good their retreat into Oudh before daylight. He acquiesced in the suggestion of his Ministers that he should relinquish to them the management of the affairs of the State and the perusal of all business documents, which work, they pointed out, was unsuitable for one of his dignified position. He was still, however, to hear certain classes of important cases and reserve to himself the affixing of the great seal to particular decisions. But too soon *all* cases, together with the power of affixing the seal, were left to the discretion of the State officials, and so the King virtually ceased to administer justice himself to his people, or even to witness its administration in his presence. Things drifted from bad to worse; and finally his misrule resulted in the annexation of Oudh by the British, particulars of which are given in Chapter I of this book. He died, at Calcutta, on the 21st September, 1887, in his 68th year.

Wajid Ali was guiltless of complicity in the rebellious proceeding which had inflicted so much injury on the country.

It was during Wajid Ali's reign that the fracas at Hanuman Garhi, in Ajodhya, took place. It originated with the Muhammadans, who, under the leadership of a fanatical Maulvi, Amir Ali by name, attacked the local Hindus for the possession of a sacred piece of ground, but they were repulsed with great loss by the tact of Raja Man Singh. The King's troops sent to quell the disturbance, were also routed by him, which serves to show the condition the Native Government was reduced to.

Nawab Ali Naqi Khan was Prime Minister of Wajid Ali Shah.

CHAPTER IV.
BUILDINGS OF INTEREST AT LUCKNOW.
(Noted on the Map.)

To enable the reader to identify the edifices described below, it will be necessary to begin from the extreme south-east side and proceed thence, without any deviation, in a westward direction.

1.—BIBIAPUR KOTHI.

This chateau is situated on the right bank of the Gumti, about a mile to the east of the Dilkusha Palace, from which a metalled road leads direct to the building, which is two-storied and English in style, General Claude Martin being its reputed architect. It was built by Nawab Asaf-ud-daula (1775-1797) who resorted thither for the chase, of which he was passionately fond.

Whenever a change of Residents took place, the incoming Ambassador, on first arrival, used to take up his abode here. Having fixed the auspicious day, the King would come with a procession and conduct the new arrival to the Residency, in great pomp, riding with him on the same elephant.* As the pageant moved along, it attracted crowds of people who thronged the roads to witness this grand and imposing spectacle of richly caparisoned elephants and horses bedecked with gold and silver trappings.

When it was decided to depose Vazir Ali (see page 146), the reputed son of Asaf-ud-daula, in favour of Saádat Ali Khan, it was in this chateau that the Governor-General, Sir John Shore, held a Darbar (levée) of all the Lucknow nobles and communicated the order of his deposition to Vazir Ali, who was afterwards deported to Benares.

The building and extensive grounds are now exclusively appropriated for all the purposes of the Government Dairy Farm for the troops in Cantonments, in proximity to which it is conveniently situated.

2.—WILAITI BAGH.

The Wilaiti Bagh was laid out by Nasir-ud-din Haidar (1827-1837) and planted with different exotics, hence its name. In the time of Wajid Ali Shah, this garden was in a very

---

* The golden *haudah* and the elephant play little part now-a-days in Viceregal pageantry; but let it not be supposed the magnificence of the office has departed. The Viceroy rushes across his vast dominions in a private train, which is nothing more or less than a sumptuously appointed Palace.

flourishing condition and formed a pleasant retreat for the ladies of the seraglio, who were entirely screened from observation by the high masonry walls that enclosed it on three sides, the fourth, facing the river Gumti, which flows past it, being left open.

The garden is contiguous to the Dilkusha Palace, but there is nothing left to convey the faintest idea of its pristine beauty. It contains the ruins of a summer house, but besides this and the graves of a few soldiers who fell in the relief, or capture of Lucknow, nothing is to be seen.

3.—DILKUSHA PALACE.

The Dilkusha Palace (heart's delight) stands on an elevated piece of ground south of La Martiniere. The approach to it was through an avenue of mighty trees, bordering a drive which led to a gateway in the wall, arched over, and ornamented by pilasters. It was built by Saádat Ali Khan (1798-1814) as a hunting box and country residence, around which he laid out an extensive park and stocked it with deer and other game. In 1830 a balloon ascent was made from this place, by an Englishman, in the presence of King Nasir-ud-din Haidar and a vast assemblage of the King's nobles. It was also a favorite resort for the ladies of the harem, who used frequently to reside here.

> "A country seat where Kings of Oudh of yore
> Fled city heat with their barbaric Court,
> Encircled by a park where Eastern dames
> Screened from strange eyes indulged in listless sport."

During the investment of the Residency this position was held in force by the rebels; on Sir Colin Campbell's advance to the relief it was captured (see para. 102).

After the Mutiny the building was, for many years, occupied by the General Commanding the Oudh Division, but subsequently the structure, being considered unsafe, was partially demolished, and no idea can be formed of its original grandeur from its dilapidated condition. Its gloomy appearance is in a great measure relieved by the surrounding grounds, tastefully laid out as a flower garden. On the south of the ruins there are a few tombs of Officers and men who fell in the capture of Lucknow. It was here that Sir Henry Havelock died on 24th November, 1857, (see para. 114).

4.—LA MARTINIERE COLLEGE.

On approaching Lucknow, *viâ* Fyzabad, this imposing edifice is the first to attract the attention of the traveller, as the Oudh and Rohilkhand Railway train passes over the Gumti Bridge, which was opened for traffic in 1872.

In the distance appear other buildings, but none can vie, in majestic grandeur, with *Constantia*, which forcibly reminds the traveller that he is entering the renowned "*City of Palaces and Gardens.*"

In front of the building is an artificial lake of considerable depth, in the centre of which stands a lofty fluted masonry column,* said to be not unlike the monument to the Duke of York, 123 feet high.

The wings on either side of the mansion, now used as class-rooms and dormitories, were constructed after the death of the General. They are built in a semi-circular form on either side of the central platform, each wing consisting of two stories.

The main building, which faces east, stands on an elevated basement forming a platform partly paved with stone in front of the entrance-hall and approached by a broad flight of steps.† The superstructure is surmounted with life-size figures of men and women and the several faces are flanked with circular towers whose crenalated tops are raised between rampant lions. The summit of the grand central tower is fitted with a staff on which is displayed the Union Jack on Sundays and on other special occasions. The interior of the building is elaborately ornamented with arabesque decorations and the ceilings of the halls with bas-reliefs illustrative of classical subjects.

La Martiniere, also known as *Constantia*, (from the College motto "*Labore et Constantia* "), was built, in the time of King Asaf-ud-daula, by General Claude Martin, who was apparently his own architect. When the building was under construction, the King, seeing the elaborateness of the design, expressed a wish to purchase the Palace, and offered a million sterling for it. The King's death occurring shortly after put an end to the negotiations; and the General dying before the

---

* The question is at times asked, whether or no there are steps leading up through this column to the summit. While the monument was under repair, Mr. T. G. Sykes, the present Principal of the College, took the opportunity of ascending the scaffolding, 16th November, 1885, and satisfied himself that the column is solid, with no internal means of ascent. Mr. Sykes is believed to be the only European gentleman who has been to the top.

† During the abnormal rise of the river Gumti, on the 13th September, 1894, which was as unexpected as it was unprecedented, the water rose to a level with the top of the sixth step leading to the platform in front of the main building, and was 4 feet 2½ inches deep in the class-rooms and Sergeant Superintendent's quarters when the flood was at its greatest height, the highest ever recorded during the memory of the oldest inhabitant.

This sudden rise of the river was attributed to the inadequacy of the waterway provided during the construction of the Oudh and Rohilkhand Railway line across the Gumti, opposite La Martiniere.

building was finished, directed Mr. Joseph Quieros, the Executor of his Will, to complete it out of the funds he left to endow a College there. This gentleman accordingly took in hand the completion of the three upper stories of *Constantia*, which were left unfinished at the time of the General's death, 13th September, 1800.*

The College was opened in 1840, and is entirely supported out of funds bequeathed by the founder, who is buried in a vaulted chamber in the basement, eighteen feet below the central tower.

His tomb is a sarcophagus standing on the floor of the vault and originally had, at each angle, the life-size figure of a soldier, in uniform, standing with musket reversed in an attitude of grief.

During the Mutiny these figures were destroyed by the rebels, who also dug up the tomb and scattered the bones, which were afterwards, however, restored to their original resting-place.

In the central vault is to be seen the great bell (see para. 23), cast by the General in 1786.

Diameter of bell, 3 feet.
Circumference of the rim, 9 feet.
Height from crown to rim, $2\frac{1}{2}$ feet.

In the garden on the west side of the main building is a bronze cannon with the words "The Lord Cornwallis" inscribed on it. This gun was cast in the year 1786 in General Martin's foundry and lent to the British Government, Lord Cornwallis using it at the storming of Seringapatam, in the third Mysore war, (A. D. 1792), against Tippu Sultan. During the year 1872, by permission of His Excellency Lord Northbrook, Governor-General of India, this cannon was set up in the College garden as a Memorial of the founder.

To the south, on the roadside, are the tombs of Captain Da Costa, of the Ferozepur Sikhs, and Major Hodson,† of Hodson's Horse (captor of the King and Princes of Delhi),

---

* General Martin died at the Farhat Bakhsh Palace, now the Station Library, which was built by him, and which was originally his residence, but according to previous instructions, his body was removed and interred in *Constantia* (La Martiniere College) as a precaution against probable confiscation of the building by native rulers.

† William Stephen Raikes Hodson, Captain and Brevet-Major, 1st E. B. Fusiliers, and Commandant, Hodson's Horse, third son of the Venerable George Hodson, Archdeacon of Stafford and Canon of Lichfield, was born at Maisemore Court, near Gloucester, on 19th March, 1821.

who was mortally wounded on the 11th March, 1858, at the storming of the Begam Kothi (now the Post Office) and was carried thence to Hayat-bakhsh Kothi the present Government House, where he expired the next day. "Parliament demanded Hodson's trial for the death of the Mogal Princes, but the bold spirit had already gone before a higher tribunal. As long as the traditions of our race last, the dauntless Hodson will hold a place in the Valhalla of heroes of English blood."

Also, in the Park, on the south side of the road, is the tomb of Lieutenant Augustus Olway Mayne, of the Bengal Artillery, who was killed on 14th November, 1857.

5.—GHAZI-UD-DIN HAIDAR'S CANAL

Originated with Raja Bakhtawar Singh. He persuaded King Ghazi-ud-din Haidar, in whose reign it was begun, that it would be beneficial to the country to bring the water of the Ganges, by means of this channel, within the reach of the local agriculturists. The King was thus induced to launch out into a costly enterprise, which proved abortive in the end, as the bed of the canal is always dry except in the monsoons, when it serves merely as a sewer to carry off the rain water. The only persons who really benefited by the undertaking were a number of rapacious contractors to whom the work was given of excavating the canal, which commences at Alamnagar and extends for a distance of about seven miles in an easterly direction, until it joins the Gumti at a point east of the Wingfield Park.* This canal was used by the rebels during the siege of Lucknow, as their first line of defence.

6.—HAYAT-BAKHSH KOTHI.

The Hayat-bakhsh (life-giving) Kothi was built in the time of Nawab Saádat Ali Khan (1798-1814). It was originally used by General Martin as his powder magazine. The building is also known as Banks House, as it was, after the annexation of the Province, occupied by Major Banks, Commissioner of Lucknow, who was killed in the Residency; after him also the public road on the south of this house is named. It was within

---

* This public garden owes its origin to Sir George Campbell, the then Judicial Commissioner, who laid it out and named it after Sir Charles Wingfield, who was Chief Commissioner of Oudh in 1860.

It occupies the site of an old native enclosure called the *Banarsi Bagh*, which literally translated means Benares Garden.

The *Baradari*, in the central part of the Park, formed a prominent ornament of *Hazrat Bagh* in the precincts of *Kaisar Bagh*, or Palace of King Wajid Ali. It was removed from thence and re-constructed in its present situation, the jewelled inlay, which had suffered in the Mutiny, being repaired with some inexpensive substitute.

the walls of this building that Major Hodson, of Hodson's Horse, expired. This position was captured on the 18th March, 1858, by General Sir Edward Lugard. The building is two-storied, and is now the Lucknow residence of the Lieutenant-Governor of the United Provinces of Agra and Oudh.

On the advance of Sir Colin Campbell to the relief of the Residency, this house was captured by Brigadier Russell and was held during the remainder of the operations by 50 men of the 2nd Punjab Infantry, under Lieutenant F. Keen.

7.—DAR-UL-SHAFA KOTHI

Was originally constructed and owned by Mr. Joseph Quieros. After his death in 1822, it was sold by his heirs to King Nasir-ud-din Haidar, who established a hospital there, hence the name Dar-ul-Shafa, or place of curing. The hospital was subsequently removed to the city and the building remained unoccupied for many years. In 1844, King Amjad Ali presented it to his wife, Malka Ahad, who owned the Begam Kothi in Hazratganj. Since 1858, or immediately after the Mutiny, the Dar-ul-Shafa has been the residence of the Secretaries to the Lieutenant-Governor and Chief Commissioner during their stay at Lucknow.

8.—BEGAM KOTHI.

This edifice, the residence of Malka Ahad, Queen of Amjad Ali Shah, was erected in 1844. It was the scene of a great battle at the final capture of Lucknow, and is the building in which the gallant Major Hodson was mortally wounded. Within two hours from the time the assault on this position began, over eight hundred of the rebels were killed in the inner court. It is now the General Post Office.

9.—KANKAR-WALI KOTHI.

This building is so named from its walls being decorated outside with *kankar* (a quarry rubble used for road-metalling). The Kothi was built by Nawab Saádat Ali Khan, who gave it to his son, Jafar Ali Khan, for his residence. It is now the abode of the City Magistrate.

10.—MAQBARA* OF AMJAD ALI SHAH.

This rectangular enclosure, situated opposite the Delhi and London Bank, contains the mausoleum of the fourth King of Oudh, and is commonly known by the name of *Chhota*

---

* Maqbara is a mausoleum.

Imambara. The *Maqbara* was originally furnished with costly fittings, all of which were plundered during the Mutiny. The structure has no architectural pretensions and after the storming of the Begam Kothi, this was the next position that was captured by Sir Colin Campbell, on 14th March, 1858, after a severe struggle. On the re-occupation of the Province by the British, and until the completion in 1860 of Christ Church,* the services of the Church of England were held in this building. The Rev. W. W. Phelps was Chaplain.

On Lord Canning's second visit to Lucknow, he attended Sunday Service in this building.

11.—NUR-BAKHSH KOTHI.

Nur-bakhsh (light-giving) Kothi was built by Agha Mir, the Prime Minister of King Ghazi-ud-din Haidar. Agha Mir having incurred the displeasure of King Nasir-ud-din Haidar, who succeeded Ghazi-ud-din, was forced to leave Lucknow, and his immovable property, consisting of several palatial buildings, was confiscated (see page 151). When Muhammad Ali Shah came to the throne (1837) he presented the house to his son, Mirza Rafih-us-Shan, who lived in it up to the time of the Mutiny. It was from the top of this house that Sir Henry Havelock, in his advance to the relief, overlooked the enemy's third line of defence and planned his way into the Residency. The building is now, and has been for many years, the residence of the Deputy Commissioner. †

---

* Christ Church is a Memorial Church, built after the Mutiny from the design of General Hutchinson. It was consecrated by Bishop Cotton, on Monday, the 26th November, 1860. It contains a large number of mural tablets to the memory of Officers who fell during the Mutiny of 1857. Enlargements and improvements to the building were recently completed at a total cost of Rs. 27,000. On 1st March, 1904, the Church was closed and handed over to the P. W. Department. The re-opening service of dedication was held on Sunday, the 14th August, of the same year, and a very eloquent sermon was preached by the Rev. G. A. Ford, formerly Civil Chaplain of Lucknow, who set on foot the scheme for the extensions to the nave and chancel. On Sunday, the 29th January, 1905, the portions of the sacred edifice that had been added, were consecrated by the Right Rev. A. Clifford, D. D., Lord Bishop of Lucknow. The clergymen who took part in the service comprised the Rev. J. P. Ellwood, Rev. Hari Narain, and the Civil Chaplain, the Rev. G. E. Oldham, to whose energetic exertions, in conjunction with Mr. W. Sullivan, District Engineer, P. W. D., all the alterations were carried out to perfection and with promptness. While the Church was closed, services were held in La Martiniere College Chapel, which was kindly lent by the Principal, Mr. T. G. Sykes.

† "La Place," from Nur-bakhsh Kothi to Chutter Munzil Palace had, in the *Nawabi* days, been a mass of lofty houses, which were demolished after the Mutiny.

12.—MEMORIAL OF THE MASSACRE OF EUROPEAN CAPTIVES.

The space in front of the north-east gate of Kaisar Bagh is fraught with melancholy and solemn recollections. On this spot two separate parties of Europeans, one consisting of those sent in by the Dhaurera Raja (Miss Jackson, Mrs. Green, Mrs. Rogers, Mr. Carew, and Mr. J. Sulivan), on the 24th September 1857, with the addition of some persons captured in the town, deserters from the Baillie Guard; and the other consisting of victims of the Mithauli Raja's gratitude and hospitality (Sir Mountstuart Jackson, Captain Patrick Orr, Lieutenant Burns, and Sergeant-Major Morton), on the 16th November, 1857, completed the tale of sickness, imprisonment, and indignity, by suffering a cruel martyrdom. The memorial has been erected to commemorate those massacres on the spot where they occurred. Both of them were chiefly owing to the fury of the defeated sepoys when they could no longer resist the advance of General Havelock and the Commander-in-Chief, but both were also instigated and encouraged by the leaders of the rebellion. One of these leaders, Raja Jailal Singh, a man of large territorial possessions in Oudh and of great influence with the mutineers, followed the first party of prisoners to the fatal scene, and mounted one of the gates (since demolished) of the Kaisar Bagh, in order the better to feast his eyes on their dying agonies, and to applaud the prowess of his sepoys. Two years had elapsed since that time; he had been received into favour; his rebellion had been condoned under the amnesty, and he persuaded himself that the memory of that deed had faded away, that even he might hope to die a natural death. But justice, though slowly, was following surely in the criminal's track, and overtook him when he least expected it from the quarter where he thought himself safest. His own confidential servants turned against him; link after link a wonderful chain of circumstantial evidence developed itself and heaped the guilt with deadly certainty on his head. On the first day of October, 1859, on the very spot where his crime was committed, he paid the extreme penalty of the law, and I witnessed the execution. This was followed, on the 12th idem, by the execution of Bande Husain and Fatteh Ali, who had hunted down and brought into Lucknow some of the poor captives massacred here.

A more particular account of this tragedy is given in page 378 of *Gubbins' Mutinies in Oudh*.

13.—TOMB OF KING SAADAT ALI KHAN.

On the north-east of the Canning College,* which is situated within the enclosure of the Kaisar Bagh, stand the two tombs of Saádat Ali Khan and of his wife Khurshaid Zadi. Both these tombs were built by their son, Ghazi-ud-din Haidar. On the spot on which Saádat Ali's tomb now stands formerly stood the house in which Ghazi-ud-din Haidar lived during his father's reign ; and it is reported that when he came to the throne and occupied Saádat Ali's place, he remarked that as he had now taken his father's house, it was nothing but right that he should give up his own to his father. Accordingly he gave orders to destroy his former abode, and raise on the site the tomb of Saádat Ali Khan.

When Havelock's relieving army was fighting its way to the Residency, it was greatly harassed at this point by the destructive fire from the enemy who held the position in great force. The firing from the top of the tombs was particularly heavy.

14.—THE KAISAR† BAGH PALACE.

Wajid Ali Shah, the last King of Oudh, bears the whole opprobrium for the erection of the Kaisar Bagh, the largest, and most debased of all the Lucknow Palaces. It was commenced in 1848, and finished in 1850, at a cost, including furniture and decorations, of Rs. 80 lacs (£800,000). Entering by the north-east gateway, which faces the open space in front of the Observatory, or *Tarawali Kothi*, the visitor passed through a court to a gate known as the *Jilaukhana*, (since demolished) whence the royal procession used to start, and through which the captives, mentioned in para. 86, were conducted to their prison. Turning to the right, through a screened gateway, he arrived at the *Chini Bagh*, so called from the China vessels which formerly decorated the gardens. A portal, flanked by green mermaids in the worst European taste of the last century, led next to the *Hazrat Bagh*. On the right hand lie the *Chandiwali Baradari* (once paved with silver) and the *Khas Mukam*, as well as the *Badshah Munzil*, the special residence of the King, erected by Saádat Ali Khan, but included by Wajid Ali in the plan of his new Palace. His Vazir (Minister), Nawab Ali Naki Khan, used to

---

* Canning College was founded in 1864, and is principally intended for the education of the sons of the native nobility, by whom the institution is mainly supported. It is governed by a Committee, under the Presidentship of the Commissioner of Lucknow. The Foundation Stone was laid by Sir John Lawrence in 1867 and the building completed in 1878.

† Kaisar is equivalent to Cæsar, a title adopted by the Kings of Oudh and used by them on the Royal seal.

reside above the mermaid gateway in order that he might be close at hand to attend any summons from the King. On the left stands a large confused pile of buildings, called the *Chaulakhi*, built by Azim-ul-lah Khan, the King's barber, and sold by him to the King, for four lacs of rupees, hence its name. It formed the residence of the Queen and the chief concubines. In this building the rebel Begam (see foot-note at page 80) held her court, while the British prisoners lay for weeks in one of the adjacent stables. The road-way proceeds past a large mulberry tree (since felled), which was paved round the roots with marble. Under its shade the King, Wajid Ali, used to sit, dressed in the yellow robes of a *Fakir*,* on the occasion of a great fair, called the *Jogia Mela*, held in August within the Kaisar Bagh square, to which all wearing the garb of a *Fakir* were admitted. The eastern Lakhi Gate, so-called from its having cost a lac of rupees, gives access to a magnificent open square, known pre-eminently as the Kaisar Bagh, the buildings surrounding which provided quarters for the Begams.

Proceeding past the Stone Baradari† (which is situated in the centre of the quadrangle, and is now the property of the Maharaja of Balrampur) and under the western Lakhi Gate, which corresponds to the eastern one abovementioned, there is on the left the building known as the Kaisar Pasand, or Raushan-ud-daula Kothi (now the Treasury, Police, and Deputy Commissioner's offices). This Palace was erected by Raushan-ud-daula, Prime Minister of Nasir-ud-din Haidar; but Wajid Ali Shah confiscated it, and gave it as a residence to his favourite concubine, Mashuk-ul-Sultan. In the under stories of this building was confined the Dhaurera party of European captives, who were killed on the spot marked by the memorial in front of the north-east gate of Kaisar Bagh (*vide* para. 86). Finally, on the right, was a second *Jilaukhana*, corresponding to the eastern one, by which the visitor entered; and turning down it in a northerly direction, he found himself outside the Palace and opposite the Sher Darwaza, or Neill's Gateway, adjacent to which has lately been erected a masonry pillar bearing a stone slab, which marks the spot where General Neill fell (*vide* page 98), whose remains were interred in the Residency Cemetery.

The buildings forming the quadrangle of the Kaisar Bagh have been made over to the Talukdars (landed proprietors), or Barons of Oudh, who occupy them on the occasion of their periodical visits to Lucknow. It is here that *fêtes* take place in honour of the arrival of any new Lieutenant-Governor,

---

* An Oriental ascetic, or begging monk.
† *Baradari* is an open arcaded pavilion, also a building with twelve doors.

Viceroy, or other exalted personage, whose visit to the capital is blazoned throughout the land by a grand illumination and a great pyrotechnic display, which the public are permitted to witness. Admission, however, to the Baradari, * where refreshments are provided, is given by tickets issued to the *èlite*, for whom the place is reserved.

THE CHUTTER MUNZIL PALACES

Are situated on the banks of the Gumti and are generally known as the block of buildings comprising the United Service Club and Library, the Registration Office and the Office of the Department of Land Records and Agriculture, and the adjacent two buildings to the south, besides the Lal Baradari, including the General's and Terhi Kothies. This architectural group, of which the side buildings are destroyed, extended from opposite the Government Telegraph Office up to the road east of the Baillie Guard. It included several other buildings, besides those mentioned above, which have since been razed.

The General's Kothi † is now the Office of the Board of Revenue.

The Tehri Kothi is the residence of the Judicial Commissioner. .

The new Court of the Judicial Commissioner is built on the site of the Paienbagh which, before the Mutiny, was a luxuriant Palace Garden. (See Appendix F.)

Chutter Munzil is a term properly applied to those buildings surmounted with a "Chutter," or gilt umbrella : of these there are two ; the greater is well-known as the United Service Club, which recently removed its Library, containing several thousand volumes of books, into the adjoining building, on the north-west side, lately vacated by the Union Club, for subordinates of the Uncovenanted Service, and known as the Farhat Bakhsh (built by General Martin) while the lesser is occupied by the Registration Office, and Office of the Department of Land Records and Agriculture.

This block of buildings is separately described in the following pages.

---

* The *Baradari*, a stone edifice of picturesque design, is now generally used for public meetings, festive parties, &c. In the centre hall is an oil-painting of the Prince of Wales, (now His Majesty the King) which was presented by His Royal Highness to the Talukdars of Oudh during his visit to Lucknow in 1876. In this building are also to be seen the marble statues of Maharaja Man Singh and Major-General Barrow, who was Chief Commissioner of Oudh in 1870.

† This was the residence of the "General Saheb," the ex-King's brother, Prince Mirza Sikandar Hashmat Bahadur, who at the time of the Mutiny was with the Queen-Mother in England (*vide* page 12.)

15.—GREATER CHUTTER MUNZIL.*

Occupied by the United Service Club for Officers of the Military and Covenanted Civil Services, is a three-storied building having *tykhanas*, or underground rooms. Both the Chutter Munzil Palaces were begun by Ghazi-ud-din Haidar and finished by his son, Nasir-ud-din Haidar, as a residence for the ladies of the harem, he himself occupying the adjoining palace called the Farhat Bakhsh. Between the two Chutter Munzils was a very pretty garden, with a beautiful marble tank, in the centre of which was an island covered with a pavalion. To convey to the reader an idea of the beauty of this place, the following description of it by the Honorable Miss Eden may not be uninteresting:—

"Such a place ! the only residence I have coveted in India. Don't you remember reading, in the Arabian Nights, Zobeide bets her Garden of Delight amidst the Caliph's Palance of pictures ! I am sure this was the Garden of Delight.

"There are four small places in it fitted up in the eastern way with velvet, gold and marble ; with arabesque ceilings, orange trees and roses in all directions and with numerous wild paroquets of bright colours flitting about. And, in one place, there was an immense *hammam*, or Turkish bath, of white marble, the arches intersecting each other in all directions, and the marble inlaid with cornelian and bloodstone ; and, in every corner of the place, there were little fountains ; even during the hot winds, they say, it is cool from the quantity of water in the fountains playing ; and in the verandah there were fifty trays of fruits and flowers laid out for us. * * * It was really a very pretty sight."

Originally there was a high wall surrounding the Palace and during the Mutiny it was strongly defended by the rebels, who were driven from the position by General Havelock on the 25th September, 1857.

16.—FARHAT BAKHSH PALACE.
(Station Library.)

Until Wajid Ali Shah built the Kaisar Bagh, the Farhat Bakhsh (giver of delight), together with the adjoining buildings, formed the principal residence of the Oudh Sovereigns from the time of Saádat Ali Khan, who made great additions and improvements to the building. It originally formed the residence of General Claude Martin, by whom the Palace was built and subsequently sold to Nawab Saádat Ali Khan for Rs. 50,000.

---

* On 13th September, 1894, when the flood, mentioned in foot-note on page 157, was at its greatest height, the water inside the Club-rooms was a foot above the level of the ball-room floor. This abnormal rise of the Gumti surpassed all other floods of which there is any record.

Gulistan-i-Eram.   Lesser Chutter Munzil.   Darshanbilas.

17.—LESSER CHUTTER MUNZIL

Is a two-storied building surmounted by a dome with a gilt umbrella, and is, at present, occupied by the Registration Office and Office of the Department of Land Records and Agriculture, United Provinces. The two buildings immediately behind it, facing the road leading to the Residency, are the Gulistan-i-Eram* (heavenly garden) and Darshanbilas† (pleasing to the sight); the former is part of the Museum and Office of the Curator, and the latter the Offices of the Executive Engineer, P. W. Department.

18.—THE LAL BARADARI.

This building, the great throne room, or Coronation Hall, was built by Saàdat Ali Khan and set apart for Royal Darbars. On the accession of a new King it was the custom for the Resident to place him on the throne and present him with a *nazar* (offering) in token that the British authority confirmed his assumption of the Government. After the death of Nasir-ud-din Haidar, the attempt on the throne by the Padshah Begam and Munna Jan, took place here, which is recorded by Sir W. Sleeman in the second volume of his journey through Oudh; and it was in pursuance of this custom that the insurgents attempted to force the Resident, Colonel Low, to present an offering to Munna Jan, as he sat on the throne, thinking thus to confirm the usurper's authority (*vide* page 151). The Resident was nearly killed in this place for setting aside the doubtful claim of Munna Jan to the throne in favour of Muhammad Ali Shah, the uncle of Nasir-ud-din Haidar. The gates of the Palace were forced, the new Sovereign, with all the English Officers who were there, were seized by the insurgents headed by the Queen in her palanquin, and the young Prince was formally installed. But the party of Muhammad Ali Shah triumphed in the end, and he remained King of Oudh under British protection.

The Lal Baradari is so named from its being washed with red ochre.

This building is now occupied by the Museum, and through the kindness of late Mr. E. W. Smith, the Curator, I am enabled to give the following information in as concise a form as possible :—

The Museum is contained in two buildings known as the Lal Baradari and the Gulistan-i-Eram.

---

* King Nasir-ud-din Haidar is said to have been poisoned in the underground rooms of this Palace (*vide* page 151).

† This building is also known as the *Chaurukhi Kothi*, a designation it derives from each of its four sides representing the façade of four different edifices, as, for example, that towards the west, is an imitation of the façade of the Dilkusha Palace.

In the Lal Baradari block the following sections are located:

(1) On the ground floor: Epigraphical, Archæological, Mineralogical, Palæontological, Agricultural, Conchological. The Model of the Residency as it was at the time of the Mutiny.

(2) On the first floor, the Art Section, Ethnological, Skeletons, Reptiles, Butterflies, Birds, Fishes, Mammals, Plaster Casts, Models, Brocades, &c.

In the Gulistan-i-Eram block the following departments are found :—

(1) On the ground floor, Art-ware Sale Depôt, Economic Section, Coin Collection,* Medal Collection.

(2) On the first floor, the Library.

(3) On the second floor, the Picture Gallery.

The Library contains a fine collection of books on Natural History, Indian History, Archæology, Architecture, Hindu, Buddhist, Jain and Muhammadan religions, Voyages and Travels, &c., &c.

There is an Art-ware Sale Depôt in connection with the Museum, where articles of Benares brass work, Moradabad metal-ware, Lucknow copper, brass and bidri ware, pottery and clay figures, Agra marble and soapstone-ware can be purchased.

PUBLICATIONS TO BE HAD AT THE MUSEUM.

Works by the Archæological Department, comprising the Department's illustrated Reports. The *Technical Art Series, the Mogal Architecture of Fatehpur Sikri*, by Mr. E. W. Smith. These are all of interest to the public. There are also some interesting Photographs of Lucknow, taken immediately after the Mutiny. The Art-ware Sale Depôt is an excellent thing, as it enables artizans to dispose of their goods to the best advantage. In addition to which there is a Library and Picture Gallery.

For the restoration and maintenance of a higher standard in the art-wares and manufactures of the Province, the Committee of Management has prepared a list of such specimens as are in the Museum; and information regarding the art manufactures of these Provinces can be had from the Curator.

The Museum is open throughout the year (with the exception of Fridays) from 7-30 A. M. to 3-30 P. M., during the months of November, December, January, and February; and from 6-30 A. M., to 3-30 P. M., during the remainder of the year.

---

* The Numismatic section contains a number of exceedingly rare coins.

(169)

The afternoon of the 15th of each month is specially set apart for *parda-nashins*. During the visit of the women in *parda* the male servants are made to retire from the building to allow the *parda-nashins* and their female attendants to have free access to the place, a privilege which is much appreciated.

The Museum is visited by people from all parts of India and the crowds who come on holidays go away filled with delight and evidently consider every section of it most interesting. Every effort is made to make the place a centre of instruction as well as recreation.

19.—THE RESIDENCY.

The Residency is far too famous a place and too generally known to require a very detailed description. It was originally a very extensive and beautiful brick building, with lofty rooms, fine verandahs, and splendid porticoes. Besides having a ground floor and two upper stories, it had a *tykhana*, or cellar, of splendid apartments, as lofty and well arranged as any in the house.

It was built in 1800, by Nawab Saàdat Ali Khan, for the British Resident at his Court; and such was the commodiousness of the house, that during the siege it afforded accommodation for many.

The building stands on an elevated spot not far from the Chutter Munzil. It was connected by a covered passage to a building on the south side having a *tykhana*, or underground rooms, which were resorted to by the Resident during the summer. These rooms, owing to their immunity from shot and shell, were occupied during the investment of the place in 1857 by the women and children of H. M.'s 32nd Foot. A room in the Residency, lately renewed, contains a model showing the defences, &c., being a facsimile of one in the Museum prepared from the design by the Revd. T. Moore, formerly Civil Chaplain of Lucknow.* For a detailed description of the intrenched position see Chapter V.

20.—THE IRON BRIDGE.†

This graceful structure consists of three cast-iron arches, supported on piers and abutments of brick masonry, the centre arch having a span of ninety and a rise of seven feet, while the two side arches have spans of eighty feet and a rise of six feet. The iron-work was received from England in 1798, during the

---

* Rev. T. Moore died in England in January 1905.

† The Kukrail Bridge, on the Fyzabad Road, is exactly 2 miles and 6 furlongs from the Iron Bridge. The village of Ismailganj 5 miles and the town of Chinhat 6½ miles (see page 46).

reign of Nawab Saàdat Ali Khan, only twenty years after the erection of the first iron bridge in England, General Martin, who was then living at Lucknow, having, it is supposed, suggested the idea to the Nawab. The bridge was designed by Rennie, being very similar to one erected by that famous Engineer over the Witham at Boston in Lincolnshire. The iron-work remained unused at Lucknow *more than forty years,* when the bridge was at length erected by Colonel Fraser, Bengal Engineers, between the years 1841-44 ; the cost of the masonry and erection having been Rs. 1,80,000 ; the cost of the iron-work is not known. The foundations are sunk on wells in the usual way. The width of road-way is thirty feet, and its height above water-mark at the centre is thirty-five feet.—*Professional Papers on Indian Engineering.*

21.—THE STONE BRIDGE.

The Gumti as it passes through Lucknow is crossed by six bridges. The stone bridge, as it is commonly called, situate near the Machhi Bhawan, is not built of stone, but of *pakka* brick work. The construction of this bridge was commenced by Nawab Mansur Ali Khan and completed by his grandson, Nawab Asaf-ud-daula, in the year 1780. The bridge, being considered unsafe, is now closed against wheel traffic.

22.—MACHHI BHAWAN.

The *Machhi Bhawan*[*] fort (now demolished) comprised a much larger area than that which was contained within the limits of the old fort of that name and which was surrounded by high walls, the side facing the river having the appearance of a castle. Towards the river front the fortifications commanded the stone and iron bridges ; to the south and west had been one of the most populous parts of the town, which was partially levelled at the time of the Mutiny ; towards the east the position commanded the Residency and overlooked some much frequented thoroughfares.

The Palace within the Machhi Bhawan faced the Gumti. It contained six principal courts, or quadrangles, surrounded by pavilion-like buildings. In the first of these were two lofty gateways. On the outer, there was a handsome chamber, called the *Naubat Khana,* or music room, forming an orchestra

---

[*] The buildings in the *Machhi Bhawan (Machhi,)* 'Fish' from the device over the gateway—and *Bhawan,* Sanskrit for 'House,' belonged to Nawab Yahya Ali Khan, from whom they were purchased by Sir Henry Lawrence for Rs. 50,000.

upon a splendid scale.* The second court, encompassed by state apartments, was laid out as a garden, having a well, or *bauli*, in the centre, round which were two pavilions, opening to the water, and intended to afford a cool retreat during the hot weather; the air was refreshed by the constant dripping of the fountains; and the piazzas and arcaded chambers beyond, within the influence of its luxurious atmosphere, were well adapted for sleeping apartments in the sultry nights of summer.

The high ground on the river side, crowned by the *masjid*, or mosque, built by Aurangzeb of Delhi, is Lakshman Tila, the site of the original Lakshmanpur. Behind the Machhi Bhawan itself, in a southerly direction, is an open space, once a Depôt for Ordnance Stores, that marks the site of the *Panch Mohalla* (now demolished,) the oldest houses in Lucknow, built by the family of Sheikhs who formerly owned territory here.

When Saádat Khan, the first member of the late reigning family, came here as Subahdar, or Governor of Oudh, in 1732 A. D., he hired the house from the owners at a monthly rental of Rs. 565; the money was paid at first, but his successors claimed the house as State property and confiscated it.

Shortly before the investment of the Residency, the fortification was strengthened and guns were planted at different points on the ramparts, but though to all appearance the place seemed impregnable, it was really not so, as it was afterwards condemned by the Engineers and had to be abandoned (see para. 43).

On the 2nd of July, 1857, this fort was blown up by the garrison who retreated to the Residency (*vide* para. 60). After the re-occupation of Lucknow by the British, the Machhi Bhawan was re-built and strongly fortified, but at the time of the great assemblage at Delhi, when the Queen was declared Empress of India, the fortification was completely demolished and the Great Imambara and its adjoining mosque, made over to the Muhammadan community. The concession was carried out in the year 1883.

---

* Much cannot be said in praise of the native music. Their orchestra is composed of small drums, called tom-toms, long shrill pipes, and a kind of cymbals : it is dreadfully loud and by no means harmonious. Like all the Eastern music, it is exceedingly monotonous to an ear accustomed to the cadences and varied harmony of our music. The natives, however, are passionately fond of it as it is, and will sit and listen for hours to the beating of tom-toms and the screaming of pipes.

23.—THE GREAT IMAMBARA.*

Within the precincts of the Machhi Bhawan is the Great Imambara, or Mausoleum of Nawab Asaf-ud-daula, which is said to have cost a million sterling (one crore of rupees). This superb edifice was started as a relief work during the terrible famine of 1784. As the great ornament of the north-western quarter of the city, it forms an architectural view pleasing from its variety of detail, as well as from the proportions and general good taste of its principal features: excepting the galleries in the interior, no wood-work has been used in its construction, and the principal apartment is said to be the largest vaulted hall in the world. The dimensions of the rooms are as follow:—

Centre Room.

Length within	163 feet.
Breadth of room	53 ,,
Height	49½ ,,
Thickness of walls	16 ,,

Octagonal Room, East. | *Square Room, West.*

Circumference	216 feet.	Square	54 feet.
Height	53 ,,	Height	53 ,,
Thickness of wall	16 ,,	Thickness of wall	16 ,,

In front of the Imambara are two courts rising with a steep ascent one above the other, and containing a splendid mosque flanked by two minarets, from the summit of which a magnificent view is obtained of the city and surrounding country.

The following is a description of the decorations of the Imambara, at the time when Bishop Heber visited Lucknow in 1824:—

"This tabernacle of chandeliers was hung with immense lustres of silver and gold, prysmatic crystals, and coloured glass, and any that were too heavy to be hung, they rose in radiant piles from the floor. In the midst of them were temples of silver filagree, eight or ten feet high and studded with precious stones. There were ancient banners of the Nawabs of Oudh, with sentences from the Koran embroidered on cloth of gold: gigantic bands of silver covered with talismanic words; sacred shields studded with the name of God; swords of Khorasan steel, lances, and halberds; the turbans of renowned commanders; and several *mimbars*, or pulpits, of peculiar sanctity.

---

* Imambara is a building in which the festival of the *Muharram* is celebrated and service held in commemoration of the death of Ali and his sons, Hasan and Husain. Sometimes it is used as a *Maqbara*, or Mausoleum.

During the *Muharram** festival the Imambara is illuminated, and one night, the sixth of the new moon, is specially set apart for European visitors at the Shah Najaf and Husainabad.

24.—RUMI DARWAZA.

The Rumi Darwaza, or Turkish Gate, is supposed to be a facsimile of one of the gates of Constantinople, but persons who have visited Constantinople declare that there is no gate standing there now which at all corresponds with this one, and the only inference to be drawn is that the Nawab Vazir, Asaf-ud-daula, was probably the victim of a deception. This gate is a structure of massive proportions, faced on both sides, with some imitation of leaves which rise from the base and radiate above the spring line forming a pointed arch. The archway is surmounted by a turret which completes the design.

Both the Rumi Darwaza and the Great Imambara were built by Asaf-ud-daula in 1784, as a relief work during the terrible famine that raged from 1784 to 1786.

25.—THE HUSAINABAD CLOCK TOWER. †

This tower, which is of recent date (1881), cost Rs. 1,17,000 from the funds of the endowment, is fully detailed below:—

At the suggestion, and through the influence of the Deputy Commissioner, Lieutenant-Colonel Norman T. Horsford, Bengal Staff Corps, the Trustees of the Husainabad Endowment, who administer the fortune of 36 lacs of rupees bequeathed by Muhammad Ali Shah, the third King of Oudh, have erected a stately tower, 221 feet high and 20 feet square, from the design of Mr. R. R. Bayne, of Calcutta, for the reception of a clock of great size and power, made by Mr. J. W. Benson, Ludgate Hill, London.

"The following is a brief description of the clock movement: The bed, or frame, is horizontal, which allows any part to be removed for cleaning or repair, without disturbing the rest,

---

* *Muharram* signifies most sacred, and is applied to a fast and solemn mourning which is observed chiefly by the *Shiahs*, one of the two sects of Muhammadans, the other being the *Sunnis*, so-called from their belief in *Sunnat*, or traditions of Muhammad as a supplement to the *Koran* (Muhammadan Bible), and almost of equal authority, which the latter accept whilst the *Shiahs* reject it. This fast is kept for 10 days and is called *Ashra*, from the Arabic signifying ten, to commemorate the death of Husain, younger son of Ali, and grandson of the prophet Muhammad. Husain was murdered at Karbala in Turkish Arabia.

The interment of Hazrat Imam Husain is commemorated on the fortieth day of *Muharram*.

† On 13th September, 1894, when the flood was at its greatest height, the water rose above the stone platform which forms the base of the tower.

whereas in the upright frame, to gain access to a particular part, the whole machine has to be more or less taken to pieces. It consists of two wrought-iron sides, having a massive pillar of the same material bolted between them at each end. The length is 6 feet and the width 3 feet. All the train wheels are of gun-metal well-hammered, the teeth being divided, cut, and polished by power, thereby insuring an accuracy impossible in hand-made work. The main wheel is 24 inches in diameter and $1\frac{1}{2}$ inches thick, and the other wheels are of proportionate size. In one of the designs for the great clock at Westminster, the main wheel was 18 inches in diameter, which, although considered too small, will show, by comparison, the size of the present clock. The pinions are of hardened steel, cut from the solid, made and finished in the same manner as the wheels.

"There are three trains of wheels, one in the centre to record the time on the dials, called 'the going part,' to the right of which is the quarter chiming train, and to the left the hour striking train. The barrels work in plummer-blocks, and the uprights, which carry the trains, are bolted on in such a manner as to be easily removable. All the bearings, which are of the best gun-metal, are screwed instead of being riveted into their respective places as is usually done. The barrels for carrying the weights, and the spindles on which they are mounted, are of wrought iron, the drums being 12 inches in diameter, fitted between caps and ratchets, by means of which the weights are wound without interrupting the motion of the great wheel. The weights are suspended by steel cords, which being much less bulky than rope, permit the barrels and frame to be greatly reduced in size, and render the general arrangement more compact.

"During the act of winding, which takes the motive power off the great wheel, it is obvious that the clock would stop, unless some means were provided to continue the action.

"This substitute, technically known as 'the maintaining power,' has been especially designed by the firm, and its working is as follows:—To gain access to the winding square, the attendant must first raise a lever, one end of which gears into the teeth of the great wheel, and the other being weighted, supplies the motion. The winding completed, the lever gradually drops with the revolution of the wheel into its old position. The escapement is Graham's dead-beat, the advantages of which are that, being so simple and made on such true principles, it is not easily deranged, and in the unlikely event of its becoming so, a man of ordinary capacity can rectify it, which is not the case with complicated gravity escapements. This is an important consideration for clocks in remote places, especially in the present instance, Lucknow being 678 miles ' up-country.'

"The pendulum is 14 feet long, and has a bob of 3 cwt. It is compensated with zinc and iron tubes to counteract the variations of temperature.

"The rate of the new clock, which has been thoroughly tested in the factory, is reported to be a losing one of two seconds per week, so that it will give the standard time for the city and district.

"Time is shown on four dials, each 13 feet in diameter, at an elevation of 120 feet. Each dial consists of twelve openings in the brick-work, 2 feet in diameter, glazed with white opal glass, on which the numerals are marked in black enamel. The centre circle is also of the same material, and measures 5 feet 9 inches in diameter. The hands are of copper, and counterpoised on inside of tower. The minute hand is 6 feet, and the hour hand 4 feet 6 inches long.

"As it is impossible, owing to the large surface of brick-work which divides the circles, to illuminate the dials from behind, a special method has been devised for the purpose. On the bell-chamber floor above the clock-room are eight copper lanterns, two for each dial, having plate-glass fronts and silver-plated halophotal reflectors. From these reflectors a powerful stream of light is thrown upon an exterior reflector placed at such an angle as will project the light on the centre of the dial. The outside reflectors are movable, all four being extended, or withdrawn, at the same time, by an arrangement of wheels and cogs worked by the attendant.

"This system of lighting, which has been thoroughly tested before adoption, is the best under the somewhat difficult condition in which the clock has to be illuminated, and its advantages are that the lanterns being within the building, they can be of larger size than if suspended on the outside, whilst the light being better protected from wind and rain, will be steadier and more effective.

"The striking part is made with all recent improvements, the hammer being raised by the great wheel, by which means a heavier blow and more sound are obtained than from the corresponding mechanism of the old construction. The system used is the rack repeating work, which is the easiest in its action, safest in its lockings and the most modern; whereas the old style of locking plate, or count wheel, was unreliable, being apt to run past its lockings and strike the wrong hours. The clock will chime the Cambridge quarters, the beauty of which is universally acknowledged, being attributed to no less a musician than Handel.

"Immediately above the dials is the bell-chamber, where, upon a teak frame, the bells are so mounted as to produce the greatest volume of sound. These five bells have been especially cast for this clock, are of the finest bell-metal, and their tones are extremely clear and musical. The hammers mounted in frames and fitted with steel counter-springs to prevent 'chattering.'

"The following are the weights and notes of the bells:—

	Cwt.	qr.	lb.	Note.
Hour bell ...	20	2	0	E♭.
Fourth quarter ...	8	3	11	B♭.
Third „ ...	8	0	12	E.
Second „ ...	6	0	12	F.
First „ ...	5	3	0	G.

"This is by far the largest clock in India."—Reprinted from the *Engineering*.

26.—HUSAINABAD TANK.

Along with the Husainabad Imambara, Muhammad Ali Shah built this magnificent pakka Tank, which is contiguous to the Clock Tower. The Tank is well stocked with fish and is said to have been connected with the river by an underground passage.

27.—SAT KHANDA.

West of the Husainabad Tank may be seen an unfinished structure called the Sat Khanda, or seven-storied tower, having been originally designed as such. It was commenced simultaneously with the Husainabad Imambara by Muhammad Ali Shah, as a watch-tower, from whence he might survey the extent and magnificence of his palatial domain, but the tower only reached its fourth storey when the King died and the work remained unfinished.

28.—DAULAT KHANA.*

Proceeding westward from the Rumi Darwaza, we have, on our right, the Daulat Khana, or old palace of Nawab Asaf-ud-daula, which is north of the Clock Tower, and to which you gain access through the gateway on the right of the Baradari facing the Tank. Under this name (Daulat Khana) is included a number of large houses, irregularly placed, which formed the residence of Asaf-ud-daula and his Court when he transferred

---

* Daulat Khana literally means the residence of a nobleman.

the seat of Government from Fyzabad to Lucknow. The principal house, the Asfi Kothi, was named after him. Saàdat Ali Khan, his successor, however, relinquished this place for the Farhat Bakhsh. The Daulat Khana is now occupied by Muhammad Jafar Ali Khan.

The Baradari facing the tank was erected by Muhammad Ali Shah, and has recently been repaired and improved at a great cost. This building is now used as a place of conference for the native nobility and also as a picture gallery, or repository for the portraits of all the Kings of Oudh, which were formerly kept in one of the side rooms of the Husainabad Imambara.

29.—HUSAINABAD IMAMBARA.

(THE PALACE OF LIGHTS.)

The Husainabad Imambara is the only architectural work completed by Muhammad Ali Shah, the third King of Oudh; and though inferior in grandeur to some of the works of his successors, it is the rival of many of them in beauty of detail. It contains the tomb of this monarch and his mother. The garden, which occupies the quadrangle, is somewhat disfigured by being crowded with a bad model of the Taj of Agra on the west, (in which is buried the King's daughter) and on the east there is a building of similar dimensions. On the right of the Taj is a small mosque for the exclusive use of the surviving heirs and successors of departed royalty. The Husainabad presents a very grand appearance when illuminated, and in the time of the native rulers it formed the chief attraction during the *Moharram*.

It is munificently endowed by Muhammad Ali Shah, who left a very large sum* to keep up the splendour of the Imambara, which is grandly illuminated on the anniversary of the King's death and for several nights during the *Moharram* festival.† By the courtesy of the authorities of the Imambara, one night, the sixth of the moon, is specially set apart for European visitors, who are admitted to all parts of the building to see the illumination up to midnight, after which the native public are allowed access to the place.

---

* The King left thirty-six lacs of rupees in trust for the maintenance of the Imambara, and for several purposes of education and charity.

NOTE—On the 1st April, 1901, the Water Works of the Husainabad Trust, close to Nawab Asaf-ud-daula's Imambara, was opened by R. G. Hardy, Esqr., Commissioner of Lucknow.

† *Moharram* is the first month of the Muhammadan year, but it is impossible to fix the festival in conjunction with any English month, as it varies with the motions of the moon.

About one mile north-west of Husainabad (see map) is the intake pumping station of the Lucknow Water Works, situated at a spot above the city on the right bank of the Gumti.*

30.—JUMA MASJID. †

The Juma Masjid, or 'Cathedral Mosque,' is used chiefly on Friday as the place of worship by the Muhammadans. This mosque lies due west of the Husainabad Imambara and can easily be identified by the two lofty minaretes and three cupolas constructed thereon. It was commenced by Muhammad Ali Shah and intended to excel in grandeur the mosque of Asaf-ud-daula in the Machhi Bhawan, but the King did not live to complete it. Subsequently the work was resumed and completed by Begam Malka Jahan, a surviving member of the Royal family, who is now dead.

The edifice stands on an elevated basement with an open platform in front, fitted with lavatories for the use of the worshippers. The walls are beautifully ornamented and the arches colored in stucco.

31.—MUSA BAGH.

Far beyond the Husainabad, in a northerly direction, is the Musa Bagh, which was laid out as a garden by Asaf-ud-daula, but the house was built by Saàdat Ali Khan, who made it his favorite country residence. In his reign wild beast fights used to take place there on the opposite bank of the Gumti. The building is in the English style, and is said to have been designed and constructed by General Martin. This was the last position held in force by the rebels of the city, and was captured by General Outram on the 19th March, 1858. The place is now in ruins.

Within the garden is the tomb of Captain T. Wale, who commanded the 1st Sikh Irregular Cavalry, killed in action on 21st March, 1858, when in pursuit of the flying enemy.

---

* The foundation stone of the Lucknow Water Works was laid by Sir Auckland Colvin, Lieutenant-Governor of the N.-W. Provinces and Chief Commissioner of Oudh, on the evening of the 8th November, 1892, and was opened by Sir Charles Crosthwaite, his successor, on the evening of the 21st July, 1894. "The water is obtained from the Gumti, and pumped through a 20-inch rising main three miles long to the three settling tanks at Aish Bagh. From the settling tanks the water is conducted through four filters to an underground clear water reservoir having a capacity of 16,30,000 gallons. The water is then pumped into the mains of the distributing system, which contains some 34 miles of pipes and 300 standposts. The scheme cost about 15½ lacs of rupees, and the annual maintenance charges (including interest on capital and sinking fund) amount to about Rs. 1,30,000."—*Morning Post.*

† In 1901 the Lieutenant-Governor, Sir Antony MacDonald, made a grant of Rs. 12,000 for the repair of the *Juma Masjid*, which, from an architectural point of view, far excels any of the other *Nawabi* buildings in the city.

32.—BADSHAH BAGH.

The road over Bruce's Bridge* east of the Chutter Munzil, leads into the Badshah Bagh, which was a Royal Garden laid out by King Nasir-ud-din Haidar. In the centre of this walled enclosure is a substantial stone edifice having an open arcaded hall, well adapted for festive gatherings (such as picnics, &c.), allowed to be held here by the kind permission of His Highness, the Maharaja of Kapurthala, to whom the property belonged. On the left of the garden, and within the enclosure, is a large building which was sacred to the ladies of the King's harem; and it is here that Kunwar Harnam Singh, Ahluwalia, C. I. E., Manager of the Kapurthala Estates in Oudh, and President and Secretary, British Indian Association, reside during his visits to Lucknow. The garden now partakes more of the nature of an orchard, but it is not altogether destitute of flowers.

The annual distributions of prizes to children of the Sunday Schools were generally held here during Christmas week. On such occasions the garden presents a very animated scene. The prizes are generally distributed towards the close of the day's entertainment, which consists of outdoor games by the children, for whom refreshments are abundantly provided. This garden was captured by General Outram on the 8th March, 1858.

33.—MOTI MAHAL PALACE.

The Moti Mahal, or Pearl Palace, so called from the fancied resemblance of one of its domes (since destroyed) to the shape of a pearl, is situated on the right bank of the Gumti, a little above the Shah Najaf. It includes three separately named and distinct buildings, now the property of the Maharaja of Balrampur. The Moti Mahal, properly so called, was built by Saâdat Ali Khan (1798-1814) and forms the northern part of the enclosure, which contains the Mubarak Munzil and Shah Munzil, or royal halls, built along the river face by Ghazi-ud-din Haidar. It was the prettiest building of the kind in Lucknow.

The Shah Munzil was the scene of the celebrated wild beast fights of the smaller animals, and the combats between tigers, &c., was also held within the enclosure of this building. But the encounter between the elephant and rhinoceros, which required to be viewed at a safe distance, took place across the

---
* This bridge was constructed after the Mutiny, about the year 1863, and is named after Mr. Bruce, the Engineer, who designed and constructed it.

About 60 yards east of the bridge, on both banks, are to be seen at the present time, blocks of masonry which formed the approach to the Bridge of Boats, over which the mutineers escaped on the advance of General Havelock after he captured the Moti Mahal Palace (see para. 91).

river on the ground in front of the Hazri Bagh, * the building now occupied by the Oudh Ice Company, the King and his court watching it from the upper storey of the Shah Munzil.

It was in the court-yard of the Moti Mahal that Doctor Bartram and Brigadier Cooper, of the Artillery, were killed on the 26th of September, and it was here that Colonel Campbell, of H. M.'s 90th, was mortally wounded. At the gateway one of General Havelock's 24-pounders stuck, but was withdrawn by the skilful exertions of Captain Olpherts. In assisting this operation a very distinguished officer of the Madras Artillery, Captain Crump, was killed. This was the advanced position taken by Sir Colin Campbell's relieving army; and it was here that the rear guard and heavy guns and wounded men of General Havelock's force halted on the night of the 25th September, 1857, *vide* page 102.

34.—KHURSHAED MUNZIL.†

The name of this building means "House of the sun." It was commenced by Snádat Ali Khan and completed by his son, Ghazi-ud-din Haidar. The Khurshaed Munzil is built in the form of a castle. It is surrounded by a moat 12 feet broad, over which there was formerly a drawbridge, but this has since been replaced by a masonry bridge (or bridges since there are now four entrances), by which access is gained to the building. It was not devoted to any particular purpose during the time of the Kings of Oudh, but, after the annexation, it was used as the Mess House of the Officers of the 32nd Regiment.

This handsome and commodious double-storied building is now the property of the Lucknow La Martiniere authorities, to whom it was made over, on 27th November, 1876, as a free gift from Government, for the use of La Martiniere Girls' High School. Extensive additions and improvements have been made to the building at a cost of more than one lac of rupees from La Martiniere "Female Education Fund," and it is now admirably suited to the requirements of a Boarding School. The situation is one of the healthiest in Lucknow, and the school grounds are extensive, affording the pupils ample scope for exercise and recreation. The instruction is in accordance with the new Code for the education of European children in India; and pupils are prepared for the Government High, or Final Standard Examination.

---

* It was here that the Kings of Oudh generally entertained their European guests to breakfast, hence the name.
† Struck by lightning on the evening of 12th March 1891, without injury to life or property.

The Khurshaed Munzil (32nd Mess House), as it appeared immediately after the Mutiny in 1857.

(181)

The building was stormed and taken on the 17th November, 1857. Shortly after its capture, it was here that Generals Outram and Havelock had their memorable meeting with Sir Colin Campbell,* (see para. 106).

35.—TARAWALI KOTHI.

The Tarawali Kothi, or observatory (now occupied by the Bank of Bengal) was built in the reign of Nasir-ud-din Haidar, under the supervision of Colonel Wilcox, astronomer royal, who had it fitted with the necessary astronomical instruments.

The Colonel died in 1847, and King Wajid Ali abolished the department. The instruments were put by, but they were all destroyed in the Mutiny. The Fyzabad Maulvi, Ahmad-ullah Shah, better known as Danka Shah, from his always having a drum beaten before him when he went out, made this place his head-quarters during the rebellion; and the rebel leaders held their meetings here, (see para. 107).

36.—SHAH NAJAF.

The Shah Najaf, or Najaf Ashraf is situated on the right bank of the Gumti close to the Horticultural Gardens. It was built by Ghazi-ud-din Haidar, the First King of Oudh, as a mausoleum, and contains the remains of this King, his wife, and other members of the royal family. It derives its name "Najaf" from the hill on which the tomb of Ali, the son-in-law of Muhammad, is built, of which this tomb is a copy. It has been largely endowed † by the King for the maintenance of an establishment to look after it, and to defray the expenses of the illumination which takes place there twice a year, once during the *Muharram* festival, and again on the anniversary of the King's death, a night being set apart, during the *Muharram*, especially for European visitors, who are admitted to the building to see the illumination up to midnight, after which the native public are allowed access to the place, (see para. 105).

37.—KADAM RASUL.

The Kadam Rasul, or "Prophet's foot-print" was a Muhammadan place of worship built in the time of King Nasir-ud-din Haidar, (1827-1837) on an artificial mound of earth to the east of the Shah Najaf. It contained a stone bearing the impression

---

* A masonry pillar, with a tablet, marks the spot where the Generals met.
† The Shah Najaf endowment consists of Rs. 1,137-11-8 per month, interest on one crore of rupees lent to the British Government in perpetuity in 1825 A. D. by Ghazi-ud-din Haidar, known as the "Third Oudh Loan."—*Lucknow Historical Monuments.*

of a foot, supposed to be that of the Prophet, which was brought from Arabia by a pilgrim as a sacred relic. During the Mutiny this stone was carried off and the place was still used by the Mutineers as a powder magazine, but the powder had been conveyed from it into the Shah Najaf, when the latter was converted into a place of defence to bar the advance of Sir Colin Camptell on the Residency.

The mosque is no longer a place of veneration and is now a crumbling ruin.

38.—SIKANDAR BAGH.*

This garden was built by Wajid Ali Shah, who gave it to one of his Begams, Sikandar Mahal, from whom it derives its name. It is a high walled enclosure of 120 yards square, carefully loopholed all round, with turrets at the angles, and originally contained a garden prettily laid out with a summer house in the centre, which is still standing. Intrinsically there is nothing now in the place deserving of notice, its fame arises from the severe retribution which here overtook the rebels at the final relief of the Residency on 16th November, 1857, (see paras. 103 and 104).

39.—LAWRENCE TERRACE.

Also known as Chaupar Stables, being originally built in the form of a cross. The building was erected by King Saàdat Ali Khan, (1798-1814), and in it were kept the choicest of the King's horses, but, after the annexation it was converted into barracks for the 32nd Regiment,(see Chaps. 11, para.11). The arms east and west were demolished after the Mutiny, and those now existing were converted into apartments and let out at moderate rents. The south end rooms are occupied by the Union Club, which is principally supported by members of the Uncovenanted Service. This place was captured by Sir Colin Campbell on the 16th November, 1857.

The road to the east of the building, leading to the Sikandar Bagh, was the route taken by the first relieving force on their advance to the Residency, hence named *Outram Road;* whilst its continuation along the west side of Government House and the Canal is named after *Havelock*.

40.—CHAUK.

The Chauk † was built in Asaf-ud-daula's time, but of the two gates at each end of it, the southern one is said to belong

---

* The Girder Bridge over the Gumti, east of Sikandar Bagh, and near the Paper Mills, was completed and opened to traffic on 1st April 1902.

† Chauk is the principal street of the city where the wealthy native tradesmen reside and transact business in person or by agents.

to an earlier date. It is called the *Akbari Darwaza* and was, probably, built by one of the Subahdars of Oudh, who named it after Akbar Shah, the founder of this Subah.

Immediately opposite the north gate of the Chauk is the Victoria Park, which was established by the Husainabad Endowment. The land was granted to the Husainabad Trustees by the Government in 1890, on the understanding that it was to be converted into a Park and pleasure ground for the inhabitants of the city. The bronze statue of Her Majesty the Queen-Empress was erected by the Municipal Board of Lucknow, in commemoration of Her Majesty's Jubilee, and was unveiled by His Honour Sir Auckland Colvin, on the evening of the 23rd November, 1892.

41.—KAZMAIN AND DARGAH OF HAZRAT ABBAS.

Proceeding westward from the Chauk we come to two singular *Dargahs*, or Muhammadan shrines, one the Kazmain, built by Sharf-ud-daula and said to be a copy of the tomb of two Imams, Musa Kazim and Raza Kazim, of Khorasan; and the other built by Dian-ud-daula on the model of the tomb of the Imam Husain at Karbala. But, except when these places are illuminated during the *Muharram* festival, there is nothing to repay a visit.

The *Dargah of Hazrat Abbas*,* which is also in the city, is another place of sanctity and resort, wherein the banner of Abbas, a relative of Ali, who was killed in the battle of Karbala is deposited. The Lucknow Muhammadans believe that they have the metal crest of the banner of Abbas, brought here by a pilgrim from the west, and the relic is regarded as peculiarly sacred. The building in which it is contained is called the *Dargah;* and thither the banners used in the *Muharram* are brought by thronging multitudes, with great display, upon the fifth day of the festival. The banners are borne through the *Dargah,* presented to the sacred crest and touched, and then taken out again at the opposite door to make room for others. Innumerable banners are so hallowed in the course of the day.

It was here that Nawab Saádat Ali Khan is said to have received a sudden awakening which converted him from a wild and vicious youth to the sober, practical statesman he became, (see page 147.)

ALAM BAGH

Is situated on the Cawnpore road about two miles southwest of the Railway station. The building in the centre of the

---

* *Dargah* is a shrine or tomb of a saint, and *Hazrat* is a term of respect used in addressing holy men.

garden was constructed by one of the Begums of Wajid Ali Shah, the ex-King of Oudh. It was captured by General Havelock on the 23rd September, 1857, and the wounded and sick, with spare stores, were left here on the General's advance to the relief of the Residency, (see para. 97). The detachment that was left in Alambagh in charge of the baggage was closely invested by the enemy during the two months that elapsed until relieved by Sir Colin Campbell on 12th November, 1857. When the Commander-in-Chief returned to Alambagh, after extricating the Residency garrison, General Outram was left here with a strong force to watch the rebels and to avoid the appearance of having abandoned Oudh, (see para. 116).

It was on the turret of this building that the Semaphore telegraph was erected, by means of which Sir Colin Campbell communicated with General Outram in the Residency, (see para. 101).

General Havelock is buried within the enclosure, on the north side of the building, which is, at the present time, in a state of disrepair. An obelisk marks the spot where repose the remains of Major-General Sir Henry Havelock, (see para. 115). To this monument an addition has been made of a tablet in memory of Sir Henry Havelock Allan, who was killed by the Afridis, on 30th December, 1897.

> " Here in this Park his sacred ashes lie,
> No more a sweet and pleasant sylvan glade,
> But now a waste of weeds and filthy wreck
> Where starveling cattle browse a scanty blade,
> Where foul and fetid odours taint the air,
> Here on his battle ground he lies forgot.
> A weeping widow, not his country, raised
> The simple monument that marks the spot. "

JOSEPH B. S. BOYLE.

CHAPTER V.

INTRODUCTION TO THE RESIDENCY.

The heroic defence of the Residency during the prolonged investment of the place by the rebels, forms an episode in Indian History as being connected with the memorable sepoy rebellion of 1857-58. It, therefore, possesses a peculiar interest to tourists and others who are attracted thither from all parts of the globe; and persons of every nationality may be seen walking through the extensive grounds of the place in contemplation of the ruins around, where a death-like stillness pervades.

On entering the Baillie Guard Gate the mind of the visitor is filled with strange emotion, and this feeling is intensified when standing beneath the battered walls—silent witnesses of fierce conflict that raged there, as already narrated.

Grateful at the deliverance of the beleaguered garrison from their perilous position, in which the finger of God is manifest, and proud of the victory achieved by the British, which was a triumph of Christianity over Heathenism, the visit is sorrowfully brought to a close at the thought of the illustrious dead who sank to rest within its sacred precincts: of brave fathers and sons; of heroic women and dear children who found an early grave amidst the ruined grandeur where they fell, and over which they shed a holy radiance.

Many will be affected reflecting on the sufferings, both in mind and body, which they endured before their dissolution, but the Christian will find comfort in the knowledge that death to them meant eternal life, and that their spirits have fled beyond the turmoil of war to that blest abode above, to which they were translated by blessed Faith and Hope in the Redeemer.

THE land you tread on is Historic ground,
Full many a Warrior here, a grave hath found.
The "Baillie Guard"—yon ivy-mantled Tower,
Is where the Rebel mock'd Britannia's power.
Where once alas! Rebellion's surge roll'd high,
And death and danger were for ever nigh!
Where Inglis fought, and Henry Lawrence fell,
" When Freedom shriek'd, and Hope e'en bid farewell!"
Indeed, awhile, there seemed no hand to save,
And dauntless men, but fill'd the yawning grave!
"Havelock's Relief," was with disaster fraught.
Heroic Neill, was 'neath yon gateway shot.
At length "Sir Colin"—destin'd to command,
Brought timely succour, to the gallant band.
Who five long months hemm'd in on every side,
Yet still undaunted, battled with the tide!
The storms now passed, behold 'tis calm again
No adverse Armies battle on the plain!
No more is heard the iron tramp of War,
Or belching cannon thund'ring from afar!
But Art and Science, Peace and Joy are here,
While sweet soft music falls upon the ear!

K. M. NICHOLSON.

RUINS OF THE RESIDENCY, LUCKNOW.

GUIDE TO THE RESIDENCY.
A.—RESIDENCY.

This was originally an imposing edifice, along the west side of which extended a wide and lofty colonnaded verandah. The main entrance was, on the east side, under a handsome portico, which, at the beginning of the siege, was barricaded with boxes filled with earth, but the building was ill-adapted for purposes of defence, as it contained numberless lofty windows which could not be effectually barricaded, and the roof was only protected by an open balustrade. On the south turret was erected a semaphore for telegraphic communication with Machhi Bhawan Fort, and subsequently with the Commander-in-Chief at Alambagh.

In the open space between the water-gate and hospital, the line of defence (indicated by the dotted line on the plan of the Intrenched Position) * ran along the irregular ridge of the high level, which was protected by a ditch and low

---

* In the Lucknow Museum there is a model, by the Rev. T. Moore, formerly (1871-74) Civil Chaplain of Lucknow, of the Intrenched Position, a copy of which is kept in the Residency for the information of visitors. It is constructed on a scale of 20 superficial feet to the inch, and, in perpendicular measurement the scale is 5 feet (for ground only) to the inch.

The distance around the Intrenched Position is 1 mile, 3 furlongs, and 433 feet. Diameter from Baillie Guard Gate to boundary near slaughter-house post (marked V on the plan) is 1,020 feet.

bank of earth made breast high by the addition of sand-bags. These served as a protection to our men, who were enabled to fire, with comparative safety, through the interstices. Within this space three guns were placed, *viz.*, a 9-pounder, an 18-pounder, and a 24-pounder howitzer, at the back of which, in the open space in front of the Residency, were planted two 8-inch mortars pointing in the direction of the city.

The Residency grounds had been most tastefully laid out in parterres and contained the choicest flowers and shrubs, but in a short time one could hardly recognize the place, which was suddenly transformed into an arsenal, piles of shot and shell having taken the place of flowers and shrubs, which were everywhere trodden down, and of which there was soon not a vestige left.

The ground floor of the Residency was occupied by soldiers of H. M.'s 32nd Regiment, under the command of Captain Low, of the same corps; the rest of the building was completely filled by ladies and children. "Besides having a ground floor and two upper stories, it had a *tykhana*, or underground rooms, which, from its immunity from shot and shell, was occupied by the women and children of the 32nd. It was built to shelter the Residency of the King's court during the summer from the extreme heat of the day."

In the upper room, on the east side, above the *tykhana*, Miss Palmer, the daughter of Colonel Palmer, 48th N. I., was wounded in the leg on 1st July by a round shot, which caused her death. On the second storey, at the east angle of the main building, on the following day, Sir Henry Lawrence was mortally wounded, and died on the 4th, in Dr. Fayrer's house. No sooner had the siege commenced, than the exposed position of the Residency (in front of which treasure to the amount of twenty-three lacs of rupees (£2,30,000) was buried began to be severely felt, and the ladies and children abandoned the upper stories. The Mess of the 32nd kept possession of a centre room, on the first floor, until several casualties occurred, when they too were obliged to abandon it (*vide* para. 70).

About the 8th August a 24-pound shot entered the centre room of the building and wounded Ensign Studdy of the 32nd, in the arm, from the effects of which he died; and on the 11th of the same month, a gust of wind struck the north-east wing, part of which fell, burying six men of the same corps. On the 24th August the entire length of the verandah along two stories on the west side fell, and buried seven of the 32nd men. On this date Mr. Ramsay, Assistant in charge of the Telegraph, was shot, and died instantly. The death rate, for many days, averaged 20. By the end of July, 170 casualties had occurred in the 32nd only.

On the arrival of Sir Colin Campbell's army on the 17th November orders were received to prepare for leaving. The women, children, and the sick were ordered to the Dilkusha encampment, but the men were obliged to stay behind for several days to guard the various posts. Only a certain amount of baggage was allowed to each person, and many valuable things were left behind. Such a scene as the Residency then presented was really sad to behold. Women's apparel, children's clothes, rich dresses, men's clothes, and all kinds of cooking utensils and plated-ware, bedding, &c., were left behind. The guns were removed from most of the Batteries, and other guns, formerly the property of the King of Oudh, were burst.* The ordnance stores and treasure, and State prisoners, were removed at the same time. Many delicate ladies had to walk six miles, over very rough ground, exposed at one place (between the Moti Mahal and Shah Najaf) to the fire of the enemy. By a General Order, dated 23rd November, the Commander-in-Chief describes this movement of retreat, by which the final rescue of the garrison was effected, as a model of discipline and exactness. The enemy was completely deceived, the force retiring by a narrow, tortuous lane without molestation.

In such a way was the evacuation of the Residency of Lucknow effected, after enduring a close siege of 87 days, during which the enemy were always within pistol shot; a further period of 60 days elapsed after the arrival of Generals Havelock and Outram, when the enemy were driven back on two sides of the position. In all 147 days of siege without parallel in history. "The story of Cawnpore is, alas! more tragical; † but for the great qualities of the heroic and the enduring, Lucknow may well challenge human history to furnish a higher example, especially when we remember the number of women who were here shut up, and how nobly they bore themselves amid risk and sufferings which only Christian women of our Anglo-Saxon race could bear to the bitter end, and yet emerge from them all in moral triumph."

B.—BANQUETING-HALL.

(GENERAL HOSPITAL.)

This building was the banqueting-hall for the British Resident at the King of Oudh's Court; but from the commencement of the siege it was converted into a hospital. It was

---

* See Chap. II, para. 13.
† See page 130.

two-storied, with very large and lofty rooms on the upper storey; it stands on the same level with the Residency, and, having numerous large doors and windows, suffered much from the enemy's bullets and shot; the openings on the exposed sides (east and north) were closed, and protected with tents and other materials.

On the 8th July the Reverend Mr. Polehampton was severely wounded, in one of the rooms on the south side, by a rifle ball fired from Johannes' house, by "Bob the Nailer," a nickname for the African Rifleman, who shot many a man in the early days of the siege, and who was stopped in his career by a mine begun from La Martiniere Post, and passing under Johannes' house, blew up the latter, thus relieving the garrison of a most deadly fire from which we had suffered (*vide* Chap. II, para. 75).

The north-east line of defence, from the hospital to the Redan, was garrisoned by the 71st and 48th Native Infantry, under command of Captain Strangways and Colonel Palmer, respectively. For a description of the scenes of suffering which occurred in this building, and the heroism of many delicately nurtured ladies in attending to the wounded and dying, I must refer the reader to Rev. Mr. Polehampton's book and Mrs. Harris' Diary of the Siege of Lucknow.

During the siege the Rev. Father Bernard, R. C. Chaplain, occupied the staircase in the east corner of the hospital.

C.—THE TREASURY AND GATEWAY.

Both these posts were garrisoned by the 13th N. I., under the command of Lieutenant Aitken. The treasury is on the right at the entrance into the Residency compound. The long room in the centre of the building served as a laboratory for making Enfield cartridges,* which Major North, of the relieving force, made from a mould belonging to Lieutenant Sewell and a second was found in the garrison. But for this the relieving force would have been virtually disarmed, as far as the Enfield was concerned, and would have had to depend on the miserable Brown Bess, which was the weapon used by the men of the 32nd Regiment during the siege (*vide* page 42).

As the gateway of the Residency is still standing it need not, therefore, be described. The gates were in good order in July, 1857; during the siege they were banked up from the inside with earth. The road leading from the Residency through the gateway to the public highway, is throughout a

---

* I have in my possession an Enfield Rifle cartridge which, among other Mutiny relics, was preserved by my father.

steep descent. Three field-pieces (two 9-pounders and a 24-pounder howitzer) were put in position on this road, and completely commanded the ascent from the gateway. On the 2nd July the enemy made an attack on the position, but was repulsed; Lieutenant Graham received a bayonet wound in the groin from one of the assailants, who was bold enough to advance to the very walls.

On the 20th August an attempt was made to destroy the gates by fire, but the flames were extinguished without causing injury (*vide* para. 74). The enemy commenced a mine against this position from buildings opposite to the gateway, compelling Lieutenant Aitken to commence a countermine, but the enemy's mine was destroyed by a heavy fall of rain. The position of Aitken's 18-pounder gun rendered the Clock Tower Gate untenable by the enemy.* A mosque close to it, which afforded shelter to two of the enemy's guns, was destroyed by Aitken. A galling musketry fire from the *Naubat Khana* made the south-east corner of this position almost untenable, and far from comfortable.

On the 25th September, Generals Outram and Havelock entered through the embrasure of Aitken's battery (*vide* para. 92). On the afternoon of the 27th a sortie was made on the buildings, which afterwards formed part of Lockhart's post (78th Highlanders), directed against a battery of the enemy known as Phillips' garden battery (opposed to our south-east angle), with the object of capturing their guns. In consequence of the paucity of men sent, not exceeding 120, the party were unable to accomplish their object, and were obliged* to return after spiking two guns.

The guard-house (since demolished) was built in a crescent shape outside the gate, and not being within the line of defences, afforded shelter to the enemy in their attacks on Aitken's, Fayrer's and the Financial posts. On the 28th September, Lieutenant Alexander, one of the few surviving Artillery Officers, while walking on the road outside the Baillie Guard Gate, was killed by a round shot.

D.—DR. FAYRER'S HOUSE

Is described as a very extensive lower-roomed building with a flat roof, protected by sand-bags all round, behind which the inmates were enabled to keep up a fire upon the enemy. There was also a large *tykhana* beneath, which served as a shelter for the ladies.

---

* There was formerly a clock above the arch-way, placed there in the time of the Kings of Oudh. The enemy's fire had been particularly fatal from this point. A masonry pillar, 150 yards in front of the Baillie Guard Gate, marks the spot where the gate stood.

This post was defended by a party of sepoy pensioners, under the command of Captain Weston, Superintendent of the Military Police. It was commanded by the Clock Tower, and was much exposed to the enemy's fire. A 9-pounder, loaded with grape, was placed in front of the building, in a north-easterly direction, to command the Baillie Guard Gate.

It was here that Sir Henry Lawrence breathed his last, on 4th July, after removal from the Residency. Here also Sir James Outram, with his staff, fixed their head-quarters on the arrival of Havelock's relieving force.

E.—SAUNDERS' (FINANCIAL) POST.

The road ran below this garrison, which was a large and extensive building of two stories, on low ground, being separated from Dr. Fayrer's house by a lane, across which was erected a barricade. There were two verandahs to the house, both were barricaded with furniture and boxes. It communicated with the Residency through the Post Office (being commanded by two 18-pounders and a 9-pounder at the latter place) and was garrisoned by a party of the 32nd Regiment and Uncovenanted Civilians, under command of Captain Saunders, 41st N. I.

It is described as a most uncomfortable position, both to hold and approach; for the only way of reaching it was by sliding down a steep and slippery descent in the rear of the building, which descent was completely exposed to the musketry fire of the enemy. It was still more dangerous to leave the position, as the noise made by the falling bricks, displaced by the departing soldier as he nimbly scrambled up the ascent, attracted the attention of the insurgents, which brought on him a sharp fire.

This was a most important post, and was one of the two great objects of the enemy's third grand attack on the 5th September. Between the 1st and 5th they ran three mines in succession against it, but were foiled in each attempt. During the attack the enemy rushed up to the barricade that ran along the front of the verandah, but were driven back by hand grenades, and by the flanking fire from the Post Office. The number of mines that were blown up in front of the Financial Garrison had so broken up the ground as to render this position quite impervious to further attacks of this kind.

F.—SAGO'S HOUSE.*

This is described as a small lower-roomed house (the property of Mrs. Sago, a school-mistress) separated by a wall

---

* This house was known as the "Sago Garrison," because it had been used as a school house, prior to the siege, by Mrs. Elizabeth Sago. With the assistance of the King of Oudh, a school for the instruction of native female Christians was established in 1837 by the British Resident, Sir John Low; and that amiable and most respectable widow lady undertook the arduous task of instructing them,

from the Financial out-post. The enclosing wall and compound were abandoned, and the defence confined to the building itself; although higher than the road yet it stood low and was much exposed. This position was commanded by the two 18-pounders and a 9-pounder at the Post Office, and was held until ruined on the 14th August. It was garrisoned by a party of the 32nd Regiment, under command of Lieutenant Clery of the same corps.

On 10th August the enemy sprang a mine against this post, which fortunately brought down only a few out-houses, and "two European soldiers who had stood sentinel at one of the out-houses picquets were blown into the air, but both escaped with their lives. One, who fell within the compound, was slightly bruised, and the other was thrown into the middle of the road which separated us from the enemy. He no sooner found himself unhurt, than he got upon his legs, jumped over our wall and made his escape in perfect safety, notwithstanding the shower of bullets that whistled past his ears."

This was one of the principal points of attack on this date. It was begun by the springing of an enemy's mine there which did no practical harm; and the mining was then continued on both sides for three days till the enemy was blown in and defeated. Finally a gallery of the enemy's fell in from the heaviness of the rain on the 29th August, and the garrison, early in the following month, completed the needful mines to foil any other such attempts that might be made there.

G.—GERMON'S (JUDICIAL) POST.

This post consisted of an extensive upper-roomed house between Anderson's and the Post Office, and was a most important position. It was barricaded on all sides with furniture, &c., and was much exposed to the enemy's fire from the east, also from the turret on Johannes' house on the west; an earth-work and a wall of fascines protected it on the roadside. It was garrisoned by Uncovenanted Civilians (whose families also found shelter here) and the Sikhs of the 13th N. I., commanded by Captain Germon of the same Regiment.

This post is described as having been almost battered out of the perpendicular, and the walls were so crumbled away, and eaten into by the incessant rain of bullets, that it is hardly too much to say that it was breached by musketry. The enemy's position was just across the road, and they assaulted frequently with great determination. More hand-to-hand conflicts took place here than in any other post in the defences. The enemy commenced an elaborate mine for the destruction of this building, but a countermine was sunk, from the well still existing which resulted in the destruction of about 20 of the rebels.

H.—POST OFFICE.

This important position was the head-quarters of the Engineers and Artillery. It commanded the *Hawalat*, Jail, (now the District Judge's Court), and mosque to the right, also Clock Tower and out-offices of the Terhi Kothi to the left, besides protecting the Financial out-post and Sago's Garrison below. It was defended by a party of the 32nd Regiment commanded by Captain McCabe of the same corps, who was killed on the 29th, of September. Mrs. Kavanagh had the calf of her leg shot away at this post, but survived. Its defence consisted of two 18-pounders and a 9-pounder, pointing in different directions; also two mortars playing on the Cawnpore road.

There was a workshop attached to it for the manufacture of tools and preparation of shells and fuses during the first siege. The wall bounding the south side communicated by breaches with the *Thagi* Jail, Native Hospital, Martiniere Post and Cawnpore Battery, as well as the Judicial and Anderson's garrisons. Major Anderson, the Chief Engineer, whose head-quarters were at this place, and from whence he directed all engineering operations, died here of dysentery on the 11th August, 1857.

I.—ANDERSON'S POST.

This building, situated on the Cawnpore road, was two-storied on high ground, and formed the south-east angle of our position. It was defended by a party of the 32nd Regiment and Uncovenanted Civilians, under the command of Captain Anderson, 25th Native Infantry. It was surrounded by a trench, within which was a stockade bound with interlaced bamboos. This was one of the most exposed outworks in the place, as the enemy, throughout the siege, were only distant forty yards on the left, and from seventy to eighty yards on the front.

It was exposed day and night to the fire of the enemy's heavy guns, and when it is remembered how close these were planted, some idea may be formed as to the effect on the building. Among the foe's heavy ordnance was an 8-inch howitzer. This piece use to throw shell clean through the walls of the house, and right into the room where the Commander and Volunteers slept, eight in number. Later in the siege nine Europeans and a Sergeant of the 32nd joined the little garrison, making in all, with the Commander and a Subaltern Officer, only twenty men! Mr. Capper, of the Civil Service, had a narrow escape in this house, having been buried in the *débris* of the verandah. Corporal William Oxenham, 32nd Foot, save the life of Mr. Capper, by extricating him from the ruins of the verandah while exposed to heavy fire.

On the 20th July the enemy advanced to the attack in force, led by a man carrying a green standard, who was shot, and fell into the trench, upon which the remainder fled. On the 10th August another attack was made with identical results. This, from its salient position, was one of the most important and dangerous of the out-posts. It was two-storied, and had also a *tykhana*, or subterranean room, from which the defensive mines were begun. The upper storey was battered to pieces, but was a valuable look-out.

The enemy sprang a mine directed at this post on the 10th August. This immediately led to the construction of a series of countermines, which were eventually united. Through their agency, a mine of the enemy's was detected and destroyed on the 9th September.

J.—CAWNPORE BATTERY.

This battery was commenced in the early part of June, under the directions of Lieutenant J. C. Anderson. It was defended by a party of the 32nd Regiment, under the command of Captain Radcliffe, 7th Light Cavalry. It mounted an 18-pounder facing the Cawnpore road, a 9-pounder commanding Johannes' house, and another 9-pounder to sweep the road leading towards Golaganj, in front of La Martiniere Post and Brigade Mess.

The platform on which the guns were placed was protected by a stockade and trench leading past Anderson's Post.

The Battory was of little use, seeing that the men could not stand by their guns on account of the heavy musketry fire directed at them from the turret of Johannes' house. Many of its defenders were shot daily in their endeavours to keep the enemy out; and even thus it must frequently have been lost, but for the flanking fire kept-up from La Martiniere Post, and the rifles of the ever-watchful defenders of the Brigade Mess.

At this post were killed, on 9th July, Mr. Bryson of the Volunteer Cavalry; on 19th, Lieutenant Arthur, 7th Light Cavalry; and Lieutenant Lewin, of the Artillery, on the 26th; Captain Radcliffe, the Commander, was severely wounded, on 25th September, from the effects of which he died.

K.—DUPRAT'S HOUSE

Was a lower-storied building, with a verandah, having a sloping room protected by a mud wall pierced for musketry. It overlooked Johannes' wall and contained three large rooms, with a *tykhana* beneath, having the same number of rooms. There was another *tykhana* under the verandah. A mud wall, about nine feet high, was constructed leading in a straight line to the wall of the next house, La Martiniere Post, protecting very imperfectly a little yard with a well in the centre.

By the 10th of August this house was nearly reduced to ruins by the incessant fire of the enemy. The verandah first came down, then the outer wall was demolished. In this house were placed the valuable library of Captain Hayes, and other property belonging to Officers, which was totally destroyed.

In August a large quantity of small picks, *phaurahs* and tarpaulins were discovered stored on the roof.

L.—THAGI JAIL

Used as a Convalescent Hospital, was a well ventilated, lofty barrack, divided into four equal sized compartments, with grated doors and spacious out-offices. The Cawnpore Battery was on the south: the Post Office on the east; and the Martiniere Post and Native Hospital on the west.

M.—MARTINIERE POST.

This was a native building belonging to Sah Behari Lal, a banker. It was a single-storied house, with a good parapet, protecting its flat roof. When the buildings about the Residency were being put into a state of defence, this house was one of those selected to be an out-post. The south front was totally unprotected and as the enemy throughout the siege was only 30 feet distant, it was one of the most exposed outworks in the line of defences. It was separated from the Brigade Mess by a broad road, which was closed by a strong stockade and bank extending along the outside front of La Martiniere Post. The Martiniere building *Constantia*, being too remote, the boys were moved into the Residency on 13th June and this building allotted for their quarters. It was defended by a party of the 32nd Regiment—masters and students of the College, under command of Mr. George Schilling, Principal of La Martiniere College.

On the 10th August a mine was sprung by the enemy in front of Johannes' house, which entirely blew down the outer room of the post, destroying also upwards of fifty feet of palisades and defences. The room adjoining, in which were the sick and wounded boys, became thus completely exposed; the outer room, which was providentially unoccupied at the moment, being blown away. The teachers discovering the danger, communicated the fact to the boys and they promptly rushed to the spot and hastily removed the sick and wounded to a secure position without any mishap. The doors connecting the inner room with the room blown up were, however, open, and through these doors the enemy, who swarmed in Johannes' house, could be plainly seen. For some minutes they neither fired, nor made any attempt to advance, so that Mr. Schilling and the boys had time to close the intervening doors securely. The enemy soon after commenced firing, and a private, who had accompanied Brigadier Inglis to the scene of the disaster, was killed by a bullet passing through the door-panels. The rebels soon occupied in force all the surrounding buildings, from which they commenced a furious fusilade ; they made several attempts to get into the Cawnpore Battery, but a steady musketry fire made them beat a hasty retreat. They managed, however, to get into the cellars of the rooms in which the guard of the 32nd was located and made it very uncomfortable in the courtyard by firing through the grating; and as it was dangerous to step forward to fire upon them, it seemed as if one of the posts was really lost. Captain McCade, of the 32nd Regiment, however, came to the rescue with a few hand grenades, which were dropped into the *tykhana*, killing three, and the remainder found things so uncomfortable that they vanished, (see paras. 71 and 72).

The garrison then made a breach at one end of the *tykhana* and so got into the end room, beginning with which they barricaded the whole of the outer doors. From this post the garrison began the mine, which, passing under Johannes' house, blew it up on the 21st August, relieving the besieged garrison of the most deadly musketry fire from which it had suffered.*

The enclosing wall of this post, on the east-side was twice breached and had as often to be replaced by a stockade.

N.—NATIVE HOSPITAL.

This was formerly the bullock-train office. It consisted of a square of low out-offices situated between the Martiniere Post, the Post Office, Civil Dispensary, and Convalescent Depôt.

O.—KING'S HOSPITAL, OR BRIGADE MESS.

This post, commonly known as the King's Hospital, was garrisoned by Officers, commanded by Colonel Masters, 7th

---
* See para. 75.

Light Cavalry. It was a lofty double-storied solid masonry structure, particularly in its outside, or south front, where the massive wall rose to a height overtopping all the neighbouring houses. In the rear of the main building were courts called the first and second squares. The body of the building was used by the Officers of the Light Cavalry and Native Infantry as a Mess ; hence its name. The two courts were surrounded by lines of low, flat roofed masonry buildings, which afforded accommodation to many families, and which were protected by high walls from the enemy's fire. It was here that Lady Inglis* and Lady Couper occupied rooms. On the 7th July Major Francis, 13th N. I., received his death wound from a round shot while sitting in the upper storey ; both his legs were fractured. Major Bruere, of the same corps, was killed here.

In the beginning of September the outer wall of the building fell, bringing down the rooms of the upper storey. It sustained a vigorous attack on the 20th July, but the rebels were repulsed. On the 10th August a mine was sprung by the enemy in front of the Martiniere Post, which blew down the stockade traversing the road leading from Johannes' house to the Residency; a few of the enemy attempted to enter, but were repulsed. On the evacuation of the Residency an officer was left behind: Captain Waterman went to bed in a retired corner of the Brigade Mess and overslept himself, (see para. 112). Some time after he awoke and found to his horror that every one had left, everything was silent and deserted, and he in an open intrenchment with thousands of rebels outside ; like a wise man, he took to his heels and ran, never stopping, until he came up with the retiring rear-guard, (see para 112).

P.—SIKH SQUARE.

This post, next to the Brigade Mess, was commanded by Captain Hardinge, Oudh Irregular Infantry. It consisted of two square enclosures, surrounded by rows of low, flat roofed buildings, known as Sikh Square, so designated, because they were occupied during the siege by the Sikh Cavalry. At the south-west angle, the native buildings, densely occupied by the enemy, closely adjoined the line of our defence, overlooking the roofs of the buildings, which were protected by sand-bags, and other materials planted for the men to fire from. The squares were separated by a lane from the eastern wall of Gubbins' compound, which was closed; but its best defence was an 18-pounder placed at the end of the lane, near Ommanney's house, so as to sweep the street. On the 18th of August the enemy sprung a mine under the outer defences of the left Sikh Square, which blew down an outhouse at the south-west corner,

---

* Lady Inglis, the wife of General Inglis, died in London, on 4th February, 1904.

sending Lieutenants Mecham and Soppitt, of the Oudh Irregular Infantry, Captain Orr, of the Military Police, and a drummer, into the air; they providentially escaped with but slight injuries. Six drummers and one sepoy were, however, buried amidst the ruins. A breach having been made in the Sikh Yard Battery of 30 feet in breadth, two 9-pounders were brought to bear on it; the embrasures were made in a wall about fifty yards in rear of the breach, and the guns were always kept loaded with grape. The breach was partially closed with doors and rafters, but any steady driver could have driven a coach and four through it without much fear of an upset. To watch this open breach was one more addition to the daily increasing work of the gallant garrison of the Brigade Mess.

Q.—BEGAM KOTHI.

This building was previously the property and residence of Mrs. Walters, her elder daughter, and only son. The younger Miss Walters was married to King Nasir-ud-din Haidar, under the title of *Mukhaddar-i-uliya*, who was paternal aunt to Nawab Mehdi Ali Khan, familiarly known as Nawab Manjbu Saheb, who is at the present time an Honorary Magistrate and member of the Municipal Board of this city. The elder Miss Walters, known as Begam Ashraf-ul-nisa, rendered valuable services to the British Government during the Mutiny in furnishing information to Captain Bruce, Deputy Quarter-Master General, afterwards Inspector-General of Police in Oudh, regarding the state of affairs in Lucknow.

A lofty gateway, nearly fronting the road leading to Johannes' house, served as the main entrance. A double range of out-offices formed a square within a square, one side of which consisted of a fine Imambara, used as a palace of Muhammadan worship. Some of these buildings contained fine and lofty apartments, which were afterwards made use of by officers and their families; others were lower roofed out-houses, having very deep foundations, and appearing from the road leading past the Post Office to Dr. Fayrer's to be considerably higher than they really were.

A fine upper-roomed house served as the Commissariat store-room. A mosque which, at the desire of the Begam, was not made use of, was within the Kothi. As the Begam Kothi was supposed to be pretty safe, being in the very centre of our defences, the inmates were required to garrison the *bhusa* (chopped straw) enclosure, in the Slaughter-house post.

Mr. Quieros' house, with the stabling, used as a canteen and liquor store-room, were, together with the main guard house behind, considered as forming part of the Begam Kothi, with which it was connected by a narrow passage.

R.—GRANT'S BASTION.

This was a high, square, flat-roofed building belonging to a native, which was taken possession of by Mr. Gubbins. On it was erected a parapet. Monsieur Duprat was wounded here through a loop-hole, and died soon afterwards.

It derived its name from Lieutenant Grant, of the Bombay Army, one of the Duriabad refugees, who commanded this post during the greater part of the siege, and who was killed by the bursting of a hand grenade in his hand.

S.—GUBBINS' BATTERY.

This is described as a half-moon battery, mounting one 9-pounder that commanded the road between Johannes' house leading down to Hill's shop by the Iron Bridge, the Golaganj Bazar, and numerous buildings to the west. The ground from which the bastion had been commenced was about 18 feet below that of the compound, and, when abandoned on account of the Chinhut disaster, the work was about ten feet high. It was constructed by Lieutenant Hutchinson, and was of great solidity.

The enclosing wall, which was 10 feet thick, was of masonry. It was strengthened by very large upright beams let into the ground, on both sides of the wall, at the distance of five feet apart; these were bound together by cross pieces of wood firmly nailed to the uprights. Within the enclosing parapet, earth had been heaped, but the parapet had not attained the height of ten feet all round when it had to be relinquished.

To complete this work a rough palisade was constructed of rafters, doors, &c., outside which the earth was scraped away as much as possible to render the assault difficult. The battery was ultimately raised to the required height, and a 9-pounder, and subsequently an 18-pounder, were mounted on it. The Civilians of the Covenanted Service, who aided in defending this post, were Messrs. M. Ommanney, G. Couper, S. Martin, G. Benson, W. C. Capper, J. B. Thornhill and G. H. Lawrence.

T.—GUBBINS' GARRISON.

This house,* which was constructed of solid masonry, consisted of two stories, "built by the King as a concert-room and cock-pit." It stood in a garden of no great extent, which sloped to the south, towards the enclosing wall, where the ground was lower than the level of the lane which divided the compound from the Goindah lines. Three sides of the roof of the building, which were exposed to the city, were barricaded. There were

---

* Gubbins' house was used as the Officers' Hospital.

two porticos; the principal one, towards the south, being much exposed, especially from what was called the "Lane Gun." This portico was overshadowed by an immense tree which intercepted many a shot, until ultimately it became quite denuded of branches. The south and west sides of the compound were bounded by out-houses, stables and servants' houses, built of masonry with flat roofs. Along the latter loop-holed parapets were erected. For about one hundred yards on the south front, a low brick wall bounded the compound.

On the 14th of July an attack was made on this post in which Lieutenant Lester was killed by a matchlock ball. Lieutenant Grant and Captain Forbes were also wounded; and, on the 21st, Major Banks, whilst approaching the position (where Gubbins was employed in keeping the lane clear between his post and the Goindah lines), received a bullet through the temple. Dr. Brydon was also wounded here on the 20th July. On the 22nd Mrs. Dorin, who occupied a room on the north side, was killed by a matchlock ball. This post was commanded successively by Captain Forbes, 1st Light Cavalry, Captain Hawes, 5th Oudh Irregular Infantry, and Major Apthorp, 41st N. I.; and was defended by a party of the 32nd Regiment, Sepoy pensioners, 48th N. I., and Gubbins' Levies. On the 26th August Lieutenant Webb, of the 32nd, was killed. Captain Fulton, of the Engineers, a most distinguished officer, also fell here.

On the evening of the 2nd September, Lieutenant Birch, 59th N. I., was accidentally shot by one of our own sentries, who mistook him for an enemy. On 20th July an attack was made, chiefly on the south side and around the unfinished south-east bastion. The enemy showed in great numbers; some ascended the south-east slope of the bastion (where the wall was incomplete) to the crest of the parapet, and were shot. A very considerable force made an attack on the 21st, undeterred by their failure of the preceding day, but were compelled to retire. On the 10th August another attempt was made to scale the south-west bastion, by bringing scaling ladders close to it. The assaulting party were, however, dislodged by hand grenades. The Goindah lines were destroyed on the 22nd July by a sortie under Colonel Inglis.

U.—Ommanney's House.

This edifice was capacious and double-storied, and was occupied by Mr. Ommanney, the Judicial Commissioner, who was killed by a cannon shot in the Redan on the 5th of July. After the death of Sir Henry Lawrence, Brigadier Inglis established his head-quarters here. The building was protected by a deep ditch and hedge of cactus, and fortified by two guns, intended to sweep the road between Gubbins' post and the Sikh Square, in the event of the former falling into the hands of the enemy. General Havelock, and such of his staff as were not wounded, took up their abode in this house. From this he used to walk, every morning, round all the posts of the place, embracing a distance of more than two miles. It was this incessant strain, on an already overstrained body, which produced the dysentery to which he succumbed, at Dilkusha, on the 24th of November.

V.—SLAUGHTER-HOUSE POST.

This was used by the Commissariat Department for the slaughtering of animals (battery bullocks) for the use of the garrison, (see para. 76) also for the custody of cattle and *bhusa*, or chopped straw. These buildings were originally the outhouse, cock-rooms, stabling, &c., of the Residency; and were entered through a gateway called the *Ghurrialie Darwaza*. At the angle stood the racquet court, filled with *bhusa*, which, in the rains, became so saturated that it pushed down the walls, crushing a score, or so, of much valued cattle on which the garrison depended for fresh meat.

W.—SHEEP-HOUSE.

This row of out-houses was used by the Commissariat Department as a depôt for the safe custody of sheep, preparatory to their removal to the slaughter-house adjacent. Many Native Christians resided in the servants' rooms in this square, and used sometimes to desert over the outer wall towards Golaganj. As, however, the enemy invariably executed all Christians, the rest thought it wiser to remain on half rations than court inevitable death at their hands by desertion.

The sheep and slaughter-houses were defended by Uncovenanted Civilians, under the command of Captain Boileau, 7th Light Cavalry.

Sheep-house Battery was begun about the 12th September, at the end of the lane between the sheep-yard and the slaughter-yard, to flank and protect that front. After a few days the work was suspended, and then resumed about the 7th October, but the battery was never brought into use.

X.—CHURCH.

This was a Gothic building, erected in the year 1810. It was converted into store-rooms for grain, but was afterwards found too much exposed, and Volunteer fatigue parties had to be obtained for the removal of the grain, oil, *ghee*, &c., which was a service of great danger, as the enemy was in possession of the native houses in close proximity to the Church on the west side. The opening through which the stores were removed is still to be seen in the east wall of the chancel.

At the gate to the east was a mortar battery to shell the whole of the western and northern buildings as far as the Iron and Stone Bridges. Near the entrance to the Church, upon the road, was placed a battery of three guns, one 18-pounder and two 9-pounders, which, from having been commanded during the siege by Captain Evans, the Deputy Commissioner of Purwah, was known as Evans' Battery.

The Church had no garrison in it. This was the weakest point in the whole defence, and one which caused the greatest anxiety to Brigadier Inglis. It was under cover of this building that pits were dug at night to receive the victims of the day's fire, cholera or small-pox.

" 'Neath the ruined Church walls, here sleep in the shade,
The mother and infant, the warrior and maid.
Their graves are sad voices, which silently tell
Of those who once suffer'd and gloriously fell.
When the Mutinous surge beat against this lone rock,
And a handful of Heroes repell'd the dread shock !
Which threatened destruction to each and to all,
When death was a solace, and welcome the call.
Affliction's dark cloud has since vanish'd at last !
But the *Ruins* remain, which still speak of the past !
The stranger now treads, with full reverence, the ground,
Where the sleepers will sleep till the last Trumpet's sound."

K. M. NICHOLSON.

Y.—REDAN BATTERY.

This Battery was commenced about the 15th June, under the direction of Captain Fulton, and was by far the best battery we possessed in the line of defences. It was defended by a party of the 32nd Regiment, under the command of Lieutenant Sam Lawrence, of the same corps, an able and gallant officer. It mounted two 18-pounders and a 9-pounder, and was placed so as to sweep the Captain Bazar, and the road up to the Iron Bridge. Here, on the 5th July, Mr. Ommanney was struck by a cannon shot in the head, which caused his death. On the 20th July the enemy made an attack on this post, by springing a mine, but fortunately missed the right direction, and the battery remained uninjured. They advanced within 25 paces of the post, but were compelled to retire under a heavy discharge of musketry. No less than one hundred of the enemy were borne off the ground by their comrades from this post alone, so tremendous and precise was the fire.

The enemy made two mines directed against the Redan. The nose of the Redan was of brick work, and I think that there was a small building abutting on it, a tool-house, or something of the kind. The point in the Bazar where the second mine was started was 203 feet from the apex of the Redan, on a bearing of 72°. The actual direction of the mine was on a bearing of 101° and its extreme length was 157, the point reached being as nearly as possible 100 feet from the point aimed at. It was blown up as a precautionary measure, by the garrison, on the 30th September.

The first mine was begun at a point 150 feet lower down the Captain Bazar than the second, and was quite wrong in direction, and short in length. It was sprung innocuously on the 20th July.

There was a constant alarm that the enemy would undermine the Redan successfully, and the ground immediately in front of it was twice reconnoitred and sounded for mines but none were discovered; and, as was known subsequently none were made that really approached the Redan sufficiently near to endanger it.

Z.—INNES' HOUSE.

This post was separated from the churchyard by a low mud wall. It was a commodious, lower-roomed house, having a sloping *pakka* roof, with a verandah to the east and north, and consisted of four large and several small rooms; in the centre room there was a staircase leading to the roof. It was only very slightly protected by palisades and the ordinary mud compound wall. At the end of one stockade existed a mud shed, with a flight of stairs leading to an upper room called the cockloft, commanding the Iron Bridge. The position was defended by a party of the 32nd, a few Sepoys of the 13th Native Infantry, and some Uncovenanted Civilians,* under the command of Lieutenant Loughnan, 13th Native Infantry, and subsequently Captain Graydon, of the 44th Native Infantry.

This extreme outpost was on the north-west, a most commanding position. On the 20th July a most fierce assault

---

* Mr. Gubbins writes:—" Sufficient justice has scarcely been done to the clerks and Uncovenanted Service. The admirable conduct displayed by this class, which contained such men as Kavanagh and Williams, during the siege, surprised us all. Several of them rendered excellent service in the Volunteer Cavalry. All behaved well during the siege, and were often very conspicuous in repelling the fiercest attacks of the enemy. They deserved better at the hands of Government than they have received, or had at least received when I left India."

was made on this post; the enemy came close under the walls with scaling ladders, but so hot a fire was kept up from our position that they were unable to plant them against the wall; after repeated futile efforts the foe was forced to relinquish the attempt. While this was going on, the cockloft mentioned above was in the most imminent danger of being taken: Mr. Erith, Corporal of Volunteers, seeing the peril, advanced amidst a shower of bullets, but was struck in the neck and fell. Meanwhile another part of the outpost was resolutely held by George Bailey (also a Volunteer) and a couple of sepoys, which resulted in the Volunteer receiving a dangerous wound in the chin. This little party was, however, reinforced, and they held their own.

Another assault, accompanied by an explosion of mines, was made on the 10th August: the enemy's fire was incessant, especially from the 8-inch howitzer lost at Chinhut, which played on this post with fatal effect, bringing down beam after beam of the roof, and making a great many breaches in the wall. Captain Graydon was shot while superintending some works on a mound in front of the outpost. In September this place, after having sustained such a severe cannonading, was pronounced unsafe, two sides having fallen in, and nearly burying the sentries in the ruins.

The following account of the post and its defence has been kindly supplied by Mr. E. Bickers, who received a severe wound at this place:—

"Innes' House was situated at the extreme end of the intrenchments and towards the north of the Church. It was regarded as an outpost and, very indifferently protected. On the south side there was a masonry wall six feet high. In this post there were a few out-offices and a wooden barricade. On the north there was also a range of out-offices, and here and there bare walls scarcely five feet high. The east of the house almost faced the Residency. There was no cannon at this post, but one was obtained for three days, with the permission of the Brigadier-General, and directed towards the enemy's gun, near the Iron Bridge, which did considerable damage to the house as well as the Residency building. But our gun only served to increase the fire of the enemy, and the General ordered it to be withdrawn, as the post was greatly exposed, and it was feared the enemy might attempt to take possession of it. The 20th July was a memorable day to the beleaguered garrison, as on that day the enemy made a most desperate attack, (see page 62).

"They sprang a mine at the Redan Battery, which was the signal for a general attack that lasted the whole day. About 2,000 of the enemy assembled towards Innes' Post, which they endeavoured to storm, making every effort to burn down the barricade, but we kept up a galling fire from the out-offices and shot several of the leading men, when they were compelled to retire. Our loss on that occasion, in killed and wounded, was about four; and it was fortunate we were protected by the out-offices or the casualties on our side would have been far greater. The Brigadier-General was so pleased with our exertions that he came to the post and thanked us in person. There was another sharp attack on the 12th August and afterwards on two or three occasions, but nothing compared to the desperate assault of 20th July."

ZZ.—RESIDENCY LOWER GARDEN.

This was abandoned on the 3rd of July as untenable, with tents standing, and about 200 unmounted guns of the late King, (see para. 13). It was a sort of neutral ground during the siege, until occupied again after Havelock's entry. On bringing in the ammunition from Machhi Bhawan, the powder was buried here, but owing to a stack of *bhusa*, or chopped straw, having caught fire in its neighbourhood, and the enemy occupying the houses on the far side of the garden, it was thought best to remove it into the Begam Kothi, where it was placed in the *tykhana*, heavy beams being laid over the floor to keep it safe, (see para. 53.)

NOTES.—The annexed plan of the Residency shews the position of the places described above as indicated by corresponding letters of the alphabet being affixed thereto, but it may be necessary to point out that this differs from the order laid down in the Rev. Mr. Moore's book and model.

In the Residency Church-yard, even up to the present time, only burials of the members of the original garrison and their families are permitted—sanction for such burials must be obtained from the City Magistrate. The defenders are interred in the ground on which the ruins of the Church stand and their families in the higher ground south-east of the Church.

APPENDIX A.

[OPINION OF THE PRESS.]
THE INDIAN MUTINY MEDAL, 1857-1858.

" This medal, which is by L. C. Wyon, Esquire, is a work of great merit. The obverse has the Queen's head with the superscription *Victoria Regina* and on the reverse Britannia is represented in an erect position, instead of being seated, and above is the word *India*; the drapery is most judiciously arranged. In her right hand, outstretched, is a laurel wreath. The usual shield with the union is on the left arm, and in the hand are other wreaths. The British Lion forms an appropriate background. The ribbon is French white, with two red stripes. It was granted to all engaged in operations against the rebels or mutineers, and was also conferred on non-military persons who had borne arms as Volunteers against them. There are five bars attached, respectively inscribed *Delhi, Defence of Lucknow, Relief of Lucknow, Lucknow,* and *Central India*. The first clasp was granted to the troops employed in the operations against, and at the assault of Delhi; that for the *Defence of Lucknow* was conferred on all of the original garrison, under Major-General Inglis, and to those who succoured them, and continued the defence under Major-Generals Sir Henry Havelock and Sir James Outram, until relieved by Lord Clyde; *Relief of Lucknow* was authorized to the troops engaged in the operations against that place, under the immediate command of Lord Clyde, in November, 1857; and the clasp *Lucknow* was awarded to the force engaged under his lordship's immediate command in March, 1858, in the final capture of the town, and in all operations connected therewith; *Central India* was granted to the column under Major-General Sir Hugh Rose, G. C. B., engaged in the operations against Jhansi, Kalpi, and Gwalior, and also to the troops, which, under the command of Major-Generals Roberts and Whitlock, respectively, performed such important service in Central India."—*Medals of the British Army.*

APPENDIX B.

[OPINION OF THE PRESS.]

Extract from the speech of H. H. Risley, Esq., C. S. I., C. I. E., at the Lucknow Martiniere Prize Day, on 26th March, 1904.

" You, like the Winchester College (to which I have just referred) have what so few schools in India can lay claim to—a continuous and distinguished tradition, a part to live up to, an ideal to maintain. And among those traditions you can point to the unexampled distinction, the badge of honour that no other school in the world bears, of having taken part in the historic struggle of the Lucknow Residency—wherever the history of that heroic defence, to use the fine expression of the oldest Roman poet, *Volitat viva per ora virum,* flies alive from mouth to mouth among men, there will the courage and endurance of the little Martiniere Post be had in everlasting remembrance. And if for some struggle of the future another Martiniere Post is called for, the School Volunteer corps are here ready to defend it at a moment's notice with better weapons than their predecessors'."

Extract from Major-General Sir E. Locke Elliot's address at the Lucknow Martiniere Prize Day, on 14th February, 1905.

" In connection with the question of including public schools in a system of National Defence, we consider ourselves as not only in the front rank, but as pioneers of the movement. What College or school can beat our record of 1857 ?

"The present companies of Martiniere Volunteers, B., G. and H., aggregate more than four times as many as the Volunteers who were in the Residency in 1857, and are, of course, incomparably better trained and armed. Since 1872, about 2,000 Volunteers have left the Martiniere, so that in addition to the 230 now in the Martiniere Companies, there are many hundreds of men in all parts of India who started their Military education and proved their Military efficiency before leaving the school."

APPENDIX C.

(PAGE 129.)

THE LUCKNOW MEMORIAL.

[*Extract from " The Express."*]

"As the present generation know only by tradition what led to the erection of the Memorial in the Residency grounds: 'In Memory of Sir Henry Lawrence, K. C. B., and the brave men who fell in defence of the Residency in 1857'—*vide* the Inscription on the Memorial—it has occurred to us that it would be of considerable interest to our readers of the present day, if we reproduced the principal paragraphs of an account of the ceremonial of laying the foundation-stone of the Memorial, which took place on the 2nd of January, 1864, and is related, in detail in the *Oudh Gazette and Samachar Hindustani* of Wednesday, January 6th, 1864.

"The narrative opens with a statement of the measures taken to erect the Memorial. From the date of the re-occupation of Lucknow, to the middle of 1860, nothing whatever, it would appear, was done towards erecting a Memorial of any kind. But then the Chief Commissioner of Oudh " having assured himself of the support and aid of the Government," invited a meeting of all interested in the commemoration of the Defenders of the Lucknow Garrison. The first meeting was held on the 30th of June, 1863, the third anniversary of the battle of Chinhut. The object of the Memorial, as at first defined, was to have included not only those belonging to the Garrison, but also those attached to the several Forces during the subsequent reliefs under Outram and Havelock even to Lord Clyde's campaign. This wide interpretation of the Memorial was, we find, considerably modified and made to apply only to those who perished in the actual siege, and in the first relief of the Residency under Outram and Havelock. In other words—to all who fell between the 30th of June and the 22nd of November, 1857. Every exertion was made to obtain a monster meeting, but whether successful or not, we fail to learn from the account before us. Sir R. Walpole proposed that the Memorial should be placed " in London, either in one of the public Squares, or in Westminster Abbey, or in St. Paul's." This was amended on a Resolution by Colonel Abbott and Captain Ouseley, proposing Lucknow as the site of the Memorial. Both proposition and amendment being separately put to the meeting, the votes for each were found to be equal. Thereupon an adjournment took place; the sense of the whole subscribing community in the three Presidencies was taken, and the question of the site generally ventilated through the Press. These measures resulted finally in the following Resolution, carried unanimously at a meeting, held at the Chutter Munzil, Lucknow, on the 10th of July, 1860 :— " That the said monument be erected on or near the site of the Residency."

"The important point of locality being thus disposed of, the next question appears to have been the design, the funds, and the range over which subscriptions were to extend. It was not unnaturally assumed that money, for such an object, would flow in with unprecedented rapidity; and that 'the Delhi Bank and all its branches' would be put into active employment in the receipt of subscriptions. But whether from the delay in starting the proposition, from want of zeal in the Committee, or from the unsettled state of things in consequence of the amalgamation, the project seems to have hung fire, and at a meeting held on the 12th February, 1861, it was announced that the total sum then subscribed, after paying incidental expenses amounted to only Rs. 5,831. The next meeting, held on the 1st July, 1861, showed a continued apathy regarding subscriptions, the sum available amounting to only Rs. 7,521. On the 22nd of October, however, mainly owing to the increased activity and energy infused into the project by the new Secretary, Mr. Wyllie, the subscriptions amounted to Rs. 15,547. The Masons of the Province donated Rs. 1,000.

"Funds being thus in a satisfactory condition, designs were called for. The design adopted was that of a Column, forty feet high, surmounted by an Ionic Cross, and ornamented by scroll sculpture. The design was originally intended for Cawnpore; and was estimated by Mr. Thornhill, Commissioner of Allahabad, to cost Rs. 12,000. It was from the studio of Messrs. Gilbert Scott and Co. The next step in the proceedings was the receipt of a model, prepared by Mr. Thornhill, on which a Resolution was passed, on the 29th of May, 1862, that the work be commenced at once. After many delays and disappointments, measures were taken for laying the foundation-stone of the Memorial. Then difficulties arose as to which of several officials should be invited to lay the stone. The local paper, from which we quote remarks on this head, wrote :—'It was intended to have waited till Mr. Wingfield might return, or Sir Charels Trevelyan arrive on his announced visit. The movements of Mr. Wingfield being contingent on the arrival of Sir Charles, which was very uncertain, it being considered a favourable opportunity during the Christmas holidays, when many of the Garrison were assembled, including Mr. George Lawrence, nephew of the late Sir Henry, who was present at his uncle's death, and was himself wounded during the siege, preparations were hurried on. The absence of the Chief Commissioner was commented upon, but, when it is remembered that Sir George Couper was a member of the Lucknow Garrison, and is one of the Craft, it may probably have been the delicate intention of Mr. Wingfield to assign to him the honour of officiating at this, to him, peculiarly touching ceremony; which he could not have done, had not Mr. Wingfield's absence constituted him, for the time-being, the Chief Officer of the Commission in the station.

"In the result, Sir George Couper laid the foundation-stone, and it was generally understood at the time that no one could have been more appropriately selected for the honour, nor have performed it more gracefully.

"The Committee was composed of General MacDuff, C. B., Commanding; Colonel Christie, Commanding Royal Artillery; Colonel Barwell, A. A.-G.; Colonel Patton, Commanding H. M.'s 107th; Major Aitken, V. C., Inspector-General of Police; Major Chamberlain, City Magistrate; W. Lane, Esq., C. S, Deputy Commissioner; Captain Pemberton, Executive Engineer; D. Blenman, Esq., Superintendent, City Police; and W. C. Capper, Esq., C. S., Honorary Secretary."

(iv)

The following troops were in attendance, under the command of Colonel Patton :—

Three Horse Artillery Guns of Colonel Bruce's Battery, under Captain Percival.

100 Mounted Artillerymen, under Captain Wyllie.

100 Troopers of H. M.'s 5th Lancers, under Captain Chaffy.

250 Rank and file of H. M.'s 107th Regiment, under Major Kemp.

The three Horse Artillery Guns led the procession. The remainder of the troops formed a street, from the Baillie Guard Gate to the site of the Memorial, through which the procession passed in the following order, at 4-15 P. M.

The Masonic fraternity, after having opened Lodge in due and ancient form in the Lal Baradari.

Bro. I. G.

Brethren of other Lodges.

Members of Lodge "Morning Star."

Captain Pemberton with the Plans.

M. M. Bearing Cornucopia with corn., M. M.

M. M. Bearing ewer of wine.

M. M. Bearing ewer of oil.

Secretary, with Book of Constitutions.

M. M. Treasurer with coins, M. M.

J. W. with his column.

S. W. with his column.

M. M. { W. P. M. MacGrennan, bearing the volume of the Sacred Law. } M. M.

W. P. M. Capper, with the Square.

M. M. The W. Master's column, borne by M. M. M.

The Standard, borne by a M. M., Bro. Gillford.

J. D. { W. M. Bro. Major Baring and W. Bro. Sir G. Couper, Bt. and C. B. Tyler Brethren of the Lodge. } S. D.

Next followed the Clergy, represented by the Rev. M. R. Burge, M. A ; Rev. T. Moore, B. A. ; Rev. Fr. Paul ; Rev. Fr. Felix ; Rev. J. P. Menger ; Rev. J. Baume ; General MacDuff and Staff ; the Civil and Military Officers of Government.

Members of the " Illustrious Garrison " of Lucknow.

The Europeans preceded by Colonel Barwell, A. A.-G ; and the Natives under Major Aitken, V. C. ; Colonel L. Barrow, C. B.; Major Chamier ; Messieurs G. Lawrence, C. S. ; S. J. Williams ; R. C. Joyce ; M. Nazareth ; W. Brown ; J. Best ; W. Ewart ; W. C. Phillips ; A. Hyde ; F. J. Quieros ; A. Quieros ; E. Quieros ; J. Braganza ; W. Hilton ; E. H. Hilton ; E. Medley ; J. Holt ; W. Reed ; C. J. Best ; T. Villoza ; J. H. Todd ; W. Samuells ; J. H. Gordon ; F. Lincoln ; R. Grant ; E. FitzGerald ; J. Graham ; D. Lucksted ; E. M. Potter ; D. W. Forbes ; J. Jones ; A. Owen ; G. Bailey ; G. Swaries.

The procession closed with a large concourse of the members of the community, and marched in slow time from the Lal Baradari. The street was kept by the District Police, under Captain E. Hill, and by the City Police, under Mr. Prince, as far as the gate of the Baillie Guard; from whence it was taken up by H. M.'s 5th Lancers, Troopers of the Royal Horse Artillery, and men of H. M.'s 107th Regiment, all in double ranks, and standing at attention.

The arrangements, at the spot itself, were excellent. On the platform, erected to the North, the ladies took their place; those who had been in the Lucknow Garrison being in the front row, among whom we observed—

Lady Couper.

Mesdames Barwell; Aitken; Lincoln; Chick; Grant; Dubois; Hyde; DeRozario; MacGreunou; Gordon; Hilton; Joyce; Alone; Senior; Phillips; Misses Johannes; E. Gardiner; S. Hilton.

As the procession reached the site of the Memorial, three guns turned off to the left, towards Gubbins' Post, and unlimbered, ready to fire the Salute at the conclusion of the ceremony.

The band formed up on the South, and the Members of the Lucknow Garrison, passing to the right, took their position on the East.

The Masons, proceeding to the left, formed ranks on the West, through which the Worshipful Master with his Officers, the General with his Staff, and the Clergy passed to the positions assigned to them, the band playing the whole time.

Sir George Couper, the General and his Staff, the Chaplains and Clergy of all denominations, and the Memorial Committee, standing to the West, the Worshipful Master to the North-East, Worshipful Past Master Capper to the East, supported by the Architect and the Officers of Lodge 'Morning Star,' the Revd. M. R. Burge, Civil Chaplain of Lucknow, read the service selected and arranged by him for the occasion.

At the conclusion of the service, the Worshipful Master, receiving from the Architect the plan of the proposed building, made it over to Sir George Couper, together with a silver trowel, the handle of which was made of wood taken from the Residency building and in which was embedded a musket ball. The Treasurer of the Lodge, by order of the Worshipful Master, deposited in the bottle (that already contained a copy of the inscription, plan, and usual papers), specimens of all the current coins of the year. Sir George Couper then laid the cement, the workmen were called for, the band commenced playing, and the Stone was lowered with three marked stops. The Worshipful Master having in ancient form, with the assistance of the Worshipful Past Master and the Wardens of his Lodge, proved the stone, called on Worshipful Brother Sir George Couper to conclude the work. Thus requested, Sir George in a calm, clear tone, and with impressive accent, addressed the assembly as follows:—

"I find myself placed in a very trying position and I hope that you will bear with me if I falter as my thoughts revert to the past; as I call to mind the intimate relation which I once bore to many of those whose memory we have met this day to perpetuate; as I remember how often I have strolled around this very place, which was formerly the garden of the Residency, with Lawrence, with Outram, with Inglis, and with Banks.

"It is hardly necessary for me to recount at length to a Lucknow audience, assembled within sight of these riddled walls, the events of the well-known past. For all will remember, or at least will have heard of, the glorious bearing of the handful of Volunteer Cavalry on the disastrous morning of Chinhut, and many of those who now hear me can themselves tell of the consternation and grief which pervaded the Garrison on the sudden and unexpected fall of Lawrence.

They can recollect the fire which raged around these walls on the day of the twentieth of July; a fire so close and searching that the very birds, which chanced to be within these precincts, fell, perforated, from the trees.

"They can recall the ceaseless tour of a soldier's duty by night and by day. They can recall the perils which were incurred in repelling the incessant attacks of a pitiless and blood-thirsty enemy. They can recall the labours in the mines and on fatigue duties; and they can bear witness to the gallantry and cheerfulness displayed by those who were engaged in that unwonted and that unfamiliar toil. They can also bear testimony to the indomitable resolution and calm courage evinced by the troops of all arms, both European and Native.

"They can remember how the comrades, in honour of whose Memory we have met on this occasion, fell beside them day by day, and hour by hour. They can remember the round shot crashing into the defenceless hospital: and they can remember the feelings of despair and anguish with which the intelligence of another woman or child, killed or maimed, in the only places which afforded even a chance of safety, was received by the entire Garrison.

"They can speak of the heroic constancy and self-denial displayed by women—their eyes big with hunger, and sparkling with that light which hunger only can kindle—while listening with the compressed lips which stifle the emotions of a bursting heart, to the wailing of their little ones for that bread which they had not to give.

"They have experienced the sickness of hope deferred while watching for the oft-promised, but long delayed relief; and they can call to mind that hour of wild rejoicing which ensued on the opening of those gates to admit the wearied and wounded Outram, and his gallant and devoted followers.

"I have already referred to the revered and lamented name of Henry Lawrence, to whose far-seeing wisdom, self-sacrificing zeal, and chivalrous devotion every surviving member of the Lucknow Garrison owes the fact that he is not also sleeping in a bloody grave. Many of those whom I now see around me can bear personal testimony to the heroism and kindliness of heart of Outram, and to the soldierly qualities of Havelock, of Inglis, and of Neil. They can tell of the bravery displayed by Banks, by Ratcliffe, by Hardinge, by Case, by McCabe, by Bryson, by Simons, by Francis, and by Hughes. They could confirm all I might say of the skill and genius of Anderson and Fulton, of the gentle virtues of Polehampton, and of the self-devotion of Thornhill. But it is not for me to dwell upon this subject, for the names and actions of the more distinguished among the illustrious dead, have already been recorded in the annals of contemporary history; while the names of the rest, who bore a humbler though, each in his own sphere, perhaps a not less noble part, will be saved from oblivion, from which no words of mine could save them, by being inscribed at the base of the column, the foundation-stone of which we are now placing in the ground.

"In the name of the promoters of this undertaking, I thank you for your kind attendance here upon this occasion. It will hereafter be a source of pleasure to us all to reflect, that we took part in laying the foundation-stone of a monument which will, one day, and that not far distant, be a household word among the homesteads of our English land. For we may be well assured, that every traveller of the Anglo-Saxon race, who may in future visit this Empire, will turn aside hither to linger a while around this hallowed spot, and will go back to tell his children, with pride and reverence, of the pillar which stands at Lucknow in honour of the fallen brave, and in memory of the true and tender and devoted souls, who passed away from earth, when fighting for their God, for their country, and for their kindred in the desperate defence of these ruins."

"At the conclusion of the above address, the Worshipful Master consecrated the stone with corn, wine and oil (the emblems of plenty) and invoked the usual blessing. The Rev. Mr. Burge then read the remaining services arranged for the occasion."

The local paper of Wednesday, January 6th, 1864, goes on to say :—

"The Artillery fired a salute of 13 guns, that being the number to which the late lamented Sir Henry Lawrence was entitled, at the time of his decease.

"The Masons returned to the Lal Baradari in procession, the troops to their barracks, and the spectators to their respective homes.

"Thus concluded a ceremony that will not soon be forgotten by those who witnessed it.

"Sir George Couper's speech did full justice to the occasion, and that is saying much; for it is difficult to imagine a position more trying than that on which it was spoken, or a subject that required such delicate treatment. With the object of being more generally heard, the speaker was deliberate in his enunciation; and the language of his address is, it must be confessed, chaste, elegant, and to the point, as was to be expected from his well-known powers of English composition.

"Some have regretted that the services of H. M.'s 32nd, a detachment of H. M.'s 84th, the 13th N. I., a part of the 48th N. I., the 71st N. I., and the pensioners, present during the siege of Lucknow, were not prominently and specifically noticed. It should, however, be borne in mind, that out of the few names mentioned, three belonged to. H. M.'s 32nd Regiment : Colonel Inglis, and Captains Case and MacCabe. In a speech of necessarily limited scope, it would have been difficult—perhaps invidious—to go through, in detail, all out of the vast number who distinguished themselves. Of this, however, we are quite certain, that no intentional slight was implied in the omission; or any desire to depreciate the value and importance of those who are well and universally known to have constituted the chief part and mainstay of the "Illustrious Garrison." The address throughout is full of kindly feelings, and touching recollections; and bears no trace of any desire to depreciate the services of a single branch or individual member of the gallant corps who bore themselves so nobly in all that time of unceasing anxiety, endurance, and fatigue ; and who met "day by day, and hour by hour," peril and death with that unflinching patience and self-abnegation that British soldiers know so well how to exercise. Still, had Sir Henry Lawrence's well-known love for the soldiers who were in the Garrison, his care and unceasing anxiety to spare them unnecessary fatigue and exposure been remembered, the recollection, at such a time and in the presence of so many British soldiers, would have added the crowning grace to a speech that in every other respect was all that could be desired.

The boom of the guns, as the *Requiem* over the good and the great Sir Henry Lawrence, must have echoed upon the battered ruins of the Residency with a strange new sound to those who, as is well-known, felt the stillness that succeeded the incessant cannonade of the siege painful. It must, we doubt not, have inspired feelings of wonder and gratitude to the Great Preserver of men, that they have been spared to be present, on the 2nd of January, 1864, to assist in the sacred duty of rescuing from cold oblivion, the heroes and heroines, the sufferers and the slain, of the painful, yet in Lucknow victorious, year 1857.

THE foregoing is an account of laying the foundation-stone of the Lawrence Memorial in 1864, which was originally erected on a mound recently removed, and particulars relating to the lowering of the monument are given below :—

LOWERING THE LAWRENCE MEMORIAL AT THE RESIDENCY, LUCKNOW.

There had been for some time a feeling among those who were interested in the history and preservation of the Lucknow Residency, that the unsightly mound on which the Memorial stood, should be removed, as it greatly obscured the view of the Residency and adjoining buildings as one approached from the Baillie Guard Gate, and gave visitors an entirely incorrect impression of the place as it existed in 1857. By order of Government the mound has been removed and the column re-erected immediately over the spot where the foundation-stone was originally laid. The shape of the mound was a truncated pyramid, each side of the base measuring 136 feet, while the top was a square of 26 feet; the height from ground level to the base of the Monument was 16 feet, while the height of the Monument itself, including the stone footings, is 35 feet. The top of the Monument therefore was 51 feet above ground level. The mound was largely composed of dismantled fragments of buildings within the intrenched position, which were pulled down and destroyed by the Mutineers after the evacuation of the Residency in November, 1857. The work of removing the mound began in April 1904, and the column was placed in its present position on ground level in August of the same year. On removing the mound the bases of two Gate pillars were discovered on the south side. These marked the position of the entrance to the Residency proper as it stood during the siege and have not been demolished, as they will be of interest to those who saw them originally. The re-laying of the foundation-stone of the Memorial Monument took place on the morning of the 21st July, 1904, when there were present the following gentlemen :—

Messrs. G. K. Watts, Superintending Engineer; W. Sullivan, District Engineer; A. R. Ross-Redding, Secretary United Service Club; Captain W. Routleff; E. E. Baker, Agent, Delhi and London Bank; E. H. Hilton; and W. Ireland, Residency Keeper.

The honour of replacing the bottle in its former position, containing the original coins, to which were added a few more of the present time, was conferred on the compiler of this Guide, as he happened to be the only one present who had witnessed the laying of the foundation-stone on the 2nd January, 1864.

The removal of the mound was not undertaken without due deliberation, and it may be added that through the exertions of Mr. Leslie-Porter, Chief Secretary of the United Provinces Government, the consent of the Viceroy, Lord Curzon, the Lieutenant-Governor, Sir James Digges La Touche, and the Lawrence family were obtained to the same.

The work of removing the mound and lowering the Monument was successfully carried out under the immediate supervision of Mr. W. Sullivan, District Engineer, Public Works Department.

Group of loyal native defenders of the Garrison who were present at the inauguration of the 32nd (Duke of Cornwall's Light Infantry) Memorial in the Residency, Lucknow, 5th April 1899.

APPENDIX D.
(PAGE 72.)

INAUGURATION OF THE 32ND MEMORIAL IN THE RESIDENCY, LUCKNOW, APRIL 5TH, 1899.*

Extract from Supplement to "One and All," Lucknow, April, 1899.

"It was just three years ago, when the 1st Battalion, Duke of Cornwall's Light Infantry, arrived in Lucknow, to be quartered once more, after an absence of nearly 40 years, that all of us who visited the Historic Grounds of the Residency, and gazed with awe and reverence upon the carefully preserved remains of buildings, the battered evidences of its glorious and never-to-be-forgotten defence, were struck with a feeling of disappointment that no memorial stone was there to be found, recording the important part borne by the 32nd Foot during those terrible 87 days. It was at once decided to start a fund to which all ranks, past and present, of the Regiment should be invited to subscribe, in order to erect a Memorial in the grounds of the Residency, which should be a lasting witness, and a fitting Monument, to the bravery and devotion to duty of our gallant predecessors in the Regiment. Time has passed, subscriptions have flowed in, plans of the Memorial have been made, the great blocks of Cornish granite have been laboriously wrested from their native beds in the Bosahan Quarry, they have been carved into shape, despatched by rail, road and sea, until they have at length arrived at their final resting-place in the beautiful Residency Grounds of Lucknow, and we have attended the ceremony of their inauguration at the hands of the one person most fitted of all others to perform it, the brave and devoted Lady Inglis, who shared with her noble husband, the gallant Sir John Inglis, the Colonel of the 32nd, all the dangers and trials of those memorable days.

"What scene could be more impressive? What occasion more momentous?

"The Regiment which, in their white hot-weather uniform, has marched in from their barracks some three miles away, and has entered the grounds by the Baillie Guard Gate to the stirring strains of "Trelawney," is drawn up in hollow square, the Colours facing the position of the Memorial, which is gaily draped with flags, and the base built round with a platform covered with red cloth. At the base of the Memorial is a magnificent wreath presented by Mr. E. H. Hilton, on behalf of the survivors of the defence, bearing the following inscription "From the Survivors of the Garrison. In deep reverence and affectionate remembrance of the gallant deeds of the Officers and Men of the 32nd Regiment who fell during the memorable siege of the Residency, 1857." At the back and sides are many spectators, both Civil and Military, and friends of the Regiment, and on the right are grouped and seated in chairs some gallant old pensioners of the native army covered with medals, who fought so gallantly side by side with their British brothers in arms, " true to their salt ", though their dearest friends or relations might be on the other side. It may be appropriately mentioned here that a telegram was received by the Commanding Officer, just before the ceremony, from the Officer Commanding 16th, (Lucknow Regiment), now stationed at Cawnpore, expressing from all ranks respectful homage to Lady Inglis, and congratulations to all ranks of the old 32nd, on the auspicious occasion. This Native Infantry Regiment helped to defend the Residency.

"Here we see Mr. Hilton, well-known for his history of the Residency, who was present in the defence, himself a Martiniere boy at the time,

---

* A monument is erected in Exeter Cathedral to the memory of the Officers, Non-Commissioned Officers, and men of the 32nd Regiment, killed and died during the Mutiny, 1857.

here too Mr. Lincoln, who bore his part in all the fighting, as a gallant volunteer, and Mrs. Lincoln, who, with their little boy, now the well-known Barrister, was with her husband, and also the following survivors of the Garrison :—

                Captain W. Routleff.
                Mr. E. Quieros.
                  „ A. Quieros.
                  „ M. Joyce.
                  „ Peters.
                  „ W. Morgan.
                Mrs. S. Sutton.
                  „ A Routleff.
                  „ J. DeCruz.

Presently, the Honourable Lady Inglis and her daughter, Mrs. Ashton, arrived with Mrs. Turnbull, Major-General and Mrs. Jennings, and then Sir Antony MacDonnell, Lieutenant-Governor of the North-West Provinces and Oudh, with his Private Secretary, Mr. H. R. C. Dobbs.

The Rev. R. M. Kirwan, M. A., now Chaplain to the Forces at Meerut, formerly stationed at Lucknow, and well-known to the Regiment, who is supported by the Rev. Father David, and the Rev. W. Dyson Frater, Wesleyan Chaplain, now steps forward, and special prayer; composed by the Bishop of Lucknow, is read :—

Form of prayer drawn up by the Lord Bishop of Lucknow :—

Let us pray—

                Lord have mercy upon us !

                Christ have mercy upon us !

                Lord have mercy upon us !

Our Father, which art in heaven, Hallowed be thy Name. Thy Kingdom come. Thy will be done, in earth as it is in heaven. Give us this day our daily bread. And forgive us our trespasses, As we forgive them that trespass against us. And lead us not into temptation ; But deliver us from evil ; for Thine is the kingdom, the power, and the glory, For ever and ever. *Amen.*

Almighty God, who art from generation to generation the refuge and strength of Thy people, Who both turnest man to destruction, and sayest, return ye children of men : Regard, we humbly beseech Thee, our supplications, and grant, that, as in the past, so now and always, Thy mercy and goodness may rest upon this Regiment. Accept and bless this stone which we place here in perpetual memory of those who gave their lives for the honour of our Nation, and in defence of this place; and grant us Grace so to follow the good example of their constancy, endurance, patience and valour, that we with them may have our part at last, in Thy Eternal and Glorious Kingdom, through Jesus Christ our Lord, to whom, with Thee and the Holy Ghost, be all honour and glory, world without end. *Amen.*

Prevent us, O Lord, in all our doings with Thy most gracious favour, and further us with Thy continual help ; that in all our works begun, continued, and ended in Thee, we may glorify Thy holy Name, and finally by Thy mercy obtain everlasting life, through Jesus Christ our Lord. *Amen.*

The short service ending with a hymn : " O God our help in ages past."

HYMN 165.

" Lord, Thou hast been our refuge from one generation to another."

O God, our help in ages past,
  Our hope for years to come ;
Our shelter from the stormy blast,
  And our eternal home.

Beneath the shadow of Thy Throne,
  Thy saints have dwelt secure ;
Sufficient is Thine Arm alone,
  And our defence is sure.

Before the hills in order stood,
  Or earth received her frame ;
From everlasting Thou art God,
  To endless years the same.

A thousand ages in Thy sight,
  Are like an evening gone ;
Short as the watch that ends the night,
  Before the rising sun.

O God, our help in ages past,
  Our hope for years to come ;
Be Thou our guard while troubles last,
  And our eternal home. *Amen.*

The grace of our Lord Jesus Christ, and the love of God, and the fellowship of the Holy Ghost, be with us all evermore. *Amen.*

The above short service being ended, Lieutenant-Colonel C. F. A. Turnbull said:—

"Your Honour, Lady Inglis, General Jennings, Ladies and Gentlemen—

"Before I ask Lady Inglis to perform the ceremony of inaugurating this Monument, I propose to say a few words with reference to it.

"Nearly forty years had elapsed since the heroic defence of this Residency before the 32nd, now called the 1st Duke of Cornwall's Light Infantry, were again quartered in Lucknow. We found that there was no Memorial of the service rendered by the Regiment at that momentous time. It was agreed that we should take the initiative, and with those who had previously served in the Regiment, erect a suitable Monument recording the gallant defence—and in memory of those of the Regiment who lost their lives in the noble discharge of their duty.

"Officers, Warrant Officers, Non-Commissioned Officers and Private Soldiers of the Regiment, past and present, alike readily subscribed to erect this Memorial. The monument consists of two blocks of Cornish granite from the Bosahan quarry, near Penryn (Cornwall). The form selected is that of an obelisk, which may be considered specially appropriate, the obelisk from earliest times having been the accepted emblem of strength and dominion.

"These massive blocks of unpolished granite also carry with them the idea of strength and power.

"We are fortunate in having present to-day the representative of Her Most Gracious Majesty the Queen, His Honour the Lieutenant-Governor of these Provinces.

"In the name of the Officers, Warrant Officers, Non-Commissioned Officers and Private Soldiers of the Regiment, which I have the honour to command, and absent subscribers, I thank Your Honour for your presence here to-day, testifying thereby that the years which have passed, have in no way dimmed the memory of the great deeds of 1857, when no less than fifteen Officers, four hundred and forty-eight Non-Commissioned Officers, and Private Soldiers of the 32nd perished in Lucknow, Cawnpore, and the subsequent operations in Oudh.

"We are all indeed glad to see here to-day so many who fought side by side with the old 32nd, in that unparalleled defence, and also those who took part in that determined relief.

"It is extremely gratifying to us all, that you Lady Inglis have come here to perform this ceremony, adding as it does so immensely to its interest, both as having been the wife of the great and gallant Colonel of the 32nd, Brigadier-General Sir John Inglis, of whose memory this Regiment is so justly proud, who, with a handful of men, so ably and successfully conducted the defence, and also as one who shared the perils and dangers of those eighty-seven days of endurance, constancy and devotion to duty.

"Thanking you all for your presence here to-day, I will now ask Lady Inglis to inaugurate this Monument."

At the conclusion of this speech Lieutenant-Colonel Turnbull requested Lady Inglis to inaugurate the Memorial, which she did by mounting the platform, and, addressing the Regiment in clearly audible words, said : "Before performing this ceremony I want to thank Lieutenant-Colonel Turnbull, and the Officers of the Regiment, for the great honour they have done me in asking me to assist at this most deeply interesting ceremony. It is indeed the greatest pleasure to me, after so many years, to see this handsome Monument about to be inaugurated in memory of those brave men who laid down their lives in defence of this place forty years ago. My husband would rejoice to see this day. He loved his Regiment and was very proud of it. He served in it for twenty-five years, and died its Colonel, and he took the deepest interest in every member of the Corps. I know this Regiment always has upheld and will uphold the name it has gained in this and other lands, and that whenever good and brave men are wanted, the Duke of Cornwall's Light Infantry will ever be to the fore. I again thank you very much and wish the dear old 32nd, for I can think of it by no other name, every prosperity and success in future."

Then lightly tapping the huge base block of granite with an ebony and silver hammer, she declared it duly inaugurated.

Lieutenant-Colonel Turnbull then ordered the Regiment to present Arms, and the Colours were lowered, as the Band played "God save the Queen."

When Arms had been again shouldered, Sir Antony MacDonnell addressed the Regiment as follows :—

"Colonel Turnbull, Officers and men of the 32nd Regiment—I ask your permission for the moment to address you by your old and famous name, and to offer you on behalf of all here present our grateful thanks for permitting us to assist at this most interesting and significant ceremony. It is a ceremony that none of us can forget. Perhaps there is no spot of Indian soil which is so much endeared to Englishmen as the ground on which we stand. It is endeared to our feelings by unfading memories of suffering, of fortitude and of triumph. There are other places that will readily occur to you, around which cling recollections of greater sadness ; there are places which we identify with swifter triumphs. But to no place on Indian soil do we attach the blended memory of suffering, of unfailing endurance, of devoted bravery and of final triumph which we attach to the Lucknow Residency. With these memories and with every ennobling thought which they inspire, the name of your famous Regiment is inseparably entwined. Many great victories are inscribed on your colours, from Dettingen to Waterloo, from the Punjab to the Nile; yet I doubt whether any name in the long list means to us what Lucknow means. For it was here above all other places that "Your persevering constancy" (I quote from Sir Colin Campbell's general order after the Relief) "was, under Providence, the means of adding to the prestige of the British Army and to preserving the honour and lives of your countrywomen." In the years to come, you will doubtless add fresh laurels to your already ample crown, and fresh names to the long roll of fame emblazoned on your flag. But strive as you will, it will be hard for you to beat the record of Lucknow.

> God send you fortune; yet be sure,
> Among the lights that gleam and pass,
> You'll live to follow none more pure,
> Than that which glows on yonder brass.

"To perpetuate the fame of your greatest achievement, it needed no Monument or brazen tablet.

"You have built in the nation's heart for all time a Monument *aere perennius*. But yet it is right and becoming that on this historic spot, a Memorial should be raised in memory of the men who, with their comrades in arms, held it against a whole country. It is said that all things come to those who know how to wait. You have waited, and you now realize your wishes amid dramatic surroundings. It would be difficult to conceive a more striking picture than is at this moment presented to our gaze. These war-worn walls: these honoured graves, eloquent of duty done; this famous Regiment now marshalled on this hallowed ground, for the first time since they left it on that November night over forty years ago; this remnant of the comrades, Native and European, who stood by you, shoulder to shoulder, through the siege; and finally this most pathetic figure, a gracious link between the present and the past, the sharer of your struggles and your triumph, vividly recalling the gallant soldier who led you to victory—all these appeal powerfully to the imagination.

"It is a scene worthy of a great painter's brush; to find a parallel for it we must abandon the records of prosaic life, and search through the pages of romance. It is a scene never to be forgotten; and we all thank you with full hearts for allowing us to participate in it, and for giving us one more inspiring memory which can only fade with life itself."

At the conclusion of this speech the Regiment formed fours, and marching past the Memorial with shouldered Arms, led on through the Water Gate, and so back to Barracks whilst the Band played the Regimental March "One and All." *

---

* "It may not be generally known that the Regimental March of the Duke of Cornwall's Light Infantry is "One and all." It is stated to have been written by a lady residing near Bodmin, and to have been adopted by the Regiment early in the year 1811."

"The Cornish arms and motto, "One and All," are supposed to have originated during the time of the Crusaders. The story is, that a Duke of Cornwall was taken prisoner by the Saracens and held to ransom for fifteen bezants; on the news reaching Cornwall, the whole of the population subscribed. The fifteen bezants are represented by fifteen balls on the shield of the Cornish arms, with the motto "One and All," meaning, it is presumed, that all subscribed."—*Historical records of the 32nd Cornwall's Light Infantry.*

A memorable day indeed ! and a memorable event, and none we may be sure who were privileged to be present on this occasion, will ever forget the impressive scene they witnessed, or the stirring words they heard.

Of those who materially assisted in the many arrangements, the following stand prominently forward, viz. :—

Major Morris, who, as President of the Memorial Committee, had all the correspondence with reference to every detail of the Memorial itself and its conveyance to India on his hands ; Captain Chapman taking it over when he went home on leave. Colonel Stopford and Major Hammans, who helped to forward the affair at home. The British India Steam Navigation Company, who patriotically brought out the stones to Calcutta free of charge. Mr. Hartwell, of the Oudh and Rohilkhand Railway, who obtained for us a special low rate both over his own and other railways, and who with Mr. Pope gave much general assistance. Major Dickie, R. E., and his assistants, who kindly undertook the final setting up of the monument in the Residency grounds. And last, but not least, Captain Trethewy, who undertook, and most successfully carried out, the arrangements for the ceremony, receivin much valuable assistance from Colonel Pulford, R. E., and Mr. Pope.

On the following evening, April 6th, Lady Inglis and her daughter, Mrs. Ashton, dined at the Officers' Mess, there being invited to meet them, His Honour the Lieutenant-Governor and his Private Secretary, Mr. H. R. C. Dobbs, Major-General and Mrs. Jennings, Lieutenant Jennings, A. D. C., Mr. and Mrs. Hardy, Colonel Prickett, A. A.-G., Lieutenant-Colonel and Mrs. Wilson, Major and Mrs. Dickie, Rev. R. M. Kirwan, Mrs. Turnbull, Mrs. Chapman, and Mrs. Hearsey.

Extract from the "Pioneer," 10th April, 1899.

"As already reported in your telegraphic columns, a ceremony of historic interest took place in the beautiful grounds of the ruined Residency at Lucknow on Wednesday evening, when in the presence of the Lieutenant-Governor and nearly all the local notabilities, besides many from afar, a permanent monument in memory of the deathless slain of the old 32nd Foot was with sacred pomp declared to be "inaugurated." Memorials of the heroic past are not few in Lucknow, but Wednesday's ceremony was linked with certain romantic coincidences, that rendered it in a sense unique. Firstly, the monument perpetuates the fame of a by-gone generation of the 32nd Foot ; and it is the new generation of that grand old regiment—now known by its honor-title of the Duke of Cornwall's Light Infantry—supported by surviving veterans of the corps, who have raised this tribute of honor to the dead. Secondly, in 1857 the 32nd Foot were the defenders of Lucknow ; and now after the lapse of nearly half a century they are again doing garrison duty in the ancient Oudh Capital. Thirdly, the principal venue of the splendid story which the Monument will recall to posterity was the Lucknow Residency ; and it was the powder-blackened and cannon-crumpled ruins of the famous building which formed the melancholy yet proud back-ground of Wednesday's scene. Fourthly, it was Brigadier Inglis of the 32nd Foot on whom, in July, 1857, devolved suddenly and without warning the seemingly hopeless task of commanding the small remnant of defenders ; and it was Lady Inglis, the honored widow of that fine old fighter and the companion of his Mutiny days, who was the central figure in Wednesday's gathering. Fifthly, the Chief Commissioner of Oudh during the Mutiny, Henry Lawrence—a name never uttered by Englishmen in indifferent tones—recieved his death-wound from one of the enemy's shells within hailing distance of the green sward whereon his present-day successor, Sir Antony MacDonnell, stood bare-headed on Wednesday to do him and his soldiers' reverence.

" It has been said that the ceremony was an impressive one. In cold print adjectives have sometimes a way of staring at one strangely ; I will forbear, therefore, to multiply words to describe how deeply moved were all present, soldiers and civilians, by what they saw and heard. Suffice it to say that the Lieutenant-Governor's concluding sentence—" the memory of this day will surely abide with us till life itself departs " was no idle rhetoric (as indeed few of His Honour's words at any time are) but were the last words of a peroration to which his obvious emotion and the prevailing tone of the whole proceedings irresistibly led him.

" It was half-past five o'clock in the evening-when the glare of the sun had softened and the hot west wind had died quite away—that a long string of carriages, tum-tums, and gharries deposited their *tamasha*-apparelled occupants at the gates of the Residency gardens, where they were joined by a motley throng of pedestrians—motley, because including in large numbers every variety of the Mutiny veteran.

"Sikhs, Mussulmans and Hindus, some grey, some white, some walking proudly upright, some bent double and limping on crutches, some without arms, some without legs, some without eyes, all of them wrinkled and scarred, and all honourably associated with the suppression of the Mutiny (no other natives being present) were to be seen trudging along the gravel walks, now and then conversing with the many sympathetic Europeans who elbowed them. Many were decorated, some profusely ; and never were medals more proudly worn.

" The telegraphic report has already made it known that the Monument is in the form of an obelisk. The base is a cube of unpolished granite, weighing 7½ tons ; and the obelisk, or " needle," weighs 5½ tons.

"Both were appropriately hewn from the Cornwall granite quarries not very far from Penryn ; and the designing and the sculpturing were executed by Mr. Howard Ince of Lincoln's Inn Fields, who has certainly done his work well. It would require an artist to reproduce on paper the strong and enduring appearance of the monument, to paint in its simple dignity and isolation in the centre of an always green lawn, and to illustrate the grace of its proportions.

" The cubical base of the monument is 4 feet in height and is 5 feet 6 inches broad and some 4 feet deep. The "needle" rises from the base cube to a height of 14 feet 6 inches and is 3 feet broad. The whole monument, including the foundation block, which is 8 feet 6 inches broad, reaches a height of 21 feet 6 inches. A panel let into the base on the obverse side bears the following inscription :—

" This Monument of granite, from the Bosahan quarry, Cornwall, was erected by the Officers, Warrant Officers, Non-Commissioned Officers, and men, past and present, of the 32nd Light Infantry, now the 1st Battalion, Duke of Cornwall's Light Infantry, while the Battalion was garrisoned at Lucknow in 1899."

" It is backed on the reverse side by a corresponding panel, which thus complements the inscription :—

" To commemorate the gallant part taken by Her Majesty's 32nd Foot in the heroic defence of the Residency during the Indian Mutiny of 1857 ; also to the memory of the Officers, Non-Commissioned Officers, men, women and children of the regiment, who perished during the Mutiny here and at Cawnpore."

"The choral responses and the hymn "O God, our help in ages past" were accompanied by the fine band of the Cornwalls. At the conclusion of the service Colonel Turnbull invited Lady Inglis to perform her part of the ceremony, and in a short speech, delivered with parade-ground clearness, he explained, in greater detail of circumstance than possibly was in the recollection of everyone present, the full significance of the occasion. Lady Inglis responded with gentle dignity to the invitation, and taking a mallet, which the Colonel handed to her, struck the base of the Monument and declared it" Inaugurated." Her pathetic speech—during which, though her voice faltered from emotion, she was never inaudible—you have already published; it was the crowning grace of the ceremony, leaving the audience in a frame of mind to appreciate every word of the high-spirited and lofty address with which the Lieutenant-Governor brought the verbal part of the proceedings to a close. His Honour's speech like the others, has already appeared in your telegraphic columns, and it only remains to be said of it here that it was as eloquent in the manner of its delivery as in its language, and was in all respects an utterance worthy of the ruler of the province on an occasion that may well live in history.

"Following His Honour's address, the Cornwalls, responding to the martial voice of their Colonel, suddenly presented arms, and a thrill of pride was felt when the Band struck up the National Anthem and the regimental colours were lowered in loyal allegiance, at the same time that hats were doffed and voices hushed. Resuming thereafter the attitude of "attention," the battalion "formed fours," turned left, and with the band playing the good old march of the regiment, wheeled round and passed in its whole length in front of the Monument, each Company saluting in turn. A proud man must Colonel Turnbull have been as he stepped out in front of his corps. Continuing their onward march the gallant Cornwalls passed smartly out of view among the trees; and we knew then that the ceremony had come to an end. The enclosure was at once invaded by the crowd who were anxious to get a closer view of the monument, and to decipher the inscription card attached to a handsome floral wreath hung upon the granite base—which informed the reader that this tribute had been placed there by the "Survivors of the Defenders of Lucknow."

"The following is a list of those whose presence was specially invited; and very few of them were absent:—Major General Sir W. P. Symons, Major-General R. M. Jennings (Commanding Oudh), Lady Gaselee; the Officers Commanding the 3rd Hussars, B. Battery, Royal Horse Artillery, the 41st Field Battery, Royal Artillery, the 1st Battalion Scottish Rifles, the King's Own Scottish Borderers, the Black Watch, the Northamptons, the Argyll and Sutherland Highlanders, the Cameronians, the 1st Bengal Lancers, the 7th Bengal Cavalry, and the 8th and 16th Bengal Infantry; Colonel W. B. Slaughter, R. A. M. C. and Mrs. Slaughter, Lieutenant-Colonel G. Hall, I. M. S., Major Dickie, R. E., Major Rennell, the Chutter Munzil Club, the Mahomed Bagh Club, the Revs. R. M. Kirwan, H. W. Nelson and Father David, the Nursing Sisters, Sir Kunwar Harnam Singh, K. C. I. E., Mr., Mrs. and the Misses Hooper, Mr. and Mrs. Crosse, Miss Williams, Mr. and Mrs. Miller, the Deputy Commissioner of Bara Banki, Messrs. G. Roberts, C. Dodd, T. O'Donnell, Owen E. Quieros, A. Quieros, W. B. Thompson, Mr., Mrs. and Miss Hilton, Captain and Mrs. Routleff, W. Morgan, Messrs. J. Sutton, J. W. Walsh, Head, Fayrer, Deas, Hardy, Hopkins, T. Edwards, Lomax, Richardson, Meares, Lincoln, Ryves, McDowell, St. G. Jackson, J. Jackson, Mackintosh, Roberts, de Jersey, Sidney Hartwell, Cockerell, Butler, Cordeux, de Gruyther, Peart, Jesse, Sykes, Kennedy, Rynd, Prior, Freeland, Green, Kortwright, Ross-Scott, Spankie, Robertson, C. B. North, Woolgar, Staines, Wingfield, McConoghey, Father Bartholomew, Newell, Simpson, Dixon, Prickett, Gardner, Tytler, A. W. Trethewy, Birnie, Owen, De Cruz, Darrah, Palmer, Cardew, and Cunliffe.

APPENDIX E.

(Page 29).

Extract from "A Particular Account of the European Military Adventurers of Hindustan, from 1784-1803.

Claude Martin was a Frenchman. He was born in the year 1735 at Lyons, where his father carried on the business of a silk manufacturer. It was intended that he should follow the same calling, but his adventurous spirit would not submit to so tame a career, and running away from home at an early age, he enlisted in the French army. He soon distinguished himself by his activity and energy, and was advanced from an Infantry to a Cavalry Regiment. In 1757 Count de Lally was appointed to the Government of Pondicherry, and requiring volunteers for his body-guard, Martin made application to be enrolled, and was accepted. Accompanying Lally to India, he arrived there in 1758, but had not been long in the country before he began to experience trouble. Lally's ideas of discipline were inordinately severe, and his behaviour and manners towards his subordinates harsh and tyrannical. His treatment might have been necessary, for a large portion of his body-guard had been recruited from Military criminals and deserters under sentence, who were drafted into it as a punishment. But Lally's sternness had the effect of increasing rather than diminishing the insubordination, and when, a little later, Coote advanced and laid siege to Pondicherry, the whole of the Governor's body-guard deserted *en masse* to the English, by whom they were well received. On the return of the British troops to Madras, Martin volunteered to raise a corps of French chasseurs from amongst the prisoners of war, for service under the Company's flag. His proposal was entertained, and he received a commission as Ensign. Shortly afterwards he was ordered to Bengal with his corps, but, during the voyage, the ship in which he sailed sprang a leak, and it was only with the greatest difficulty that he saved his men in the boats, and eventually landed them safely in Calcutta. In due course he was promoted to the rank of Captain, but in 1764 his men mutinied, notwithstanding his exertions to keep them faithful, and the corps was broken up. Martin's conduct on this occasion was greatly commended by the authorities, and, being an able draughtsman, he was rewarded by an appointment in the North Eastern Districts of Bengal, where he was sent to survey the country. His work was so satisfactory that, on its completion, a similar appointment was found for him in the Province of Oudh.

This was the turning-point in his career, which had hitherto been more eventful than profitable. Having fixed his head-quarters at Lucknow he employed his leisure in exercising his ingenuity in several branches of mechanics, and amongst other things, manufactured "the first balloon that ever floated in the air of Asia." This brought him under the notice of the Nawab, who conceived so high an opinion of his abilities, and especially his skill in gunnery, that he solicited permission from the Bengal Government for Martin's services to be transferred to him, and this being granted, the adventurer was appointed Superintendent of the Nawab's Park of Artillery and Arsenal.

Martin did not neglect the opportunities thus opened out to him, and speedily ingratiated himself with his new master, whose confidential adviser he became. In the many political changes that took place in Oudh during the next twenty years, the Frenchman always contrived to remain on the right side, making himself indispensable in negotiations between the Nawab and the Company. At the same time he was careful not to push himself forward into public notice, preferring to remain the power behind the throne; and although he seldom appeared at Darbar, he had more real influence than the Nawab's ministers in shaping the course of events.

Martin's salary was largely increased, and he enjoyed, in addition, extensive sources of emolument, such as were always open to men in positions of confidence in the Native Courts. He became the recognised channel for petitions from all who desired any favour from the Government, and in this capacity enormous sums of money and presents of great value found their way into his hands. He educated the Nawab into an appreciation of the products of Europe, and then acted as his agent in procuring them.

He established extensive credits with the Native bankers, and so obtained a large share in the profitable public loans made to his master. Finally his position at Court was esteemed so secure that, in a country distracted by war and internal troubles, he soon became a sort of "safe deposit" for the valuables of the Nawab's subjects, charging a commission of 12 per cent. for the custody of articles committed to his care. By these and similar methods he acquired an immense fortune during his long residence at Lucknow.

Martin's pleasure in life seems to have been limited to the mere accumulation of riches, for he derived none for spending them. In his peculiar way he was sufficiently hospitable, but his table was not calculated to attract guests either by the elegance of the entertainment, or the geniality of the host. Of his private bounty during his life very few instances are recorded, though it is known that from time to time he assisted his family at Lyons. The principal object of his ambition or vanity seem to have been the attainment of Military rank, a fact the truth of which is emphasised by the epitaph he wrote for his own tomb. During the time he resided at Lucknow his promotion in the Company's service continued: for although he relinquished his pay and allowances, he retained his Commission. In 1790, at the commencement of the first war with Tipu Sultan, he presented the Company with a number of fine horses to mount a troop of Cavalry, and in return was gazetted to the rank of Colonel, thus achieving the object for which the gift was made. Six years later, when the Company's Officers received brevet rank from the King, Martin's name was included in the *Gazette*, and to his infinite satisfaction he became a Major-General. Lord Teignmouth described him in 1797 as a man of much penetration and observation, whose language would be elegant if it corresponded with his ideas; but he talked very broken English, interlanding every sentence with "What do you call it?"—"Do you see?"

Amongst the most remarkable points connected with Martin was his house at Lucknow, which was a castellated edifice built on the banks of the river Gumti, and designed for defence if necessary. It was constructed strictly on hygienic principles, for it contained a series of rooms—or flaats, as we should call them in these modern days—adapted to the varying temperature of the different seasons of the year. Thus in the hot season he resided in a subterranean suit of chambers, which were always cool and sheltered from the fierce glare and heat outside. When the rainy season came on, he ascended to an upper storey high above the ground level and its malaria. In the cold weather he changed quarters again, and descended to the ground floor. The house was fitted with many curious mechanical contrivances for comfort; the ceilings of the different apartments were formed of elliptic arches, ornamented most elaborately, whilst the exterior decorations were equally fanciful and florid. The furniture was on a par with the building, and the walls of the rooms were covered with glasses, prints, and pictures, estimated at many thousand pounds in value. Not the least curious feature in this building—which was called *Constantia*, from the motto *Labore et Constantia* carved on its front—was a room containing a vault designed for Martin's place of sepulchre. He built this because the Nawab refused to pay him the price he asked for the edifice; whereupon, in a fit of picque, he declared that his tomb should be handsomer than any palace in the kingdom. His subsequent interment therein had the effect of desecrating the place in the eyes of the Muhammadan, for no followers of the Prophet can inhabit a tomb.

For the last fifteen years of his life Martin suffered greatly from stone. He cured himself once by a successful though crude and painful course of treatment; but a recurrence of the disease terminated his life in the year 1800, at the age of sixty-five. On the 1st of January of the same year, he executed an extraordinary Will, which he drew up himself. It contained over forty clauses, and began by acknowledging with penitence that self-interest had been his guiding principle through life. His fortune, amounting to nearly half a million sterling, he bequeathed in innumerable legacies. Amongst them were three to the poor of Calcutta, Chandernagore, and Lucknow, the interest of which was to be doled daily at certain fixed places, distinguished by tablets bearing an inscription in English, French, or Persian, according to the location, and notifying that the alms distributed were the gift of General Martin, and to be so disbursed in perpetuity. He left a large sum in trust to the Government of Bengal for the establishment and endowment of a school to be called La Martiniere, which still exists, and where, on the anniversary of his death, a sermon was to be preached, followed by a public dinner, at which the toast of "The Memory of the Founder" was to be drunk in solemn silence. To his relatives and the town of Lyons he bequeathed large legacies, and two separate sums to that city and Calcutta, their interest to be devoted to releasing poor debtors from goal on the anniversary of his death. He left directions that his house 'Constantia' should never be sold, but serve as a mausoleum for his remains, and he committed it to the care of the ruling power in the country for the time being. Such were the elaborate precautions taken by this eccentric man to keep his memory alive and hand it down to posterity.

The thirtieth clause in his Will was perhaps the most remarkable of all. It ran as follows:—" When I am dead, I request that my body may be salted, put in spirits, or embalmed, and afterwards deposited in a leaden coffin made of some sheet lead in my godown, which is to be put in another of sissoo wood, and then deposited in the cave in the small round room north-east in 'Constantia', with two feet of masonry raised above it, which is to bear the following inscription :—

MAJOR-GENERAL CLAUDE MARTIN,
Born at Lyons, 5th January, 1735,
Arrived in India as a common soldier, and died at Lucknow,
(the 13th of September, 1800), a Major-General;
and he is buried in this tomb.
Pray for his Soul,"

His wishes were faithfully fulfilled, and when Lady Fanny Parkes visited the tomb in 1831 she mentions that a bust of the General adorned the vault; lights were constantly burning before the tomb and the figures of four soldiers, as large as life, with their arms reversed, stood in niches at the side of the monument. In the centre of the vault was a large plain slab bearing the inscription above recorded.

Perchance it sufficiently summarises Martin's life, and after the lapse of nearly a hundred years, one cannot help reflecting on the achievements of the man epitomised in the few terse words. Dynasties have died out, thrones have tottered and fallen, kingdoms have crumbled into dust and been forgotten since this private soldier sought to perpetuate his name; and it is not an unpleasing thought that the atonement of his testimentary charity still keeps alive the pious memory of the founder of *La Martiniere*.

" 'Tis said that memory is life,
And that, though dead, men are alive.
Removed from sorrow, care, and strife,
They live because their works survive."

NOTE.—" Mr. S. C. Hill, Officer in charge of the records of the Government of India, has just published an extremely interesting monograph on the life of Major-General Claude Martin, the extraordinary French adventurer, who left the greater part of his large fortune to further the cause of Anglo-Indian education in India. It is so curious that so little material exists for the life of the soldier who later on became one of the most important persons in Oudh. Claude Martin has hitherto been known as an extraordinary French adventurer, who played important part in the history of Oudh and to whose munificence the two institutions at Lucknow and Calcutta, bearing his name owe their existence. Mr. Hill contradicts the popular story that Claude Martin was a deserter from the French army and that his gains were ill-gotten. His collossal fortune is said to have been gained partly by trade, partly from banking, and partly from indigo."—*Indian Daily Mail.*

APPENDIX F.
(PAGE 9.19)

NEW JUDICIAL COMMISSIONER'S COURT.
LAYING OF THE FOUNDATION STONE.

Extract from the " Indian Daily Telegraph," Lucknow, 3rd April, 1900.

Lucknow has many large buildings, constructed in Nawabi days as " lordly pleasure houses " and residences, and put by the more utilitarian Government of these times to less luxurious use as public offices and Courts. But places built for pleasure cannot always be successfully converted into resorts where litigants seek for justice or Departmental Chiefs or District Offices do their business. Amongst the failures in this respect is the old somewhat delapidated-looking building occupied by the Chief Court of Oudh--it is neither convenient, or comfortable, and is not calculated to inspire the public with a sense of the dignity of the law. The law was regarded by Mr. Bumble as a "hass," and perhaps this is the explanation why it has in Oudh put up for so long a time with discomfort and inconvenience, while only a stone's throw away buildings much more imposing from without and much more comfortable within, have been appropriated for other purposes, administrative, archæological and social. But after all the law has a knack of sooner or latter getting the best of the bargain, and the long run it has done so in Oudh, where it is now to have a habitation specially constructed for and adapted to its own needs, instead of being located in a building designed for totally different purposes.

The question of providing better accommodation for the Judicial Commissioners' Court has engaged the attention of the local Government many years, but it has been left to Sir A. MacDonnell to meet the need. His intentions in this respect were thwarted by the famine of 1897, but about two years ago a preliminary estimate on the basis of plans furnished by the Judicial Commissioner was presented, but the plans were found defective in several respects, and Mr. LaTouche being acting Lieutenant-Governor, action was deferred until the return of Sir Antony MacDonnell. As His Honour was desirous of including accommodation for the subordinate Judicial officials, fresh plans were called for. It was finally decided at the close of 1898 that the accommodation should be for the Judicial Commissioner and two Additional Judicial Commissioners, the Small Causes Court Judge and two Munsiffs' Courts. Further plans were drawn up and submitted, and they were finally settled at a conference held in July last.

The site chosen is the open piece of ground to the left of Neill Road running from the Telegraph Office to the Residency and opposite the Museum. The existing District Judge's Court, which is to be retained, also lies to the left of this road, but nearer to the Residency, the intervening space being occupied by a hetrogeneous collection of old buildings, including the Club stables, Museum workshops, sweepers' houses and delapidated dwellings. These buildings will be demolished and the new Courts will then be separated from the District Court house by an open space of 600 feet in length. The site is a very convenient one, but the soil is not particularly good for building purposes, as it is covered with from eight to twelve feet of made earth, necessitating the provision of deep foundations and thus enhancing the cost.

The main building will consist of a central office block with two wings, one occupied by the Judicial Commissioners' Court and the other by the Courts of the two Munsiffs and the Small Causes Judge. An upper storey would, it is needless to say, have given a better architectural effect, but the ornate is very rightly to be sacrificed to the convenient and the economical. To break up the great length of the blocks as compared with the height, the central office block will be provided with a double-storied porch, and the other blocks will have towers at the corners. The latter will be utilized for stair-cases to give access to the roof and to carry wrought iron water cisterns for the fire protection supply, while the room in the central porch will be available for large conferences or gatherings, being $41\frac{1}{2}$ feet by $38\frac{1}{4}$ feet in size.

In the Central Office block the accommodation will include waiting-rooms for Advocates and assistants, an extra committee room, stamps, copyists' room, form, nazir and inspection-rooms and offices for vernacular records. To the right of the stair-case will be located a tiffin room for Advocates, Government Pleaders' room, Privy Council room, waiting hall for parties, vernacular office, club rooms, and Deputy Registrar's and Translators' rooms.

These rooms are to be ranged on each side of a central eight feet passage running the whole length of the block, and of the central stair-case chamber and of an eight feet passage at right angles to the central longitudinal passages. Each room is to be 21 feet broad by 21 feet high. The passage will be roofed by a segmental arch and lighted by clerestory windows at each end, by the stair-case chamber in the centre and by two domed skylights, which will also serve as ventilators. There, as elsewhere throughout the building, all rooms will have clerestory windows and ventilators, and the floor will be of stone slabs, while all verandahs will be nine feet in width.

In the Judicial Commissioner's Court block, situated to the right or west of the Central Office block, the three Courts (provision being made for the Judicial Commissioner and two Additional Judicial Commissioners) are 40 feet by 25 feet and are 25 feet high. They are each provided with a retiring room and bath-room, direct access to which is gained by the Judge from the porch without passing through the Court Room. The rooms of the Registrar and the Head Assistant will be so placed as to be readily accessible to the Judicial Commissioner, to each other and to the English Office and Library. Besides the three Court rooms the Registrar's office and relieving rooms and bath rooms are also to be 25 feet high, the remaining rooms in the block being 21 feet in height.

In the Subordinate Judge's Court block the north of the central passage is occupied by the Small Causes Court, 35 feet by 25, retiring and bath rooms for the Judge, Munsarim's room and office, and by the pleaders, records, library, inspection, nazir and tiffin room. South of the central passage are the courts of the two Munsiffs, 30 feet by 25 feet, each of whom has his retiring and bath rooms, office of nazir, all connected with each other. There is a central passage, as in the Judicial Commissioner's Court block, and there are also to be two porches, one in the centre of the east side and the other in the centre of the south end. It is worthy of note that in no part of the building will the verandahs be blocked by bath rooms or other out-offices, so that they will be traversable the entire round without having to be left.

The style of architecture will be the Muhammadan, made to suit the requirements of such a building, the outside being lime pointed and the inside lime plastered. The architectural features of the building will be principally the *chajjas* or deep stones supported on carved stone brackets and the ornamental parapets. Every effort has been made to make the building as effective as possible at a minimum cost, and the total estimate does not greatly exceed 2¼ lakhs of rupees. The plans as finally approved were drawn up by Mr. Wood, personal assistant to the Hon. Mr. Odling, the Chief Engineer, and the work is being carried out under the supervision of Mr. G. K. Watts, Superintending Engineer, 2nd Circle, Mr. McDowell, Divisional, and Mr. A. B. Gale, District Engineer, by Sub-Overseer Bahal Singh. It is anticipated that the building will be ready for use two years hence.

LAYING OF THE FOUNDATION STONE.

The ceremony of laying the foundation stone of the new building was performed on Saturday afternoon by the Lieutenant-Governor, in the presence of the Judicial Commissioner (Mr. Ross Scott), the Additional Judicial Commissioner (Mr. G. T. Spankie), the Chief Secretary (Mr. J. O. Miller, C. S.), the Divisional and District officials, the officers of the Public Works Department, the members of the subordinate Judicial Service resident in Lucknow, and the local members of the legal profession, European and native. By the express desire of His Honour, who was met on arriva by the Hon. Mr. Odling, C. S. I., and Mr. Ross Scott, the proceedings were of a somewhat informal character. His Honour first entered the *Shamiana* where the guests were awaiting him, and then, followed by the latter, walked along the path, (specially made for the occasion and edged with plants in pots) to the north-east corner of the central office block of the proposed building, where, suspended by pulleys, was a large stone bearing the inscription:—

"This foundation stone was laid by the Honourable Sir A. P. MacDonnell, G. C. S. I., Lieutenant-Governor and Chief Commissioner, 31st March 1900."

In an aperture below the place where the stone was to be laid, Mr. Gale, the District Engineer, placed a large drying bottle containing a copy of the *Indian Daily Telegraph* of that day and all the Indian coins from the rupee (not the sovereign) downwards. His Honour then took a silver trowel of Lucknow design bearing the inscription "Presented to the Honourable Sir A. P. MacDonnell, G. C. S. I., Lieutenant-Governor and Chief Commissioner, on the occasion of his laying the foundation stone of the Judicial Commissioners' Court, Oudh, 31st March 1900."

With this trowel the Lieutenant-Governor spread the mortar and the stone having been let down, he declared it well and truly laid.

THE LIEUTENANT-GOVERNOR'S SPEECH.

Having returned to the *Shamiana* with the assembled company, His Honour said : " Gentlemen, when I accepted Mr. Odling's invitation to be present on this occasion I bargained that the ceremony should be an informal one and that much should not be required of me in the way of speech-making. Mr. Odling undertook that it would only be a small function, but I am agreeably disappointed to find it has assumed a certain amount of importance and significance by the presence here to-day of so many influential residents of Lucknow and its neighbourhood. I am not dissatisfied that it should be so, because I think the occasion has a certain significance that should not pass altogether unobserved. One of the first things, gentlemen, which struck me on my arrival in Lucknow, and in going through the town, was the poverty, not to say squalor, of some of the buildings in which Civil Justice is administered in this the chief city of Oudh. I noticed that some of the chief Civil Courts were housed in ill-ventilated and badly lighted buildings, that the remains of Nawabi palaces have been laid under contribution, and that some Courts were accommodated in buildings that were in no way adapted for their reception. Indeed, up to the present time, the Munsiffs' Courts share, with gentlemen's horses and their grooms and conservancy bullocks, the privilege of occupying that tumble-down building across the way. It struck me that even the Judicial Commissioners' Court was not housed in a proper and becoming manner. A certain amount of dignity may have attached to the building it occupies on account of its previous history* but in going through the Court, as I have had the opportunity of doing more than once, I found it was ill-adapted for the purposes of the highest Civil Appellate Court in Oudh. I determined that when the opportunity offered I would, if I could, supply the city of Lucknow with a habitation for its Civil Courts worthy of the purpose, and worthy of the city. You are acquainted with the history of the past few years, and you know that until quite recently it was impossible for me to carry out that intention. Provincial finances in 1897 were completely bankrupt ; during that year we lived altogether on the charity of the Government of India—the greatest pauper in the Provinces was the Provincial Government.

---

* This was the residence of the "General Saheb," the ex-King's brother Prince Mirza Sikandar Hashmat Bahadur. See Note on page 165.

FINDING THE MONEY.

"In 1898, my absence on leave owing to ill-health prevented me from taking the work in hand, and it was not until last year that I could do so. After careful consideration, plans and estimates were drawn up, which I believe have met with the approval both of the Judicial Officers interested and of the Bar. Last year, however, we were threatened with a certain amount of distress, and for some time I was unable to make up my mind as to whether the money would be available or not. Fortunately we have been saved from the difficulties which have overwhelmed other parts of the Country. Having the money we have made a beginning, and the rest of the sum required is practically ear-marked, so that there is every reason to hope that funds will be available until the building is carried to completion. I trust, Gentlemen, that the building will afford comfortable accommodation to Bench and Bar, and that it will also have some pretensions to architectural beauty. The city of Lucknow, though possessing several buildings of great magnitude, is singularly lacking in architectural beauty. The Public Works Department have now the chance of immortalizing themselves. They have a fair field, and if they cannot justify their claims to artistic feeling and execution it will be for you to award them the blame which they will merit.

THE CLAIMS OF LUCKNOW TO THE CHIEF COURT.

"These were the few remarks which had occurred to me to say on this occasion, but I have no doubt that many of you are anxious that I should go a little further than bricks and mortar and give you a pronouncement on the question of the future of the Chief Court of Appeal for this Province (Hear, hear). That is a laudable curiosity, and I only wish I could gratify it (Laughter). But this much I can say without any fear of being indiscreet that I think the Chief Court of Oudh should always be situated in Lucknow (Cheers). Whether that Court should be composed of a Bench of the High Court sitting permanently in Lucknow or of Judicial Commissioner, forming a Chief Court, is a matter on which I express no opinion. There are arguments on both sides of the question, but in my own personal opinion there ought to be either a Chief Court in Lucknow or a permanent Bench of the High Court (Cheers). The matter is not an urgent one, and it is not for me to decide it, but I am certain that whatever authority does decide it or contribute to its decision it will bear in mind the public feeling of Oudh and its Talukdars, whose opinions on all matters connected with Oudh, cannot but weigh very considerably with any representative of Her Majesty's Government. Whatever be the ultimate decision, whether it be a Chief Court or a Bench of the High Court, it is only right the tribunal should be properly housed and that the accommodation for the Judges, for the Bar, and for the suitors should be such as befits the capital of the Province. I wish a more spacious site could have been found for the purpose of providing this accommodation, but this was impossible without going far afield. It is desirable that the new building should be near the Criminal Courts and within reasonable reach of the Civil Lines and the city. It is my intention when the building has reached a certain degree of completion to pull down those stables you see opposite, so as to have direct connection and an open space between the new Courts and the Judges Court. It may be desirable to add a wing to the Judges' Court to bring it somewhat into harmony with the new building, but that will be a matter for subsequent arrangement and consideration. I only now ask you, Gentlemen, to join with me in good wishes for the completion of the work. (Cheers.)

The ceremony then ended.

APPENDIX G.

(PAGE 101)

[*Extract from the "Homeward Mail."*]

A complete nominal list of the European members, including women and children, of the Lucknow Garrison in 1857.

Abbott, Mrs., and child (*child dead*).
Aitken, Lieutenant and Quarter-Master, 13th Native Infantry, and wife.
Alexander, Clare, 1st-Lieutenant, Artillery (*killed*).
Alexander, J., 2nd-Lieutenant, Artillery (*wounded*).
Allnut, Clerk in Delhi Bank ; wife (*dead*), and four children (*one dead*).
Alone, Mr. A., (*wounded*), Innes' Out-post, and sister.
Alone, B., Uncovenanted Service, Innes' Out-post, and mother (*wounded*).
Anderson, Major, Chief Engineer (*dead*).
Anderson, R. P., Captain, 25th Native Infantry ; wife (*dead*), and two children (*one child dead*).
Anderson, J. C., Lieutenant, Officiating Garrison Engineer.
Anderson, Mrs.
Anthony, David, Uncovenanted Service, Financial Garrison.
Apthorp, Major, 41st Native Infantry ; wife and child (*child dead*).
Archer, Mr. G., Head Master (Martiniere) ; wife and two children.
Arno, Miss.
Arthur, Lieutenant, 7th Light Cavalry (*killed*).

Ball, Mrs., and child.
Baptist, Ellis, Volunteer.
Baptist, Peter, Volunteer.
Baptist, Adam, Volunteer, (*wounded*).
Bailey, G., Volunteer, (*wounded*).
Balley, Mrs., and two children.
Banks, Major, Provisional Chief Commissioner (*killed*) ; wife and child.
Barbor, Adjutant, 2nd Oudh Cavalry (*killed*), and wife.
Barfoot, Mrs.
Barlow, Captain, Brigade-Major, Oudh Irregular Force (*dead*), and wife.
Barnard, Rev., R. C. Chaplain.
Barnett, Mrs., and child.
Barrett, Uncovenanted Service (*dead*) ; wife and three children (*one child dead*).
Barry, Mr., Uncovenanted Service.
Barsotelli, Signor, of Calcuta.
Bartrum, Mrs., and child (*child dead*).
Barwell, Lieutenant, Fort Adjutant, Officiating Major of Brigade ; wife and child.
Bassano, Captain, Her Majesty's 32nd (*wounded at Chinhut*).
Bates, A., Uncovenanted Service, and wife
Bax, Lieutenant, 2nd in Command, 1st Oudh Cavalry (*killed*).
Baxter, Conductor, Ordnance Department (*dead*) ; wife and three children (*one child dead*).
Beale, Uncovenanted Service (*killed*) ; wife and two children (*all dead*).
Bell, Overseer, wife and child ; mother-in-law (*killed*).
Benson, Mr., Deputy Commissioner of Duriabad wife and child (*child dead*).
Best, Uncovenanted Service, Judicial Garrison ; wife and child (*child dead*).
Bickers, Uncovenanted Service (*wounded* wife and three children.

(xxvi)

Birch, F. W., Lieutenant, 71st N. I., Aide-de-Camp (*slightly wounded*).
Birch, Mr. H. H., Uncovenanted Service, and Miss Birch.
Birch, Lieutenant, 59th Native Infantry (*killed*), and wife.
Bird, Dr., Assistant Surgeon.
Bird, Major, 48th Native Infantry.
Bird, Mrs., and two children (*one child dead*).
Blaney, P., Sago's Garrison (*wounded*).
Blaney, C., Bhusa Garrison (*wounded*), Uncovenanted Service ; wife and nephew.
Bleuman, Uncovenanted Service (*wounded*), and mother.
Blunt, Clerk, Judicial Garrison, and wife.
Blythe, Uncovenanted Service ; wife and child (*child dead*).
Boileau, Mrs., and four children (*one dead*).
Boileau, Captain, T. F., 7th Light Cavalry, 2nd in Command, Volunteer Corps, (*wounded*) ; wife and three children.
Bonham, 2nd Lieutenant, Artillery (*wounded three times*).
Boulderson, Mr., Assistant Commissioner, Lucknow, (*slightly wounded*).
Boulton, Lieutenant, 7th Light Cavalry (*killed*).
Bowhear, Miss.
Boyd, Assistant-Surgeon, 32nd Regiment.
Brackenbury, Lieutenant, 32nd Regiment (*killed*).
Brandoff, Mrs.
Brett, Mrs., and child (*child dead*).
Brown., C., Clerk, Sago's Garrison (*killed*).
Brown J., Clerk, Anderson's Garrison (*killed*).
Brown., W., Uncovenanted Service, and wife.
Brown, Apothecary, Her Majesty's 32nd (*wounded*).
Brown, C., Lieutenant, 32nd Regiment (*killed*).
Browne, Oswin, Uncovenanted Service (*dead*) and wife.
Browne, Miss.
Bruere, Major, 13th Native Infantry (*killed*), wife and four children.
Bryce, 2nd Lieutenant, Artillery (*wounded, since dead*).
Brydon, Surgeon, 71st Native Infantry (*wounded*) ; wife and two children.
Bryson, Alexander, Uncovenanted Service, Sago's Garrison (*killed*) ; wife and four children (*one child dead*).
Burmester, Captain, 48th Native Infantry (*killed*).
Burnett, Mrs., and child.

Cameron, Mr., of Allahabad (*dead*).
Cameron, Mr. R., of Calcutta (*dead*).
Campagnac, C., Uncovenanted Service ; wife and daughter.
Campagnac, Lieutenant, late King's Service ; wife and daughter.
Campbell, W., Ensign, 71st Native Infantry.
Campbell, C. W., Lieutenant, 71st Native Infantry (*wounded*).
Campbell, Surgeon, 7th Light Cavalry.
Cane, Mrs., and three children.
Capper, Mr., Civil Service, Deputy Commissioner, Mullaon.
Carnegie, Captain, Provost-Marshal.
Case, Lieutenant-Colonel, 32nd Regiment of Foot (*killed*) ; wife and her sister.
Casey, Uncovenanted Service (*dead*) ; wife and five children (*one child dead*).
Catania, C., Volunteer.
Catania, T., Uncovenanted Service, and mother.
Chambers, Lieutenant, Adjutant, 13th Native Infantry (*wounded*).
Charlton, Ensign, 32nd Regiment (*wounded*).
Chick, late Sub-Editor of *Central Star*, Judicial Garrison ; wife and two children (*one child dead*).

Chrestien, Uncovenanted Service, and wife.
Clancey, Mrs., and two children.
Clancey, Uncovenanted Service, Judicial Garrison (*killed*).
Clarke, Stanley, Lieutenant, 1st Oudh Infantry, and wife.
Clarke, Mrs., and child (*both dead*).
Clarke., J., Longueville, Lieutenant, 2nd in Command, 2nd Oudh Irregular Infantry (*killed*).
Clarke, Miss.
Clery, Lieutenant, Her Majesty's 32nd.
Collins, Mr. R. M., Uncovenanted Service, Civil Dispensary ; wife and child (*both dead*).
Collins, W., Assistant to Monsieur F. Duprat.
Connell, Mrs. and child.
Cook, Lieutenant, 32nd Regiment (*wounded*).
Cook, Mrs., and four children (*one child dead*).
Couper, Mr. G., Civil Service, Secretary to Chief Commissioner ; wife and three children.
Court, Mrs., and two children.
Crabb, Uncovenanted Service (*killed*).
Crank, Mr. W., Assistant Principal, Martiniere.
Crowly, T., Bandsman, King's Service (*dead*).
Cubitt, Lieutenant, 13th Native Infantry (*wounded*).
Cunliffe, 2nd Lieutenant, Artillery (*killed*).
Cunliffe, Mr., Civil Service (*killed*).
Curtain, Mrs., and three children.
Curwan, Mrs., and child.

Darby, Assistant-Surgeon, 10th Oudh Infantry.
Darrah, Lieutenant, 41st Native Infantry ; wife and two children.
Dashwood, Lieutenant, 48th Native Infantry (*dead*) ; wife and three children (*one child dead*).
Dashwood, Ensign, 18th Native Infantry (*killed*).
Dacosta, Mrs.
Dallicott, Hospital Apprentice, Her Majesty's 32nd (*killed*).
De Rozario, Mrs.
De Verinne, Monsieur, Superintendent, La Martiniere Estate.
D'Ravara, Mr. A., Steward, La Martiniere : wife and child.
Dias, M., Uncovenanted Service, and wife.
Dinning, Captain, 71st Native Infantry.
Dodd, Mr. C., Master, La Martiniere.
Donnithorne, Uncovenanted Service, Financial Garrison wife and two children (*one child dead*.)
Dorin, Mrs. (*killed*).
Dorett R., Uncovenanted Service, Financial Garrison.
Dubois, H., Uncovenanted Service, and wife.
Dudman, E·, Uncovenanted Service ; mother, wife, and three children (*two children dead*.)
Duffy, Mrs. and child.
Duhan, Mr., Volunteer.
Duprat, Monsieur, F., Merchant (*killed*.)

Edgel, Captain, Military Secretary ; wife and one child.
Edmonstone, Lieutenant, 32nd Regiment (*twice wounded*).
Eldridge, Riding Master, 7th Light Cavalry (*killed*).
Elliot, Mrs.
Erith, Mr., Railway Contractor (*killed*), and wife (*wounded*).

Evans, Captain, Deputy Commissioner of Purwah (*wife and children were killed at Cawnpore*).
Ewart, Clerk, Judicial Garrison.

Farquhar, Lieutenant, 7th Light Cavalry (*wounded at Chinhut*).
Farquharson, Lieutenant, 48th Native Infantry (*killed*).
Fayrer, Mr., Volunteer, Oudh Irregular Force (*killed*).
Fayrer, Residency Surgeon ; wife and child.
Fernandes, Uncovenanted Service.
Fitzerald, W.E., Ucovenanted Service ;
wife, mother, and three children (*one child dead.*)
Fitzerald, Mrs., and child.
Fletcher, Lieutenant, 48th Native Infantry (*wounded*).
Forbes, Captain, 1st Oudh Cavalry (*slightly wounded*) ; wife and three children (*two children dead.*)
Forbes, Uncovenanted Service, and mother.
Forder, Mr. W., Postmaster, Post Office Garrison.
Forester, Clerk (*wounded*).
Foster, Lieutenant, 32nd Regiment (*wounded*).
Francis, Major, 13th Native Infantry (*killed*)
French, Uncovenanted Service.
Fullerton, Lieutenant, 44th Native Infantry (*dead*) ; wife and child (*child dead*).
Fulton, Captain, Garrison Engineer (*killed*).

Gabriel, Uncovenanted Service ; wife and three children.
Gall, Major, 2nd Oudh Cavalry (*killed*), and wife.
Gamboa (*deserted*), and mother.
Gardner, Miss (wounded)
Garland, Mr. R., Uncovenanted Service, Extra Assistant Commissioner (*dead*) ; wife and child.
Garrett, Mr. ; wife and two children.
Germon, Captain, 13th Native Infantry, and wife.
Giddings, Paymaster, 32nd Regiment, and wife.
Gordon, Mr. J., Uncovenanted Service, Judicial Garrison ; wife and two children.
Graham, Lieutenant, Adjutant, 1st Oudh Cavalry (*dead*) ; wife and two children (*one child dead*).
Graham, Lieutenant, 3rd Oudh Irregular Cavalry (*twice wounded*).
Grant, Lieutenant, 71st Native Infantry (*killed*).
Grant, Lieutenant, Bombay Army, 2nd in command, 5th Oudh Infantry (*killed*) ; wife and child (*both dead*).
Grant, Sergeant, and wife.
Graves, Lieutenant, 41st Native Infantry (*dead*).
Gray, Brigadier, Commanding Oudh Irregular Force.
Graydon, Lieutenant, Commanding 7th Oudh Infantry (*killed*).
Green, Captain, 48th Native Infantry, and wife (*wife dead*).
Green, Ensign, 13th Native Infantry (*dead*).
Greenhow, Assistant Surgeon, Oudh Irregular Force.
Griffiths, Mrs., and three children.
Gubbins, Mr. M. R., Financial Commissioner, and wife.

Hadow, Assistant-Surgeon, Oudh Irregular Force.
Hale, Mrs., and child (*both dead*).
Halford, Colonel, 71st Native Infantry (*dead*) ; wife and daughter.

Hamilton, W., wife and three children (*two children dead*).
Hampton, Miss.
Handscomb, Brigadier, Commanding Oudh Brigade (*killed*).
Hardinge, Lieutenant, Oudh Irregular Force, Deputy Assistant Quarter-Master General (*twice wounded*).
Hardingham, F., Uncovenanted Service, and mother.
Harmer, Lieutenant, 32nd Regiment (*wounded*)
Harris, Rev. H. P., Assistant Chaplain, and wife.
Hawes, Captain, 5th Oudh Infantry (*wounded*).
Hay, Lieutenant, 48th Native Infantry (*wounded*).
Hayes, Captain, Fletcher, Military Secretary (*killed*) ; wife and child.
Hearsey, Captain, W., Oudh Military Police, and wife.
Haly, Veterinary-Surgeon, 7th Light Cavalry (*killed*).
Hembro, Uncovenanted Service ; wife and three children.
Hernon, Mrs., and four children.
Hewitt, Ensign, 41st Native Infantry (*wounded*).
Higgins, Apothecary, Her Majesty's 32nd; wife (*dead*) and two sisters.
Hill, Mr., James, Merchant.
Hilton, Mr., William, Martiniere Garrison ; wife and daughter.
Hilton, E. H., Student, La Martinere College (*wounded accidentally*).
Hoff, Edward, Uncovenanted Service, Sago's Garrison ; wife and child (*child dead*).
Horan, Mrs., (*killed*), and three children (*one child dead*).
Horn, Mrs., and three children.
Howard, B., Volunteer.
Hughes, Captain, 4th Oudh Infantry (*killed*).
Hutchinson, Lieutenant, Aide-de-Camp (General Staff).
Hutton, Uncovenanted Service.
Huxham, Lieutenant, 48th Native Infantry (*twice wounded*) ; wife and two children (*one child dead*).
Hyde, Apothecary (*wounded*) ; wife and two children.

Ideodatus, Rev. Fr., R. C Chaplain.
Inglis, Brigadier Commanding Garrison ; wife and three children.
Inglis, H., Lieutenant, 41st Native Infantry (*wounded*).
Inglis, Ensign, 13th Native Infantry.
Innes, Mcleod, Lieutenant, Engineer ;
Ireland, G., Uncovenanted Service ; wife and child.
Ireland, W., Volunteer.

James, Lieutenant, Deputy Assistant Commissary-General (*wounded*).
Jeoffroy, Monsieur, of Calcutta.
Johannes, Merchant ; wife and child.
Johnson, Uncovenanted Service.
Jones, Uncovenanted Service, and wife.
Jones, T. E. (*deserted*).
Joseph, Mrs., and three children.
Joyce, M., Uncovenanted Service, Judicial Garrison ; wife and child.
Joyce, R., Uncovenanted Service, Judicial Garrison.

Kavanagh, H., Uncovenanted Service ; wife (*wounded*) and four children (*one child dead*).
Keir, Lieutenant, 41st Native Infantry.
Kemble, Captain, 41st Native Infantry (*wounded*).
Kendall, Mrs., and child (*child dead*).
Kennedy, Mrs., and Miss.

Keogh, Sergeant Major, 7th Light Cavalry ; wife and five children (*three children dead*).
Kight, Mr. Fitz-Herbert, Editor of *Central Star*, Financial Garrison.
Kingsley, Mrs., and four children.

Langmore, Lieutenant, Adjutant, 71st Native Infantry.
Lawrence, Sir H. M , Brigadier-General and Chief Commissioner of Oudh, K. C. B. (*killed*.)
Lawrence, Mr., Civil Service, Deputy Commissioner of Gonda (*wounded*).
Lawrence, Lieutenant, H. M.'s 32nd.
Lawrence, John, Uncovenanted Service ; wife and two children (*one child dead*).
Leach, Mr. F., Apothecary, Civil Dispensary.
Leslie, Uncovenanted Service, and wife
Lester, Lieutenant, 32nd Native Infantry (*killed*).
Lewin, 2nd Lieutenant, Artillery (*killed*) ; wife and two children.
Lincoln, Uncovenanted Service ; wife and child.
Longden, Mrs.
Longton, Mrs., and child.
Loughnan, Lieutenant, 13th Native Infantry.
Lowe, Major, Commanding 32nd Regiment (*twice wounded*).
Luffman, J., Student, Martiniere (*severely wounded*).
Luxted, Pensioner, Uncovenanted Service ; wife and daughter.
Lynch, Mrs., and child.

MacManus, Uncovenanted Service (*killed*).
Mahar, Mrs., and two children.
Mansfield, Captain, Her Majesty's 32nd (*killed*).
Manton, Mrs.
Marley, Mrs. and child.
Marriott, Major, Pension Paymaster, and wife.
Marshall, W., Opium Contractor (*killed*), and wife.
Marshall, Miss
Marshall, Mr. J., Supervisor, wife and child, Post Office Garrison.
Marshall, Mrs., and two children.
Martin, Lieutenant, 7th Light Cavalry (*killed*).
Martin, Mr., Deputy Commissioner, Lucknow ; wife and two children (*two children dead*).
Martin, Bandmaster, P. O., and wife.
Martiniere College boys about fifty (*three wounded and two died of disease*).
Master, Lieutenant-Colonel, 7th Light Cavalry.
May, W., Uncovenanted Service, Engineering Department.
McAuliff, Uncovenanted Service (*killed*).
McCabe, Captain, Her Majesty's 32nd Foot (*killed*).
McDonald, Surgeon, 41st Native Infantry (*dead*).
McDonnough, Mrs., and two children.
McFarlane, 2nd Lieutenant, Artillery (*wounded*).
McGrath, Ensign, Her Majesty's 84th Regiment.
McGregor, Ensign, 41st Native Infantry (*dead*).
McGrennan, Uncovenanted Service, and wife.
McLean, Captain, 71st Native Infantry (*killed*).
Mecham, Lieutenant, Adjutant, 7th Oudh Infantry.
Mecham, Clifford H., Lieutenant, Oudh Irregular Cavalry.
Mendes, Uncovenanted Service (*killed*), and wife (*dead*).
Miller, Mrs., and four children.
Mitchell, Uncovenanted Service.

Molloy, Mrs., and five children.
Morgan, J. J., Uncovenanted Service, Artillery *(wounded)*, and wife.
Morgan, W., Uncovenanted Service, Sago's Garrison.
Morton, Mrs., and child *(child dead)*.
Morton, Mrs. and two children *(both children dead)*.

Nazareth, M., Uncovenanted Service ; wife *(dead)* and two children.
Need, Captain W. W., Merchant, *(killed)* ; wife and three children.
Nepean, Miss.
Nugent, Mrs., Senior.
Nugent, Mrs., Junior, and three children.

O'Brien, Lieutenant, Her Majesty's 84th *(wounded)*.
O'Dowda, Ensign, 48th Native Infantry *(wounded)*.
Ogilvie, Surgeon, Superintendent of Jails, and wife.
Oliver, Overseer, Magazine *(wounded)* ; wife and two children.
Ommanney, Mr., Judicial Commissioner *(killed,)* and wife.
Ommanney, two Misses.
Orr, Captain Adolphe, Oudh Military Police ; wife and child.
Ouseley, Lieutenant, 48th Native Infantry ; wife and three children *(two dead)*.
Overitt, Apothecary, 32nd Regiment.
Overitt, R., Hospital Apprentice, 32nd Regiment.
Owen, Uncovenanted Service.
Owen, Alfred.

Palmer, Lieutenant-Colonel, 48th Native Infantry, Commanding Machhi Bhawan ; and daughter *(daughter killed)*.
Parry, Secretary to the Delhi Bank ; wife and four children.
Partridge, Assistant-Surgeon, Oudh Irregular Force.
Pearce, Uncovenanted Service ; wife and two children.
Pedron, Mrs.
Pelling, Mrs.
Peters, Mrs.
Peters, J., Bandmaster *(killed)*.
Pender, Mrs., and four children.
Pew, Senior, Uncovenanted Service, and wife.
Pew, A, Junior, Uncovenanted Service ; wife and four children *(two dead)*.
Phillips, J., Uncovenanted Service, Judicial Garrison, and wife.
Phillips, W., Uncovenanted Service, wife and child.
Pidgeon, Uncovenanted Service, Judicial Garrison *(killed)*, and wife.
Pitt, Surgeon, 13th Native Infantry ; wife and child.
Polehampton, Rev. H. S, Assistant Chaplain *(dead)*, and wife.
Potter, Clerk, Judicial Garrison.
Power, Captain, Her Majesty's 32nd Regiment *(killed)*.
Purcell, Mrs., and child.

Quieros, F., Uncovenanted Service ; wife and child.
Quieros, Edward, Uncovenanted Service.
Quieros, Alfred.

Radcliffe, Captain, 7th Light Cavalry, Commanding Volunteer Corps *(killed)* ; wife and three children *(one child dead)*.
Rae, Pleader *(wounded)*, and wife.
Raleigh, Lieutenant, 7th Light Cavalry *(killed)*.
Ramsay, Telegraph Assistant *(killed)*, and wife.

Rees, Mr. L. E., late Teacher, La Martiniere, Innes' Outpost.
Reilly, Mrs. L. E., and child (*child dead*).
Rennick, Mrs.
Roberts, Miss.
Roberts, H. J., Bandmaster, 48th Native Infantry (*killed*).
Robinson, Miss.
Rodgers, Miss.
Routleff, W. J., Artillery; wife and child.
Ruggles, Lieutenant, 41st Native Infantry, and wife.
Rutledge, Uncovenanted Service (*wounded*); wife and two children.
Ryder, Mrs.
Sago, E., Mrs., School Mistress.
Samson, Mrs.
Sanders, Captain, 41st Native Infantry.
Sangster, Uncovenanted Service; sister, wife and two children.
Savaille, Miss.
Schilling, Mr G., Principal, Martiniere, and sister.
Schmidt, R. (*wounded*).
Scott, Surgeon, 32nd Regiment.
Scott, Mrs., and child (*child dead*).
Sewell, Lieutenant, 71st Native Infantry.
Sequera, J., Uncovenanted Service and wife (*killed*).
Sequera, Edwin, Uncovenanted Service (*killed*) and sister.
Sequera, H., Uncovenanted Service.
Sequera, C., Bhoosa Garrison (*wounded*).
Sexton, Mrs.
Shepherd, Lieutenant, 2nd in Command, Oudh Irregular Force (*killed*).
Simons, Captain, Artillery (*killed*).
Sinclair, J., Merchant (*wounded*), and mother.
Sinclair, Pensioner.
Smith, Adjutant, 48th Native Infantry, (*wounded accidentally*).
Smith, Mrs., and three children.
Smith, J., Student, Martiniere (*wounded*).
Soppitt, Lieutenant, 4th Oudh Infantry, and wife.
Soule, J.
Staples, Captain, 7th Light Cavalry (*killed*), and wife.
Stevens, Captain, Her Majesty's 32nd Regiment (*killed*), wife and daughter.
Strangways, Captain, 71st Native Infantry (*wounded slightly*); wife and four children (*one child dead*).
Stribbling, Quarter-Master, 32nd Regiment.
Stuart, Captain, 3rd Native Infantry; wife and child.
Studdy, Ensign, 32nd Regiment, (*killed*).
Sullivan, Hospital Steward, Her Majesty's 32nd Regiment.
Swaries (*wounded*); wife and three children.
Symes, Mr. W., Anderson's Garrison.

Thain, Lieutenant, 13th Native Infantry.
Thomas, 1st-Lieutenant, Artillery; wife (*dead*), and child.
Thomson, Lieutenant, 32nd Regiment (*killed*).
Thompson, Apothecary, Oudh Irregular Force; wife and three children.
Thornhill, Mr. H. B., Deputy Commissioner of Sitapur (*killed*); wife and child (*child dead*).
Thriepland, Clerk, Judicial Garrison; (*wounded*).
Todd, Clerk, Judicial Garrison; wife and child.
Tolloch, Lieutenant, 48th Native Infantry, Engineering Department.
Twitchem, Mrs.

Vanrenen, Lieutenant, 9th Oudh Infantry.

Vaughan, Uncovenanted Service (*wounded*) ; wife and two children.
Velozo, Clerk, Uncovenanted Service ; wife and sister.
Virtue, Mrs. and Miss.

Wall, Mr. J., Master, La Martiniere College *(wounded accidentally)*.
Ward, Ensign, 48th Native Infantry.
Ward, Uncovenanted Service.
Ward Mrs., and child.
Warner, Lieutenant, 7th Light Cavalry.
Waterman, Captain, 13th Native Infantry (*wounded*).
Watson, widow of Sergeant Watson, and child.
Watson, Lieutenant, 2nd in Command, 7th Oudh Irregular Infantry ; wife and child.
Webb, P. C., Lieutenant, 32nd Regiment (*killed*).
Wells, Surgeon, 48th Native Infantry (*wounded slightly*) ; wife and child.
Wells, Uncovenanted Service (*killed*) : wife and child.
Weston, Captain, 65th Native Infantry, Oudh Military Police.
Wharton, T., Clerk, Sagos' Garrison.
Wilkinson, Mrs. (*dead*).
Williams, F., Clerk, Sagos' Garrison ; wife and child (*child killed*).
Williams, St. Clare, Extra Assistant Commissioner, Sagos' Garrison.
Wilson, T. F., Captain, Deputy Assistant Adjutant-General (*wounded*).
Wiltshire, Uncovenanted Service (*dead*).
Wittenbaker, Senior, Uncovenanted Service, Financial Garrison ; wife and eight children.
Wittenbaker, Junior (*killed*) Financial Garrison.
Woods, widow of Sergeant Woods, and three children (*one child dead*).
Worsley, Ensign, 71st Native Infantry.

Yerbury, Commissariat Department ; wife and two children.

I would note here, that the Veterans who took part in the Defence and Relief of Lucknow in 1857, were very kindly invited by H. E. the Viceroy, Lord Curzon, to the Coronation Durbar, in Delhi, in January 1903.

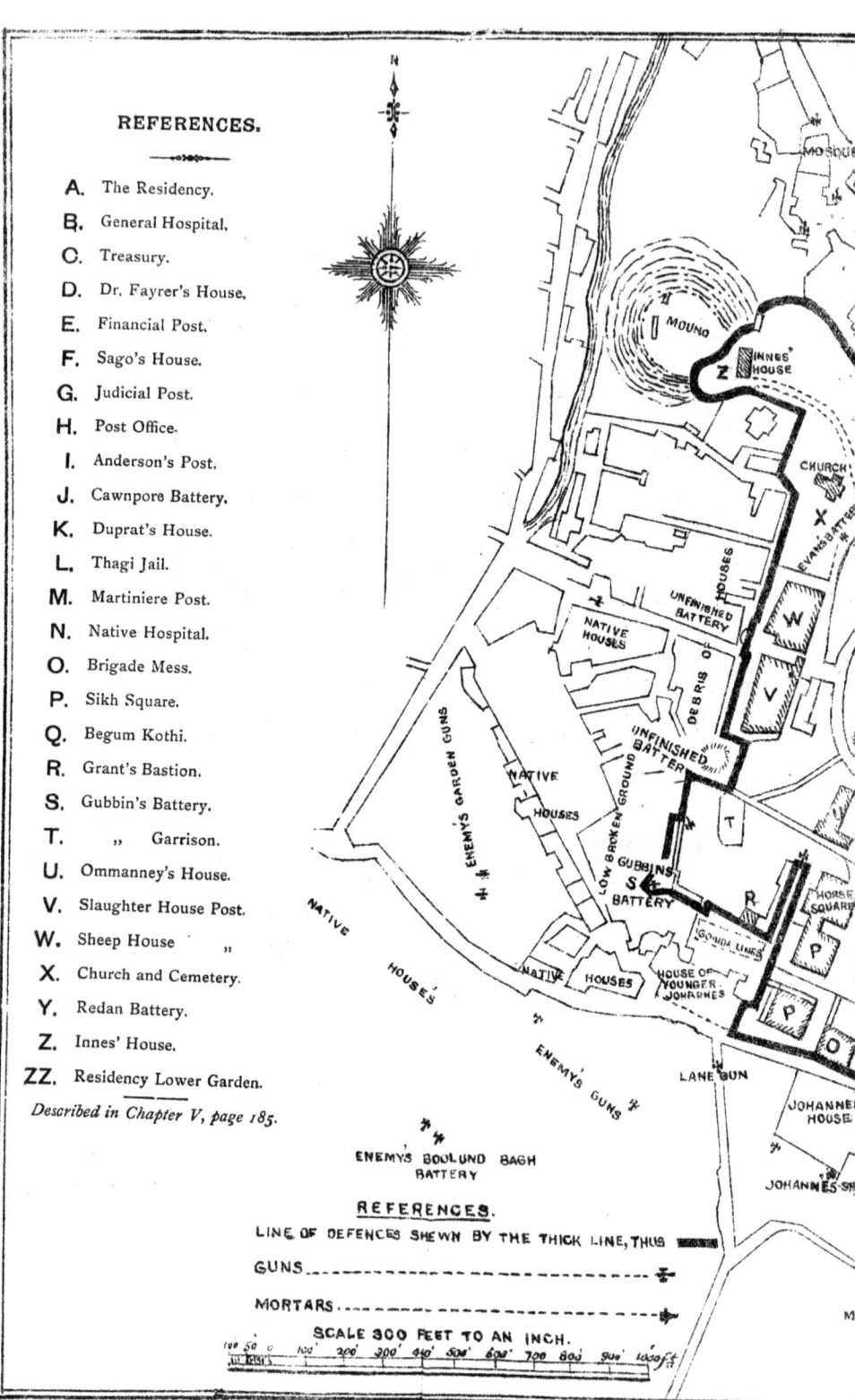

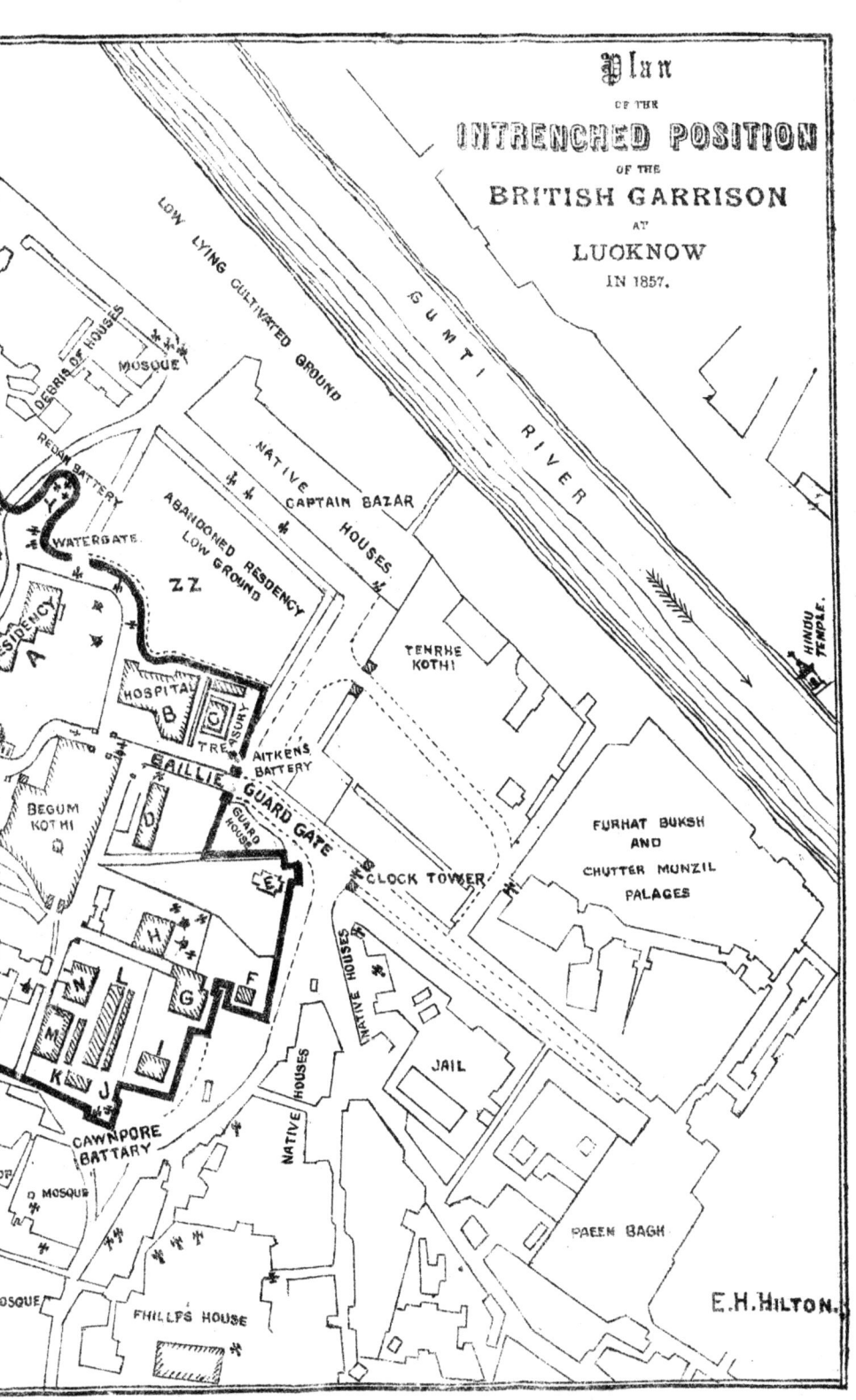

www.ingramcontent.com/pod-product-compliance
Lightning Source LLC
Chambersburg PA
CBHW070838160426
43192CB00012B/2232